CHRIST'S ETERNAL GOSPEL

CHRIST'S ETERNAL GOSPEL

Do the Dead Sea Scrolls,
the Pseudepigrapha,
and Other Ancient Records Challenge
or Support the Bible?

O. Preston Robinson
Christine H. Robinson

Published by Deseret Book Company
Salt Lake City, Utah
1976

©1976 by Deseret Book Company
All rights reserved
ISBN 0-87747-616-0
Library of Congress Catalog Card No. 76-44650
Printed in the United States of America

CONTENTS

PREFACE

The accidental discovery, over a quarter of a century ago, of the Dead Sea Scrolls has raised a number of perplexing questions and has generated some astonishing, speculative answers with respect to the origins of Christianity.

As archaeologists, translators, and interpreters of religious documents have struggled over the meaning of these important records, the confusion and differences of opinion that were widespread at the outset appear now to have centered upon at least one startling conclusion. This conclusion, which seems to be the considered basic judgment, with few exceptions, of numerous authors of hundreds of articles and books written about the Dead Sea Scrolls, is that Jesus of Nazareth did not originate the gospel teachings now known as Christianity. These authors point to the fact that most of the religious concepts and principles advanced by Jesus and his disciples were taught, believed, and practiced by others long before the Christian era. Consequently, they argue, Jesus must have borrowed many of his doctrines from already existing sources.

The prime reason for this conclusion comes from the translated Dead Sea Scrolls. The organization that kept these records, the Dead Sea Covenantors, or Essenes, as Josephus named them, was a dissident religious sect that had separated from the body of Judaism and was practicing many ordinances and teaching many concepts similar to those of Christianity long before the time of Jesus and his disciples.

Another significant reason that has prompted this speculative conclusion regarding the origins of Christianity is the fact that the scrolls have focused renewed interest and attention upon other ancient religious documents and archaeological discoveries, some of which had been virtually forgotten, which also contain significant portions of Christianlike teachings. These pre-Christian sources, combined with the authoritative translations of the Dead Sea Scrolls, appear to provide persuasive evidence that many of the principles taught by Jesus were not original with his ministry but were in existence many generations prior to his time.

The authors take no issue with the first part of the conclusion arrived at by these scriptural analysts. This conclusion of the earlier existence of Christianlike concepts is accepted as established fact. The contention, however, that Jesus and his disciples borrowed their teachings from these earlier sources is, herewith, categorically challenged. If such a conclusion is accepted and allowed to stand, the very foundations of Christianity are shattered.

With respect to the gospel presented by Jesus during his ministry, the scripturally documented material discussed in these chapters will show that this same gospel was actually presented and taught anciently to Adam, Enoch, Noah, Abraham, and all of the Old Testament patriarchs and prophets.

Unfortunately, due to the experiences, pressures, and burdens that the Israelites were forced to endure during their long captivity in Egypt, the people had largely apostatized from this original gospel. They did not respond to the exhortations of Moses as he endeavored so valiantly to call them to repentance and bring them back to the concepts and practices of the pristine gospel that had been taught by their illustrious ancestors.

According to Paul, in his letter to the Galatians (3:24-25), the law of Moses was given to the people as a "schoolmaster" to bring them back to this original gospel. Jesus himself, during his ministry, and his disciples who followed him attempted to persuade the people of their time to return to the original teachings. Jesus taught "as one having authority" and consistently maintained that this authority and these original teachings had come directly from his Father in heaven.

Any conclusions that he had merely searched out already existing religious principles, had adopted them, and had expanded upon them would automatically mark him as a false teacher who had misrepresented the truth. No teacher's reputation, built on such sand, has ever endured. Yet Jesus' exemplary life and sublime teachings have not only endured, but time itself is measured from his birth.

Despite the seemingly logical conclusion in the many articles and books about the meaning of the scrolls and other ancient religious records, there is another even more logical and obvious conclusion about Jesus and his teachings that must be considered by every believing Christian: the conclusion that Jesus of Nazareth is the Christ. According to the scriptures, under the direction of his Father he was the original author of the gospel, not only long before his birth, but also in the preexistence before the world was organized.

It is astonishing indeed, as the scriptures so clearly attest, that this conclusion should have been overlooked by so many of those who have written about the meanings of the Dead Sea Scrolls, the Pseudepigrapha, and the other ancient records that contain Christianlike concepts.

The objective of the material presented in these chapters is to analyze these ancient records and demonstrate that rather than raise doubts about Jesus' originality and divinity, they actually support and confirm the biblical account and provide additional evidence that the gospel, God's plan for the salvation of all his children, is eternal.

This study and analysis, the authors hope, will also demonstrate, according to biblical and other ancient scriptures, that all of us born on this earth preexisted as spirits before our birth here. This important scripturally supported fact raises the following challenging questions:

In the preexistence, as recorded in ancient records, were we subjected to laws, principles, and commandments, and did we enjoy our own free agency to accept or to reject this guidance?

Do these old records testify that before the world was formed a great council was convened in heaven and that at this council a plan of salvation was devised for all mankind and presented to all of us?

Was the plan of salvation presented in this heavenly council the same plan, or gospel, that was taught by Jesus and his disciples during their ministries?

The answers to these important questions are researched and analyzed on the pages of this book.

Although the authors are active church members and have their own deep religious convictions, they have endeavored conscientiously to avoid allowing their private beliefs to color or in any way influence their interpretation of the scriptures quoted and discussed throughout the book. The materials and conclusions presented herein are based exclusively on the Bible, the Dead Sea Scrolls, the Pseudepigrapha, and other generally accepted authentic ancient religious documents.

It is the authors' sincere hope that these chapters will provide the reader with additional, convincing proof that Jesus is the Christ, the long-expected Messiah, and that in the last days, as the apostle Peter declared, God again "shall send Jesus Christ, which before was preached unto you: Whom the heavens must receive until the times of the restitution of all things, which God hath spoken by the mouth of all his holy prophets since the world began." (Acts 3:20-21.)

Sincere appreciation is expressed to Dr. R. A. May and Mr. Collin Harris of the Bodleian Library, Oxford University, and to Mr. J. Claydon of the Cambridge University Library for their helpful and gracious assistance given the authors in research at the libraries during separate visits over a period of two years. Our kindest thanks also to Dr. Joseph Rosenwasser, head of the Department of Oriental Manuscripts and Printed Books, British Museum, for his help in giving us access to ancient documents, and to Eliav Simon of Israel for introducing us to Dr. David Flusser and other scholars at the Hebrew University who were most helpful and cooperative.

We further express our gratitude to Elder Mark E. Petersen

and to David L. McKay for their careful reading of the manuscript and for their invaluable suggestions, and to Elder Thomas S. Monson for his personal encouragement in the accomplishment of this project. We also are deeply indebted to Beth W. Brian for her expert typing of the manuscript, and for the editorial and design staff of Deseret Book Company for the final form of the book.

O.P.R.
C.H.R.

THE CONTROVERSY RAISED BY ANCIENT RECORDS

During recent times a significant number of ancient religious documents have been discovered or have come to light that focus on serious, troubling questions about the origins of Christianity. Most Christian churches had accepted as fact that Christianity began during the ministry of Jesus of Nazareth and was perpetuated and organized into a worldwide church by his followers and disciples.

These ancient documents, which are not contained in the canon of the Bible, have been discovered in various parts of the world during the past two centuries or have been translated or deciphered from previously untranslated records discovered during earlier times.

The most important of these discoveries of ancient records is undoubtedly the Dead Sea Scrolls, which were accidentally found in the fall, possibly September, of 1947 by two Arab boys who were looking for a lost goat. The story is told that the boys, not finding the goat in the open areas around the Dead Sea, began to throw stones into caves on the steep sides of nearby wadis. Hearing what seemed to be the shattering of pottery or glass, they investigated and found some earthen jars in which had been stored parchment manuscripts. Later, after much uncertainty and difficulty, these manuscripts were recognized by qualified authorities as ancient, extremely valuable religious records.

During the years since this remarkable discovery, scores of

books have been written about the Dead Sea Scrolls in an effort to analyze them, to pinpoint them in history, and to interpret their meanings, particularly with respect to the new information they bring about the origins of Christianity. Due to the intense theological questions these old records have raised, concerted efforts have also been made by some religionists to literally sweep the contents of the old manuscripts under ecclesiastical "rugs" and firmly nail down the edges. Nevertheless, despite abortive attempts to hide or minimize the scrolls, the burning questions they have ignited still smolder and continue to burst into full flame, demanding reasonable and acceptable answers. To the thoughtful Christian, regardless of church affiliation, these important, still-troubling questions are:

1. *Did Jesus, during his short ministry, originate Christianity, or did he borrow many of his teachings and religious concepts from already existing sources?* Were he and his disciples well acquainted with the Dead Sea sect and did they, as so many modern authors claim, select those of their teachings and practices which appealed to them, combine them with already existing pagan and Hebrew religious doctrines, and then present them as their own original theological concepts?

2. *Did Christianity, as is so generally claimed by the Jews, evolve out of Judaism as an ascetic, dissident Hebrew sect?* Was Christianity, as taught by Jesus and his disciples, merely another of those many Hebrew sects established by groups that sought to reform Judaism and bring it back to its original concepts and teachings?

3. *Was the gospel Jesus taught, as the New Testament declares, God's original plan of salvation for all of his children — a plan that was presented in a council in heaven before the world was organized?* Was this plan actually presented by Jesus in his spiritual, preexistent state, and did he himself then, in his preexistent state, also teach this gospel plan to Adam, to Enoch, to Noah, to Abraham, to the patriarchs, to Moses, and the other prophets throughout Old Testament history?

4. *Was Jesus the Jehovah of the Old Testament who later was born*

2

on the earth half-God, half-man, for the purpose not of establishing a new religion, but of restoring God's plan of salvation to the world during the meridian of time so that this plan would be universal for all of God's children who had accepted it regardless of when, where, or how they were born upon the earth?

These questions are the vital problems raised by the Dead Sea scriptures and the other ancient, recently translated records. Their answers affect the sincerity of religious beliefs of every individual upon the earth, whether theistic, atheistic, Christian, or non-Christian.

The fundamental reason behind the controversy is the fact that in these ancient records are found doctrines and principles plus church organization and practices that are so similar to those established later by Jesus and his disciples that thoughtful students are forced to conclude that these documents exerted a tremendous influence upon Christianity. For example, in the Dead Sea Scrolls alone there are tremendously significant resemblances to Christian doctrines and church organization.

The writings on the old Dead Sea caves manuscripts, authoritatively judged to have been composed before the advent of the Christian era, reveal that a religious organization of searchers after truth existed and was known by Flavius Josephus as the Essenes, or, now, as the Dead Sea Covenantors.[1] This religious group was practicing many ordinances and teaching many principles similar to Christianity long before and possibly during the lifetime of Jesus and his disciples. These old records were originally written in ancient Hebrew and Aramaic, and scholars who have worked on them authoritatively date them at least two hundred years before the Christian era.

According to the translations, some of the records' most important Christian similarities were:

1. Their concept of the nature of God.

[1]William Whiston, trans., *Josephus: Complete Works* (Grand Rapids, Mich.: Kregel Publications, 1960).

3

2. Their church organization structure.

3. Their religious rites, such as baptism by immersion preceded by faith and repentance.

4. Their noon-day communal meal conducted in form like the Christian sacrament.

5. Their emphasis on the importance of personal knowledge and free agency.

6. Their concept of sin and the personality of the devil.

7. Their form of communal living, much like that of the first Christians as practiced soon after the crucifixion of Jesus. (See Acts 4.)

8. Their strong emphasis on brotherly and neighborly love.

9. Their indications that the people had united into a new covenant and believed they were a chosen people, so designated by the Lord.

10. Their belief in the ultimate personal advent of a Messiah.

11. Their belief in the need of direct and continual revelation from the Lord in the conduct of their religious activities.

12. Their own scriptures, which are replete with religious ideas and concepts similar to those of Christianity.

The Essenes' mode of living and their attitudes toward each other and toward the stranger within their gates were so close to those advocated by Jesus that modern authors who have written about the Dead Sea sect and the meaning of their records have almost uniformly concluded that John the Baptist was a member of the group and that Jesus and his disciples had intimate knowledge of their teachings and practices.

THE CHRISTIAN DISTURBANCE

Because most Christian churches are founded on the concept that Christianity originated during the ministry of Jesus and his followers, it is not difficult to contemplate the depth of concern and controversy aroused through the discovery of the ancient records and the resulting questions about Christian origins that they present. Some evidences of these concerns are indicated in observations from some of the well-known authorities who have studied the Dead Sea scriptures.[2] For example, the late Professor William F. Albright, formerly of Johns Hopkins University, wrote, in reference to the Dead Sea Scrolls: "The new evidence with regard to the beliefs and practices of Jewish sectarians of the last two centuries B.C. bids well to revolutionize our approach to the beginning of Christianity."[3]

Professor A. DuPont Sommer, of the University of Paris, observed: "All the problems relative to primitive Christianity henceforth find themselves placed in a new light, which forces us to reconsider them completely."[4]

Many additional, similar observations about the effect and meaning of the Dead Sea Scrolls could be given. Perhaps these might be summarized, however, with these statements:

> Christianity, we must now see, instead of being a faith "once for all delivered to the saints" in the Judea of the First Century, is a development of one branch of Judaism into a religion which presently, when it mingled with other religions in the Gentile world, developed by a natural evolution into the religious system, widely divergent within itself, that we know today.[5]

> And now that the proven Mother of Christianity is known to have been the prior community of the New Covenant commonly called the Essenes, the momentous question challenging the conscience of all Christendom is whether the child will have the grace, courage, and honesty to acknowledge its own mother.[6]

> The Scrolls from the Salty Sea caves fit right into the emerging new pattern restoring the Man Jesus to the world, the Great Teacher who learned from the Hebrew prophets, from the Essene teachers, from the great thinkers of the Greek Alexandrian culture of his time. He thought it all over and

---

[2]See the Bibliography for a list of books on this subject.

[3]Basor Supplementary Studies, unpublished report of Hebrew University, nos. 1-12, 1951, p. 58.

[4]A. DuPont Sommer, *Dead Sea Scrolls, A Preliminary Survey* (Oxford: Basic Blackwell, 1950), p. 100.

[5]A. Powell Davies, *The Meaning of the Dead Sea Scrolls* (New York: The New American Library, 1956), p. 120.

[6]Charles Francis Potter, *The Lost Years of Jesus* (New Hyde Park, N.Y.: University Books, 1963), p. 13.

created his own message from the best of all he had studied and finally dramatized it as a Suffering Servant Savior Son of Man, who was also a Teacher of Righteousness and the Messiah of the coming great millennial Kingdom of Righteousness and Peace, to be ushered in when the Prince of Peace should lead the Sons of Light to a victory at Armageddon over the Sons of Darkness.[7]

OTHER RECORDS FOUND IN THE CAVES

As observed above, in addition to the Essene records, other ancient religious manuscripts have been discovered in the Dead Sea caves. In establishing the fact of Christianity before the ministry of Jesus, these records are probably as startling and as important to the present Christianity-origin controversy as are the Dead Sea Scrolls.

From the caves, in addition to the Essene literature, have come forth Old Testament canonical scriptures — copies of fragments of all of the books of the Old Testament except Esther. In addition, the caves have produced fragments of other books or scriptures that have never been included in the canon of the Bible.

These other scriptures are now known as the Pseudepigrapha; details of the contents of these old documents are presented in Part 2 of this book. It is important, however, to consider that the pseudepigraphic records were as meticulously prepared for storage and as carefully hidden in the caves as were any of the other records that were found. This would seem to indicate that the Qumran librarians were as keenly interested in preserving these "other scriptures" as they were their own records and the records that later became a part of the canon of the Old Testament.

In anticipation of the imminent destruction of their community by the approaching Roman legion, the Essenes apparently planned carefully. As a part of their preparation, they wrapped and packed their library for storage and for secret preservation either in expectation of their own return, or, possibly, in the forlorn hope that at some future time their records would be

7Ibid., p. 43.

found and appreciated. All of the records were wrapped in linen cloth, then covered with wax and stored in handmade earthen jars; then, before the invaders approached, they were carefully hidden in the natural caves near the Essene community on the plateau above the Dead Sea. The community now has been archeologically excavated and its buildings and contents studied. Fragments of the extensive library are still being found and many of them still have not been fully assembled and interpreted.

After years of scholarly work there is no question that the old religious records — the Dead Sea Scrolls, the Pseudepigrapha, and other ancient documents — contain many similarities to Christianity. There is also no doubt about whether or not they predate the Christian era or were written before the New Testament was composed and long before the King James Version of the Old and New Testaments was assembled in the form of our present Bible.

THE CRITICAL QUESTION

On the basis of these facts, the most important, vital question is that which has been asked innumerable times since the ministry of Jesus, a question that lies at the very heart and foundation of Christianity: *Is Jesus the Christ?*

This question is asked here in the present tense because if Jesus *was* the Christ during his ministry, he is *still* the Christ, the Messiah, the Savior, the Redeemer — then, now, and throughout all eternity.

If, on the other hand, he is *not* the Christ, then the entire Christian world is left with neither anchor nor foundation. It is true that he was a master teacher and that the sublime concepts, principles, and example he gave the world have miraculously changed lives for good and have brought peace and solace into the hearts of millions. Yet, throughout the New Testament, both he and his disciples claimed that he was the expected Messiah, the Redeemer, the Son of God; and if these fundamental claims can be proved false, as sublime and noble as his life and teachings might have been, surely no teacher's reputation could endure and remain great on a foundation of falsehood.

Those unbelievers who would remove Jesus of Nazareth from his sublime, royal position as the Savior of mankind, the Redeemer, the Messiah, the Son of God, and who would attempt to restore him to the world as a great teacher who learned from the Hebrew prophets and others, are building their convictions on foundations of sand.

There can be only two questions with respect to Jesus of Nazareth: Is he the Christ? Is he *not* the Christ?

Based upon the record in the New Testament, there can be no halfway answers to these questions. Regardless of the endless stream of studies and books on biblical criticism that purport to present scholarly analyses of the life and teachings of Jesus of Nazareth — most of which question the authenticity of the nativity story, and some of which even attempt to cast doubt on Jesus' historicity — the New Testament record stands solid, undisturbed, and permanent.

QUESTIONS, DOUBTS, BELIEFS

Questions about the truth of Bible stories are not new. They arose during the earliest times and have never ceased. Since the birth of Jesus, millions of sincere as well as insincere individuals have repeatedly raised the vital question about whether or not he is the promised Redeemer. Millions have believed; other millions have doubted. Today the controversy is even more intense, sophisticated, and widespread. One of the more searching articles on the subject of biblical criticism was featured on the cover of a popular news-magazine.[8] In the article, titled "How True Is the Bible?," the author surveyed the background of biblical criticism and pointed out areas in both the Old and New Testaments that have been and are being questioned, including the nativity story, the actuality of Jesus' supernatural birth, a number of his miracles, and the actuality of his resurrection. For example, on the miracle of the loaves

[8]*Time*, December 30, 1974.

and fishes, the article points out: "These critics would be apt to seek a naturalistic explanation for Jesus' multiplication of loaves and fishes — for instance, that he inspired the crowd to share food they had hidden for themselves." On the resurrection, the author quotes Rudolf Bultmann, who claims that the resurrection "was not an historical occurrence but an existential one, a 'coming to faith' by which the first Christians believed that Jesus was somehow victorious over death."

Despite this continuing body of criticism, however, the author of this article concludes that as far as the Bible is concerned, believers are gaining faster than nonbelievers.

Determined doubters of Jesus' Messiahship developed at the moment of his first claim to this divine appointment. As recorded in Luke's account, soon after Jesus had returned from his sojourn of fasting and prayer in the wilderness where he had experienced the severe temptations of the devil, he returned to his hometown of Nazareth, entered the synagogue, as was the custom, and was handed a book from which he read a passage from the prophet Isaiah. This passage predicted that the servant of the Lord would come, upon whom the Lord's spirit would be placed, and he would be anointed to preach the gospel to the poor, to heal the sick and the brokenhearted, to recover the sight of the blind, to deliver the captives, and to set at liberty those who were crippled or disabled.

After reading this scripture, Jesus put down the book and declared that this prophecy was fulfilled in him. Naturally, those who heard him were astounded. At first some believed, but as he went on to explain the prophecy, all who were in the synagogue rose up and thrust him out of the city to a brow of a hill, where they were about to cast him headlong to his death. Although this threat did not materialize, it is evident that their disbelief erupted into violence. (Luke 4:13-29.)

Another one who doubted his claim of Messiahship was a man who later became one of his most devout followers. This was Nathanael of Cana, who, when he heard about Jesus from his friend Philip and learned that Jesus was from Nazareth, asked, "Can there any good thing come out of Nazareth?"

(John 1:46.) After meeting and talking with Jesus, Nathanael immediately recognized that Jesus was the Son of God and the expected Messiah and King of Israel.

A significant instance when his disciples affirmed Jesus' Messiahship is recorded in Matthew 16. On this occasion, Jesus himself asked his disciples who their acquaintances claimed that he, the Son of Man, might be. His disciples answered that some thought that he was John the Baptist, others Elias, or Jeremias, or one of the prophets. Jesus then asked his disciples who *they* thought he was. Peter answered, "Thou art the Christ, the Son of the living God." (Matthew 16:16.)

Although these accounts constitute specific affirmation of the fact that his followers believed Jesus to be the expected Messiah, the scriptures also have many expressions of doubters. Doubters became so widespread and violent among the Jews that Jesus was brought under general condemnation and, in the mockery of a trial, was condemned to death by crucifixion.

Just prior to his crucifixion, this question was twice again raised. At the trial, the high priest insisted, by the living God, that Jesus should state whether or not he was the Christ, the Son of God. His reply was simply, "Thou hast said." And when the Jews had delivered him to Pontius Pilate, Pilate asked if he was the "King of the Jews." His response was again, "Thou sayest." (Matthew 27:11.)

THE SEARCH FOR PERSONAL IDENTITY

Possibly partly due to the extensive literature that questions the very foundations of Christian faith, but probably more closely related to the profound urge of people everywhere to understand the real purpose of life, at no time in history have there been more intent and determined efforts to learn about the real Jesus and to find the answers to the real meaning of life. Since the beginning of time man has wondered and speculated about answers to three questions:

Where did I come from?

Why am I here and what is life's meaning?

After this life, where am I going?

The ever-intensifying quest for new scientific knowledge has not as yet answered these basic questions, and it probably never will. The answers may only be found in philosophy and religion.

The Bible and the other ancient documents related to it are great sources for possible answers to these questions. However, there are increasing questions and doubts with respect to the answers given by certain religious organizations and their creeds. These growing doubts and confusion are leading large numbers of persons, particularly young people, to seek for concepts on which they can hold with more security and stability.[9] This search for meaning and identity accounts in part for the success of such religious movements and programs as those conducted by Billy Graham and Oral Roberts and the work being done through the Armstrongs at Ambassador College in Los Angeles, including their publication *Plain Truth*.

At the very heart of this quest for life's meaning is the question, Who was Jesus? Was he just another religious teacher who borrowed his ideas and concepts from other sources and from these preached the gospel that we now know as Christianity? Or was he, as he and his disciples so frequently and so clearly claimed in the New Testament, the long-awaited Christ, the Redeemer, the Son of God?

Returning now to a previous question, did Jesus come into the world to reestablish God's plan of salvation, which had been presented in a council in heaven before the world was organized? Was it his mission, as the Jehovah of the Old Testament, to teach this gospel, this plan of salvation, through chosen prophets to all of God's children from Adam until the meridian of time when Jesus himself, as the Only Begotten of the Father, came to restore it and to return the gospel principles to the plan originally established in the beginning?

If the answers to these important questions are in the posi-

[9]"Young 'Jesus People' — Coming of Age," *U.S. News and World Report*, March 29, 1976, p. 49.

11

tive, then man's quest for life's meaning can be found in the gospel of Jesus Christ, which he, through his Father in heaven, originated in the first place and which is the plan of salvation for everyone who now lives, who ever lived, and who will yet live upon the earth.

In the quest for this important answer, let us consider the facts as they are available to us in the Bible and other ancient documents that support the Bible story.

During the past few years man has watched his world stretch out into an endless universe. Human beings have walked on the moon. In fact, through the marvels of television, we have watched them as they explored this previously unknown sphere. Moreover, instruments of highly sophisticated complexity have been landed on other planets, and we have seen close-up pictures of Mars, of Venus, and even of far-away Mercury and Saturn.

As man's world has shrunk and his universe has expanded, the question of his own importance has come into vivid focus. Who am I in the great scheme of things? Am I insignificant or am I important? Am I only dust, and to dust will I return? Is there purpose to life? What am I doing and where am I going?

These problems and questions are becoming increasingly important; and, interestingly, as science has discovered new truths, we have learned the important basic fact that there is infinite order in the universe. This profound, unalterable order is not haphazard happenstance. It was organized and established by an infinite intelligence. Science has discovered what true religion has always known: that there are laws irrevocably decreed upon which all successful actions and results are based, and that the discovery of these eternal laws has made possible heretofore unbelievable advancements in science during the past few years.

Where, then, is all of this leading us? Where can we find the answers to the basic, fundamental questions about the purpose and meaning of life and the identity of the individual?

In the grand scheme of things, in God's plan for his children, it is apparent that there is order and purpose. There is a divine procedure established by an all-knowing and all-loving Creator, through which *all* of his children can overcome their problems, correct their mistakes, repent of their weaknesses and sins, and return to their Creator's presence.

In this great and glorious plan, does a Redeemer and Savior have an essential, indispensable role? Is this the reason why, throughout recorded religious history, there have been consistent, prophetic predictions of the ultimate advent of such a Redeemer?

The vitally important questions with respect to Jesus of Nazareth — who he was and whether or not he is the Redeemer — demand the most careful study and consideration. The primary foundation of the answers to these questions lies in understanding the Messianic expectations of the Hebrews. Does Jesus, his life and his teachings, fulfill these expectations? In searching for these answers, thoughtful students must investigate what the Old Testament prophets and even those whose prophecies are not recorded in the Bible predicted of the ultimate advent of the Messiah and Redeemer.

PART 1:
THE WITNESS
FOR CHRIST
IN THE BIBLE

1
MESSIANIC PREDICTIONS IN THE OLD TESTAMENT

The Messianic hope, or expectation of the ultimate advent of a Savior or Redeemer, is one of the basic foundations of Jewish faith. Prophet after prophet, as recorded in the Old Testament, predicted that the time would come when Israel would be triumphant over all of its enemies and that this conquest would be divinely accomplished by one who would come through the lineage of Israel itself.

Through the ages this expectation has been so dominant that it has been customary for Jewish families to designate one of their sons, usually the firstborn, to be educated as a rabbi with the hope that this son and his family would be blessed by being designated as the Messiah, or Deliverer.

This Messiah, "one anointed" (in Greek, *Christos*), was to be selected by God himself and empowered with the ability and authority to be the Savior of his people. According to scholarly textual criticism of the Old Testament, this messianic accomplishment was to be either national or personal depending upon which prophets made the prediction and the circumstances under which the prophecy was made. For example, according to James Hastings,[1] prophets such as Elijah and Elisha felt that the nation that worshipped Jehovah, regardless of many tragic reverses, would ultimately be triumphant over

---

[1]James Hastings, et al,, *Dictionary of the Bible* (New York: Charles Scribner's Sons, 1952), p. 607.

its enemies. Their predictions did not include a superhuman deliverer, but foresaw that a triumphant Israel would include the victorious leadership of their Jehovah. Even with this, Hastings contends, the ultimate victory would be political. This same type of claim is made in the messianic prophecies of Hosea and Amos.

Regardless of whether or not this ultimate victory was to be national or personal, the fact remained, according to all of the prophets, that it could come about only if the people adhered to the commandments and teachings of Jehovah. Only, as Moses predicted, when the people would

> return unto the Lord thy God, and shalt obey his voice according to all that I command thee this day, thou and thy children, with all thine heart, and with all thy soul;
> That then the Lord thy God will turn thy captivity, and have compassion upon thee, and will return and gather thee from all the nations, whither the Lord thy God hath scattered thee. (Deuteronomy 30:2-3.)

THE EARLIEST MESSIANIC PREDICTIONS

Although it is questioned by textual critics, probably the earliest promise of the advent of a divine deliverer was given by the Lord himself to Eve after she and Adam had partaken of the forbidden fruit. This interesting statement of a curse and a promise is found in Genesis 3:14-15, where the devil is represented by the serpent who will have the power to bruise the heel of Adam's posterity, but through Eve's seed will come the power to injure the serpent's (the devil's) head. It is interesting that this promise was given to Eve alone and not to Adam nor to Adam and Eve as husband and wife. The only person in recorded religious history whose birth is from a mortal mother but whose father was God himself is Jesus of Nazareth, who, according to the New Testament, is the Only Begotten of the Father.[2]

A similar point of view with respect to the interpretation of this scripture is given in the commentary of Scott and Henry in

[2]James E. Talmage, *Jesus the Christ* (Salt Lake City: Deseret Book Co., 1972), p. 43.

the Holy Bible printed in London by W. R. McPhun, in 1862, as follows:

> Satan's cause would be ruined . . . by one emphatically called the "seed of the woman", over whom the tempter had triumphed; and the victory over the enemy would be obtained, not only by the Messiah, but by all his servants. It is remarkable that this gracious promise of a savior was given unsolicited and previous to any humiliation on the part of a man.

Although Messianic predictions are profusely scattered throughout the Old Testament, probably the most explicit and clearest prophecies of the coming of a Redeemer are recorded in the predictions of Isaiah, who was born in Jerusalem near the year 765 B.C. When he was still a young man, in his early twenties, he records that he heard the voice of the Lord inquiring about someone He might send to warn the people. Isaiah responded, "Here am I! Send me." Thus began his career as a prophet. (Isaiah 6:1, 8.)

Hebrew prophets during early Old Testament times were inspired men who not only foresaw and predicted the future, but who also fearlessly warned the people of their wrongdoings and called them to repentance. Isaiah, probably the greatest of these Old Testament prophets, lived during the period of the great catastrophe brought upon the Israelites by the Assyrian conquest. The people were under an extremely heavy burden of oppression and persecution, which Isaiah believed had been brought upon them by their own sins, and he saw their deliverance only through the miraculous advent of a Redeemer and Savior. Throughout his teachings and prophecies, he continually warned them of their unrighteousness, calling them to repentance and reminding them that their ultimate deliverance would come only after they had returned to the Lord and obeyed his commandments. He challenged them to remember the great commandments. He challenged them to remember the great blessings the Lord had given them down through the ages and pleaded with them to repent and return to obedience of the Lord's commandments. He said: "Wash you, make you clean; put away the evil of your doings from before mine eyes; cease to do evil; Learn to do well; seek judgment, relieve the oppressed, judge the fatherless, plead for the widow." (Isaiah 1:16-17; see also verses 18-20.) He also promised the people that if they would repent, the Lord would forgive them of all their sins.

One of Isaiah's specific prophecies of the coming of a Messiah is believed by Christians to be found in Isaiah 7. The essence of this remarkable prediction, in verses 14-16, is that the Lord himself would give the people a sign and that a virgin would conceive and bear a son whose name would be called Immanuel, meaning "God would be with him." This child who would lead a simple life would consistently choose the good over evil.

In chapter 9 Isaiah pronounces the prophecy that has been referred to by Christians as a specific and detailed prediction of the birth of Jesus as the Messiah. The essence of this prediction, in verses 6 and 7, is that a child, a son, would be given to the world and his name would be called Wonderful, Counsellor, even the mighty God, the everlasting Father, the Prince of Peace. He would become great and the government would be upon his shoulders — a government that would continue to increase without end and that ultimately would bring permanent peace. This son would come through the line of David and would inherit the throne of David, from which he would rule with judgment and justice forever.

Isaiah's writings are considered by Bible scholars to be the most sublime religious poetry in the Old Testament. His visions and prophecies are comprehensive, and it is evident that the Lord allowed him to see the course of history from the beginning to the end. Reading Isaiah's teachings and prophecies indicates that Isaiah saw not only the first coming of the Savior, but also His ultimate advent and triumph during the last days when peace would be established upon the earth and his kingdom would last forever. The broad scope of his vision is apparent in his predictions in chapter 9 and is also implied in a profound statement in chapter 10 where he foresees both the dispersion and the gathering of Israel:

> And it shall come to pass in that day, that the remnant of
> Israel, and such as are escaped of the house of Jacob, shall no
> more again stay upon him that smote them; but shall stay
> upon the Lord, the Holy One of Israel, in truth.
> The remnant shall return, even the remnant of Jacob, unto
> the mighty God.
> For though thy people Israel be [scattered] as the sand of the
> sea, yet a remnant of them shall return.... (Isaiah 10:20-22.)

Isaiah foresaw the specific circumstances under which the
Messiah would be born and predicted in infinite detail the
Messiah's ministry, how his teachings would be received, and
even that he would give his life for his testimony. These remarkable predictions are in chapters 11 and 53. Christians
believe that the birth, life, teachings, and crucifixion of Jesus of
Nazareth fulfilled these specific prophecies.

Isaiah predicted that the Messiah would be born out of the
lineage of Jesse, that the Spirit of the Lord would rest upon
him, that he would be full of wisdom and understanding and
righteous counsel. He would judge the poor and reprove the
wicked with justice and righteousness, the power of his teachings would smite and even shake the earth, and the breath of
his lips would slay the wicked.

This Redeemer, Isaiah declared, would grow up as a tender
plant. He would be despised and rejected of men, a man of
sorrows and acquainted with grief, and the people would hide
their faces from him and would not esteem him. Yet, he would
bear the grief and sorrows of all of the people and would be
wounded for their transgressions and bruised for their iniquities. In fact, according to Isaiah's vision, this Redeemer
would bear all of the iniquities of the world and would, if the
people would believe and follow His teachings, provide the
means through which they could overcome their sins and be
forgiven for their transgressions.

In respect to the Messiah's life, Isaiah predicted that he
would be oppressed and afflicted and would not complain as
he was brought as a lamb to the slaughter and as a sheep to the
shearer. He would ultimately face death alongside the wicked,
but would be with the rich in his death. Though there would be

no violence or deceit in his life, he would be allowed to be bruised by his enemies, but the Lord would cut short his agony.

These are only a few of the details recorded by Isaiah as he foresaw the advent of the Messiah and the sublime nature of his teachings amidst the wickedness of the world into which he would come. More than this, as already indicated, Isaiah's visions led him to see the second coming of this Redeemer, who ultimately would bring peace upon the earth during which time there would be no wars or contentions; the wolf would dwell with the lamb and the leopard lie down with the kid; "and the calf and the young lion and the fatling together; and a little child shall lead them. . . . They shall not hurt nor destroy in all my holy mountain: for the earth shall be full of the knowledge of the Lord, as the waters cover the sea." (Isaiah 11:6, 9; see also verses 1-2, 4-5, 10.)

The detailed extent to which the birth, ministry, teachings, and death of Jesus of Nazareth literally fulfilled these predictions forms the basis of the Christian conviction that the prophecies of Isaiah prove that he actually foresaw the coming of the Messiah and that Jesus is that Redeemer.

Among the ancient patriarchs after the days of Adam, probably the earliest predictions of the advent of the Savior were given to Abraham and subsequently to his descendants, Isaac and Jacob, and their children. The Lord promised Abraham that through his seed all nations of the world would be blessed. (See Genesis 12:3; 18:18; 22:18; 26:4; 28:14.) Jews and Christians alike have interpreted these promises as foretelling the coming of a Messiah, a Redeemer, who not only would save and bless Israel, but also would be the source of salvation for all gentiles. For example, to Judah, Abraham's great-grandson, the promise was given that "the sceptre shall not depart from Judah, nor a lawgiver from between his feet, until Shiloh come; and unto him shall the gathering of the people be." (Genesis 49:10.) Bible scholars generally interpret *Shiloh* to mean the Christ.

Probably one of the most explicit prophecies of the coming of the Christ was given by Moses when he was instructing the children of Israel: "The Lord thy God will raise up unto thee a Prophet from the midst of thee, of thy brethren, like unto me; unto him ye shall hearken." (Deuteronomy 18:15.)

When the apostle Peter was preaching to the people who had assembled around him at Solomon's porch in Jerusalem, he referred to this Mosaic prophecy as having been fulfilled by Jesus of Nazareth; at the same time he reminded the people that Jesus was sent to restore the gospel but that it would be necessary for the heavens to receive Him "until the times of restitution of all things, which God hath spoken by the mouth of all his holy prophets since the world began." (Acts 3:21.)

Job, the servant of God whom the Lord described as perfect and upright, was preserved in his righteousness and testimony by his absolute confidence in the ultimate advent of a Redeemer. Despite his terrible troubles, afflictions, and sorrows, he was unwavering in his conviction that his Redeemer would stand upon the earth and that he, Job, would see him with his own eyes. (Job 19:25-27.)

David also testified extensively of the coming of a Messiah. In no fewer than ten of his Psalms he predicted the advent of the Savior and even described some of the details of His person. (See Psalms 2, 21, 22, 45, 67, 89, 96, 110, 132.)

Other Old Testament prophets were explicit in their Messianic predictions. Jeremiah spoke of the days that would come when the Lord would raise unto David a righteous branch and a king who would reign and prosper. He also predicted that the time would come when the Lord would perform that good thing which had been promised unto the house of Israel and to the house of Judah. He said that this Redeemer would execute judgment and righteousness in the land and the people of both Judah and Jerusalem would be saved and would dwell in safety. (See Jeremiah 33:14-15.)

Similar prophecies of the Messianic hope were given by Hosea, Micah, and Zechariah. (See Hosea 11:11; Micah 5:2; Zechariah 9:9; 11:12; 12:10; 13.) In fact, the Old Testament is so full of the predictions of the coming of a Messiah, both a first time and then a second time in the last days, that it can be accurately stated that these predictions are among the most important subjects, if not the most important, in the Old Testament.

A Savior, Messiah, Redeemer, a Christ was universally expected to come and save Israel from its tribulations and woes. The only unanswered question was when and under what conditions he would appear.

EVIDENCES IN THE NEW TESTAMENT

The New Testament has a number of interesting passages from Old Testament prophets that add further proof to the prediction of the advent of a Savior. For example, John 5:5-15 tells how Jesus healed a man who had had an infirmity for some thirty-eight years. Jesus blessed the man and told him to take up his bed and walk. This miracle occurred on the Sabbath and the Jews attempted to persecute Jesus, even slay him, because, they claimed, he had performed this act and caused this man to carry his bed on their holy day. Jesus chided them:

> Search the scriptures; for in them ye think ye have eternal life: and they are they which testify of me. . . .
> For had ye believed Moses, ye would have believed me: for he wrote of me.
> But if ye believe not his writings, how shall ye believe my words? (John 5:39, 46-47.)

In this exchange with his would-be persecutors, Jesus was referring to the writings of Moses, who taught the Israelites about Christ and His ultimate coming.

One of the impressively dramatic experiences Jesus had immediately after his crucifixion and resurrection is recorded in Luke, where two of the disciples were walking along the road from Jerusalem to Emmaus. Luke says that as the two walked along, discussing the tragic event which had just taken place in Jerusalem, a "stranger," the resurrected Jesus, joined them, and "their eyes were holden that they should not know him."

When Jesus asked about the nature of their conversation, they expressed astonishment that he appeared not to know the sad things that had come to pass in Jerusalem during the days when "Jesus of Nazareth, which was a prophet mighty in deed and word before God and all the people," had been tried and crucified.

As Jesus listened, he chided them because they had failed to understand or believe all that the ancient prophets had predicted. He asked: "Ought not Christ to have suffered these things, and to enter into his glory?" Then Luke records this important statement: "And beginning at Moses and all the prophets, he expounded unto them in all the scriptures the things concerning himself." (See Luke 24:13-27.)

Luke's Gospel provides no further details of these prophecies that Jesus reviewed for the disciples. However, it may be assumed that this remarkable review of the predictions of "all the prophets" since Moses would include those reviewed in the earlier pages of this chapter, in addition to other prophecies of the coming of Christ recorded in scriptures then available. These would probably include not only the Old Testament prophets now found in the King James Version, but also those mentioned in the records now known as the Pseudepigrapha, which were probably available at the time of the Savior's ministry.

The Acts of the Apostles in the New Testament also contains several passages that affirm a fulfillment of Old Testament prophecies of the coming of the Redeemer. For example, Acts 3 records that after the apostle Peter astonished the people by healing the cripple at the gate of the temple, he took this opportunity to preach the gospel of Jesus Christ and to call them to repentance. In his sermon he referred to the prophecy of Moses recorded in Deuteronomy 18 and proclaimed that this prophecy referred to Jesus Christ whom they had crucified. Then, in his review of the events connected with the ministry of Jesus and his crucifixion, Peter declared: "Yea, and all the prophets from Samuel and those that follow after, as many as have spoken, likewise foretold of these days." (Acts 3:24.)

Again, as recorded in Acts 10, at the time of the conversion of Cornelius and the dramatic experience Peter had at Jericho when he was instructed that the gospel was for everyone, both

Jew and gentile, reference again was made to the Old Testament prophecies of the coming Christ. In speaking of Jesus, Peter declared:

> Him God raised up the third day, and shewed him openly;
> Not to all the people, but unto witnesses chosen before of God, even to us, who did eat and drink with him after he rose from the dead.
> And he commanded us to preach unto the people, and to testify that it is he which was ordained of God to be the Judge of quick and dead.
> To him give *all the prophets* witness, that through his name whosoever believeth in him shall receive remission of sins. (Acts 10:40-43; italics added.)

On many occasions, the apostle Paul referred to Old Testament prophecies and their fulfillment with respect to the Messianic advent. One of these important occasions occurred in Rome just prior to Paul's execution. On this occasion, he was left alone in a lodging with only one soldier as his guard. He took this opportunity to call some of the Jews together and to recount his personal experiences, to preach the gospel, and to bear his testimony of the living Christ. In so doing, the scriptures record: "And when they had appointed him a day, there came many to him into his lodging; to whom he expounded and testified the kingdom of God, persuading them concerning Jesus, both out of the law of Moses and out of the prophets, from morning till evening." (Acts 28:23.)

In expounding the scriptures, Paul must have quoted the many predictions of the coming of Christ proclaimed by all the ancient prophets.

In his general epistles to the church, Peter records a number of specific references to Old Testament prophets who predicted the Savior's birth and ministry and the salvation he would bring through his atoning sacrifice. These are recorded in the first chapter of Peter's first epistle but with even more directness in the first chapter of his second epistle, where he explained that no prophecy of the scripture is of any private interpretation and then stated: "For the prophecy came not in old time by the will of man: but holy men of God spake as they were moved by the Holy Ghost." (2 Peter 1:21.)

The significance of these scriptural references is that they provide undeniable proof that Jesus and his disciples used the Hebrew scriptures extensively and effectively to establish the fact that the Messianic prediction of all the ancient prophets had been fulfilled in his birth, ministry, and atoning sacrifice. Moreover, the scriptures used and referred to by Jesus and his disciples were not only those now found in our Old Testament record, but also must have included some of the scriptures now known as the Pseudepigrapha, which also were available at that time. (See Section 2.)

MESSIANIC PROPHECIES FROM THE PSEUDEPIGRAPHA

Prophecies of the coming of a Savior are found in several of the pseudepigraphic books. The most extensive concentration of these is in the book now known as the Testaments of the Twelve Patriarchs.[3] In this ancient book, which apparently contains the testimonies given by the twelve sons of Jacob to their families prior to the deaths of these patriarchs, are the following interesting predictions.

1. *Testament of Simeon:* "For the Lord God shall appear on earth, and himself save men. [Because God has taken a body and eaten with men and saved men.] For the Lord shall raise up from Levi, as it were, a High Priest, and from Judah, as it were,

---

[3]During England's conquest of the world, among the many treasures brought into the country was a considerable number of ancient documents and manuscripts. Most of these remained untranslated in museums and university libraries until sometime during the thirteenth century. According to information in the Cambridge University Library, Robert Grosseteste, Bishop of Lincoln from 1235 to 1253, was one of the first English scholars to translate some of these old records that were originally written in Hebrew, including the Testaments of the Twelve Patriarchs. Grosseteste translated these into Latin, much against the wishes of the Pope. Over the years other translations have been made, the most recent by Dr. R. H. Charles, who accomplished his monumental two-volume work *The Apocrypha and Pseudepigrapha of the Old Testament* (Oxford University Press) in 1913. Quotations in this chapter are taken from vol. 2, pp. 303, 305, 323, 331, 335, 339, 345, 353, and 358 of this work. All quotations in this book are taken from volume 2 and are used by permission of the Oxford University Press.

a King. [God and man]. He shall save all the [Gentiles and] race of Israel."

2. *Testament of Levi:* "And by Thee and Judah shall the Lord appear among men and there shall be given to thee a blessing, and to all thy seed, until the Lord shall visit all the Gentiles in the tender mercies forever. But the veil of the Temple shall be rent, so as not to cover your shame and ye shall be scattered as a captive among the Gentiles. . . ."

3. *Testament of Judah:* "And a man shall arise [from my seed] like the sun of righteousness, walking with the sons of men in meekness and righteousness; and no sin shall be found in him."

4. *Testament of Zebulun:* "And after these things shall there arise unto you the Lord himself, the light of righteousness, and he and ye shall return unto your land, and ye shall see him in Jerusalem. . . ."

5. *Testament of Dan:* "For the Lord shall be in the midst of it [living among men] and the holy one of Israel shall reign over it [in humility and poverty . . .]. And the things which ye have heard from your father, do ye also impart to your children [that the Savior of the Gentiles may receive you; for he is true and long-suffering, meek and lowly, and teaches by his works the law of God]."

6. *Testament of Naphtali:* "For through their tribes [Levi and Judah] shall God appear [dwelling among men] on earth to save the race of Israel and to gather together the righteousness from amongst the Gentiles."

7. *Testament of Asher:* "Until the most high shall visit the earth, coming Himself [as man, with men eating and drinking] and breaking the head of the dragon in the water. He shall save Israel and all the Gentiles [God speaking in the person of man]."

8. *Testament of Joseph:* "And I saw that [from Judah was born] a virgin [wearing a linen garment and from her] was born a lamb [without spot] and in his left hand there was as it were, a lion; and all the beasts rushed against him and the lamb overcame them and destroyed them and trod them under foot. And

because of him the angels and men rejoiced, and all of the land, and these things shall come to pass in their season in the last days. Do ye therefore, my children, observe the commandments of the Lord and honor Levi and Judah; for from them shall arise unto you [the lamb of God], who taketh away [the sins of the world] one who saveth [all the Gentiles and Israel]."

9. *Testament of Benjamin:* "Until the most High shall send forth his Salvation of an only begotten prophet [and he shall enter into the temple and there shall the Lord be treated with outrage, and He shall be lifted upon a tree, and the veil of the temple shall be rent, and the spirit of God shall pass on to the Gentiles as fire poured forth. And He shall ascend from hades and shall pass from earth unto heaven, and I know how lowly He shall be upon the earth and how glorious in heaven]."

"Then shall we also rise, each one over our tribe, worshipping the King of Heaven [who appeared upon earth in the form of a man in humility. And as many as believed on him on the earth shall rejoice with him]. Then also all men shall rise some unto glory and some unto shame."

"And there shall arise [in the latter days] one beloved of the Lord, [of the tribe of Judah and Levi] a doer of His pleasure in his mouth [with new knowledge enlightening the Gentiles]."[4]

[4]Note: Phrases set in parentheses in quotations are believed by Dr. Charles to be interpolations added by Christian editors. For a full explanation of the meaning and background of pseudepigraphic records, see page 95 in this book.

2
WHY A
REDEEMER?

S o abundant are prophetic predictions of the ultimate advent of a Savior that this expectation must be considered to be one of the basic themes of the Old Testament. With the record revealing that nearly every prophet made such predictions, one must ask, Why a Redeemer?

This is a simple, uncomplicated question. The answer, however, is neither simple nor uncomplicated. Even to approach the answer to this important question one must, first, investigate carefully the history, both temporal and religious, of the Hebrew people in an effort to understand why this Messianic hope would be predicted so prominently by their prophets, and second, understand the spiritual and supernatural elements in a just and loving Creator's plan for the salvation of his children.

Any attempt to outline even briefly the temporal and religious history of the Hebrew people must begin with the admission of a number of important uncertainties. No authentic, accurate information of the origin of the Hebrews is available. The only original source of their origin, historical development, and religious beliefs is found in the Old Testament, and even this account is limited, being somewhat contradictory and certainly complex. There are serious questions, even among the Hebrew people themselves, with respect to whether or not the Hebrews, the Jews, and the Israelites are separate peoples or one and the same. Despite these uncertainties, the biblical history is sufficiently complete to provide a picture of a nation of people who were frequently subjected to wars, conquests, defeats, deportations to alien lands, gatherings, regatherings, and slavery, so many times that the actual account is lost in history. It is no wonder that a people living under such cruel, uncertain, and torturous conditions would look forward, for their own psychological sanity, to a Redeemer who would rescue them from their miseries and bring them to an ultimate triumph. Max Dimont, in his book *Jews, God, and History*, expresses it this way: "Each crisis, they felt, would itself create a deliverer. In this deliverer, we see the roots of the messianic concepts to come."[1]

The origin of the Hebrew people is a historical enigma. The only available, generally accepted record is that which is in Genesis, but this record is extremely scanty. Other, not so fully accepted, sources help to fill in the uncertainties in the story of the origin.

THE STORY OF ABRAHAM

Bible scholars generally agree that the Hebrews, as a people, originated with a man named Abram who had a special encounter with his God, Jehovah. Abram's name later was changed to Abraham, and from various available sources[2] can be constructed an interesting, if not fully authenticated, story about this leader whose life, teachings, and descendants have exerted such a tremendous impact upon history.

Approximately two thousand years before Christ, Abraham and his father, Terah, and their families lived in the city of Ur in the land of the Chaldees, apparently near what is now Basra, Iraq. The Bible traces the genealogy of Terah back seven generations to Shem, the son of Noah. (See Genesis 11.)

[1]Max I. Dimont, *Jews, God and History* (New York: Simon and Schuster, 1962), p. 52.

[2]This historical material is combined from information in the Bible, in the Book of Abraham in the Pearl of Great Price, in Dimont's *Jews, God and History*, and in the Book of Jasher. The Book of Jasher, one of the pseudepigraphic books, is referred to in the Bible in Joshua 10:30 and in 2 Samuel 1:17-27.

According to legend, Terah was a manufacturer or dealer in idols made both of wood and of stone. Apparently, he sold these idols to the dominant pagan church in the area. Abraham was a perceptive youngster and soon concluded that these types of gods were manmade and certainly did not possess the power he expected of a real creator. Thus, he began his own personal search for a more acceptable deity.

In the course of his search, through prayer, Abraham was instructed by the Lord, Jehovah, to take his father and his family and leave the land of the Chaldees, where a famine was about to occur, and to travel north and west to a land that the Lord had selected for them. Jewish Bible analysts believe that because the family crossed the Euphrates River, they became the first people in religious history to be identified as *Ivriim* which in English means "Hebrews," or the people who "crossed over from the other side of the river." This is one concept of the origin of the word. Another is that the family descended five generations back from a man named Eber, and some historians believe that the name Hebrew is derived from this progenitor. (See Genesis 11.) In any event, the people were of the Semitic race, the genealogical background of both the Babylonians and the Sumerians.[3]

Abraham's quest for a new and more acceptable God could have been assisted by his righteous ancestors still living. Although Terah had accepted the barbarous practice of idolatry, including human sacrifice, which dominated the culture in which he was living, other ancestors of Abraham, righteous people, apparently were still living at the time.

One account states that Abraham, in his search for the truth, desired the blessings and the priesthood of these fathers, a blessing that he received along with an actual encounter with Jehovah. That some of these righteous fathers were still living at this time is confirmed in the Bible. According to the Old Testament account (Genesis 11) there were 320 years from the birth of Shem, the son of Noah, to the birth of Abraham, and Shem lived 280 years after the birth of Abraham. This would

[3]See Appendix.

mean that if Abraham were an adult when he had his encounter with Jehovah, Shem would have lived over a hundred years after this. Noah also could have been available to teach Abraham. The biblical account indicates that Noah lived 350 years after the flood. (See Genesis 9:28-29.) This being the case, Noah would have lived some 58 years after Abraham's birth.

Of course, we do not know and there is nothing in the records that indicates where these patriarchs and prophets might have been living. Yet it is not unreasonable to expect that they would not have been too far distant and would have been available to teach and to guide Abraham in his search for the true God.

When Abraham was instructed by Jehovah to leave the land of the Chaldees with his wife, Sarah, his brother's son Lot, and his father, Terah, and to travel north and west, the first stop of the party was at Haran (in what is now southwestern Turkey), where they remained for a season and where Terah died. In all likelihood, Abraham and his party knew where they were going on this first leg of their journey. Haran was the land of a Semitic people known as the Amorites. The fact that these people were friendly and welcomed the strangers, and also the fact that the city was named Haran, the name of Abraham's brother (the father of Lot), would seem to indicate that the Amorites, if not actual relatives, were close acquaintances of Abraham and his people. Is it not possible that this also could have been the area where Noah and Shem were, or had been, living?

Following the instructions of the Lord, after a short stay in Haran Abraham took his wife, Lot, and friends from Haran and traveled west and south into the strange but promised land of Canaan. Apparently he taught the Amorites about Jehovah, the all-powerful God he had discovered, and converted some of them to this concept of Deity. It would thus seem that the people of Haran were converts who had accepted Abraham's new dynamic religion. (Genesis 12:5.)

Concerning the possibility that the souls Abraham converted in Haran had actually accepted Christ's gospel, the apostle

Paul wrote in his letter to the Galatians: "And the scripture, foreseeing that God would justify the heathen through faith, preached before the gospel unto Abraham, saying, in thee shall all nations be blessed." (Galatians 3:8.)

Referring to the ancient prophets, possibly including Abraham, the author of Hebrews also gives this supporting evidence: "For unto us was the gospel preached, as well as unto them: but the word preached did not profit them, not being mixed with faith in them that heard it." (Hebrews 4:2.)

These New Testament passages not only provide a better understanding of the nature of the beliefs of these ancient patriarchs, including Abraham, but are also indicative of the thesis of this book that the gospel is eternal and that Christ was its author from the beginning.

ABRAHAM'S JOURNEY INTO CANAAN

The land of Canaan into which Abraham and his party journeyed was already inhabited by people known as the Canaanites, who had established a number of communities and fortified areas in the country through which Abraham traveled. The party's first stop in Canaan was at Shechem, where they built an altar and gave thanks to God. Then they moved south to Bethel, where another altar was constructed. When a famine came upon the land, Abraham's group went to Egypt to obtain food and supplies. After a sojourn there the party returned to Bethel and then moved south and made permanent residence in the plains of Mamra, at Hebron.

In his contact with Jehovah, Abraham had been given a special blessing that he and his posterity would inherit the land of Canaan, which would become theirs forever. This blessing also included a promise that through Abraham and his posterity all of the peoples of the world would be blessed. The fulfillment of this promise was predicated upon a covenant that he and his posterity would remain faithful to the commandments the Lord Jehovah would give them.

In the plains of Mamra, two sons were born to Abraham. Ishmael, the firstborn, was the son of Hagar, the handmaiden of Sarah. He became a hunter and a man of the desert and is believed to be the ancestor of the Arabs.

The second son, Isaac, was born to Abraham and Sarah when they were very old. He was the preferred son, and through him the Lord's blessings and covenant were perpetuated. Later Abraham sent back to Haran, from among his own people, for a wife for Isaac, and from her Isaac had twin sons, Esau and Jacob. Esau, the firstborn, later sold his birthright to Jacob, and the covenant Abraham made with God was continued through Jacob. Isaac and his son Jacob were capable agriculturists, and they prospered and multiplied extensively in the land of Canaan. Jacob, whose name was changed to Israel, had twelve sons, and from them, the twelve tribes of Israel descended.

One of these sons, Joseph, was Jacob's favorite, and because his love for this son created jealousy among Joseph's brothers, they sold him to a caravan that carried him into Egypt. There Joseph prospered and eventually became second only to Pharaoh as a ruler. Joseph's wisdom and his programs of conservation were great blessings to the Egyptians. Eventually, due to another famine in Canaan, Jacob brought his family into Egypt and there, where he was reunited with his son Joseph, the Israelites prospered exceedingly "and the land was filled with them." (Exodus 1:7.) But after many generations, Pharaohs arose who did not remember Joseph and the blessings he had brought them. The children of Israel, by now numbering approximately 6,000 souls, were put into slavery and forced to construct Egyptian cities and monuments to Egyptian gods.

MOSES AND THE GREAT EXODUS

It was under these circumstances that the great leader Moses arose, reunited the people, and, about 1400 years before Christ, led them from their captors from Egypt toward the Promised Land. Under Moses' leadership, the people escaped from Egypt, and, after some forty years of wandering in the wilderness of Sinai (until a generation that had not known the fleshpots of Egypt had arisen) reached the mountains of Moab. From here they could look down into the oasis of Jericho and into the Promised Land, a land, however, that Moses himself was forbidden to enter.

THE ISRAELITES IN THE PROMISED LAND

After the rise of Moses and the successful escape of the children of Israel into the wilderness of Sinai, Moses died. His successor, Joshua, led the children of Israel in a conquest of the country and established them with reasonable security in their Promised Land. After Joshua's death, however, no leader arose who was strong enough to hold the tribes together, and a long period of inner strife and dissensions followed. During these times, the tribes were kept intact only through the efforts of a series of wise and unusually good men and women who served as judges.

It should be observed, as contended by many Hebrew scholars, that when Joseph invited his father, his brothers, and their families to leave Canaan and come into Egypt, it is not likely that all of them accepted the invitation. Significant numbers of Hebrews remained in various communities throughout Canaan, so that when Joshua and his forces began their conquest, much assistance may have been obtained from these remote cousins. In any event, during these times this area was controlled by a number of separate, non-unified states. Joshua's strategy was to conquer these one by one without giving them an opportunity to unite. Although this strategy, with the help of his long-separated cousins, helped him achieve his remarkable victories, seeds of dissension still remained. These seeds were yet to take root, grow, and ripen into a series of continuous conflicts with victories intermingled with defeats, as the Israelites shifted their loyalties from one group to another and from one great world power to another.

Historians have pointed out that the geographical location of the Promised Land was an unfortunate one. It lay along the Mediterranean coast between the rising and declining powers of the Babylonians, Assyrians, Persians, and the great prize to the south, Egypt. Over the centuries these powers, time after time, fought each other and used the small narrow strip of land along the Mediterranean that had been promised to Abraham and his descendants as the access to each other's lands.

Space will not permit us to delineate the nature and extent of these numerous great battles. It is historically important to remember, however, that following the reign of the judge, Samuel, the people persuaded him, before he died, to appoint a king. Samuel did this reluctantly, appointing Saul as king. Then began contention and a contest between Saul and David, and at Saul's death, David became king of all Israel. A mighty general and leader, he pushed the boundaries of the land to their greatest extent in history, and Israel became a most powerful and important country.

After David's death, his son Solomon ran into trouble. Solomon did not add to Israel's land holdings; rather, he concentrated on its economic and cultural development. He improved trade, built great cities, completed construction of the beautiful temple at Jerusalem, and added much pomp and glory to the country. Nevertheless, he had to impose heavy taxation upon the people, and in order to collect his taxes more efficiently, he divided the country into administrative divisions, conforming roughly to the areas occupied by the original twelve tribes or sons of Jacob.

DIVISION AND CONQUEST

After Solomon's death, the administrative divisions he had established for taxation purposes turned out to be the downfall of the empire. His son Rehoboam became king of Judah, which consisted basically of the two tribes of Judah and Benjamin that were not accepted by the other ten tribes scattered to the north. They followed Solomon's chief general, Jeroboam, and the stage was set for conflict between the two Hebrew groups. This unfortunate division resulted in internal conflict as well as opened the gates wide for external invasion of the powers surrounding the Hebrews. These powers not only invaded and conquered the land of Canaan, but also, in order to make their conquest secure, they engaged in the dispersion of the people and their scattering throughout the then-known world.

The first extensive dispersion of the Hebrews took place under the reign of the Assyrian king Tiglath Pileser III, in approximately 734 B.C., After subjugating the eastern cities, this king turned his attention to the west, took Damascus, and placed the entire Hebrew kingdom under his control. In the process of this conquest, he took a large number of leading Israelites captive into Assyria. Then followed conquests by Shalmaneser, Sargon II, and the Assyrian king Sennacherib.

Following these conquests, and as the Assyrian kingdom began to totter, Babylonia's dynamic leader Nebuchadnezzar saw his opportunity, conquered the Assyrians, and took over all of the land and people in Israel and Judah, which once had been so powerful under the reign of David.

Jerusalem was destroyed again in two separate attacks in 598 and 586 B.C., and Hebrew leaders were again led in captivity into Babylon. Characteristic of all who conquer by the sword, the Babylonia empire, after years of supremacy, began to disintegrate from within. In line with history's ever-moving pace, a new power was ready to step in and take control. In approximately 539 B.C., Cyrus the Great of Persia completed his conquest of Babylon and took with his plunder what was left of the vassal states of Israel and Judah. Cyrus, however, was a benevolent ruler. He reversed the Syrian and Babylonian policies of deportation and instituted instead a program of restoration of captive peoples. It was under these circumstances, which continued under the rules of Darius I and Artaxerxes I, that the prophets Ezra and Nehemiah returned with groups of Hebrews to Jerusalem and the surrounding area, where they rebuilt the cities, including Jerusalem, and Solomon's temple. Thus, Hebrew life again began to flourish, but not for long.

History soon repeated itself. The Persian empire began to crumble from within and from the military pressures of Alexander the Great, the Greek who conquered the area including Palestine and incorporated it into his empire. His reign, however, was relatively short-lived. When he died in 323 B.C., his two chief generals, Seleucus Nicator and Ptolemy, fought over and divided the kingdom.

The Seleucids established their headquarters in Syria and Phoenicia, and the Ptolemies were centered in Egypt and Alexandria. Palestine lay between, and the two warring nations never ceased fighting over it. During the next twenty-five years Jerusalem changed hands seven times, and Palestine was won and lost so many times that even an estimated count is impossible. During this troubled period, thousands of Hebrews were either taken into captivity or left voluntarily to settle in the north or in the south. The historian Philo estimated that in A.D. 38-31, more than a million Jews were in Egypt.

After a short period of restoration by the Maccabees, division again erupted and the Romans took advantage of the division, defeated the Greeks, and took as their prize the land of Palestine.

THE ARAB CONQUEST

The Roman domination was a long one but, in the year A.D. 610, a new religion, started by an Arab named Mohammed, grew rapidly and spread across the area. After Mohammed's death, the Moslems pushed his doctrines forward and in a series of holy wars conquered all of the Middle East, North Africa, and across the straits of Gibraltar to Spain. Jerusalem fell to the Moslems in A.D. 638.

This was the last of the foreign conquests until after World War II, when the British dominated this area by a series of mandates. Then followed the bitter contentions between Zionism and Arab nationalism, which resulted in the Arab-Israeli War of 1948 and the establishment of a sovereign state of Israel. Contention still prevailed, however, and the natural hatred between the Arabs and the Israelis erupted in a war in 1967, now known as the Six-Day War, in which the small Israeli armies defeated the Arabs and pushed their frontiers through the Sinai to the very borders of Egypt. They also took the land from the artificial border established in 1948 by the United

Nations, a border that snaked through the very heart of Jerusalem, pushed it back to the Jordan River, occupied all of the west bank, and took the vital section to the north known as the Golan Heights.

This conquest, never accepted by the Arabs, led to the short war in the fall of 1973 in which, again, the Israelis appeared to be victorious but were stalemated by the United Nations and persuasions of other powers. At the time of this writing, tenuous ceasefire lines exist along the Arab-Israeli border in the Sinai and between the Israelis and the Syrians in the Golan Heights in the north. Whether or not a reasonably permanent peace can be established is still uncertain.

HEBREWS, JEWS, AND ISRAELITES

As indicated earlier, one of the areas of confusion lies in the distinction, if any, among Hebrews, Jews, and Israelites. Dimont[4] indicates his conclusion that they are simply three separate names for one group of people. This is also the general concept held by most Jewish scholars.

A careful study of the Old Testament, however, appears to indicate that in the division of the tribes of Israel that took place after the death of Solomon, the tribes of Judah and Benjamin remained in the south around Jerusalem and the other ten tribes, known as Israelites, occupied the northern area with their headquarters in Samaria at Shechem. Then Samaria, after three years of siege by the Assyrian king Shalmaneser, was finally conquered by his successor, Sargon II. At this time, some 27,290 prominent Israelites were taken captive into Babylonia, then scattered throughout the then-known world. Although some of these Israelites were left behind in Samaria and others later returned, this dispersion and scattering was permanent. These people are virtually still "lost" throughout the world and their ultimate gathering is predicted by Old Testament prophets.

After the conquest of Samaria, Judah in the south still re-

4Dimont, *op. cit.*, p. 37.

mained independent, although uneasy and insecure. Then followed the Babylonian conquest, the fall and destruction of Jerusalem, and the taking into Babylon of large numbers of Jews. From this time (600 B.C.) on, the Old Testament story is concerned wholly with the history of Judah, which had absorbed the tribe of Benjamin and a small portion of the tribe of Simeon. Undoubtedly there has been over the years some intermingling of descendants of all of the tribes of Israel, but these too have been absorbed into Judah. What is known now as the Ten Tribes were scattered and "lost" among other people of the world.

3
THE SPIRITUAL NEED FOR A REDEEMER

I t is not difficult to realize, with this background of turmoil, bitterness, conquest, and invasions, intermingled with short periods of victories and reunions, that the Hebrews, for their psychological well-being, would look forward to a Redeemer or Savior. Some Hebrew and Christian Bible scholars conclude that this is the temporal and historical background from which the Messianic hope was generated. Many biblical analysts, particularly the Hebrews, believe that the Old Testament prophets who predicted the coming of ultimate victory foresaw this triumph as a national and political victory, or they conceded it as being accomplished by a single, personal savior, depending upon the circumstances and conditions that existed during the times in which they lived and prophesied. This is an intellectual analysis and not the one indicated in the scriptures. The Old Testament clearly presents these Messianic predictors as prophets who received revelations directly from God and who foresaw the future as given to them directly from the Creator himself.

The need for a spiritual redeemer is founded upon the religious doctrines of eternal life and man's need for a redemption from the fall of Adam, which brought death into the world, introduced disobedience, and opened the door to individual sin.

Applied to the human race, eternal life encompasses the concepts of a spiritual preexistence, mortality culminating in death, and resurrection of the body into an everlasting existence where all will be judged and rewarded or punished according to the quality of their lives during their mortal existence. The redemption from the fall of Adam requires a spiritual or supernatural dual procedure whereby mortal man can overcome death and become immortal and also through which imperfect and sinful man can repent of his mistakes, be forgiven, and progress toward perfection.

These profound spiritual procedures and blessings constitute the foundation of both the Hebrew and the Christian religions. They constitute the fundamental reason why mankind in general reaches out for a divine Creator and seeks to believe in the existence of an all-loving and just Father in heaven from whom, in times of stress and trouble, his children can seek and find help and to whom, after this uncertain and often painful life, all can return in peace and security.

These divine procedures and lofty hopes are founded solidly in basic religious doctrine and are fully supported for Hebrews and Christians alike in the Old and the New Testaments of the Bible.

Both the Bible and other ancient religious scriptures provide evidence of acceptance throughout religious history of the principle of the preexistence of the human spirit. For example, in the book of Numbers, the fourth book of Moses, when the Lord instructed Moses and Aaron to separate themselves from the congregation, they fell upon their faces and said, "O God, the God of the spirits of all flesh, shall one man sin, and wilt thou be wroth with all the congregation?" (Numbers 16:22.)

In another place, it is recorded that Moses spoke to the Lord and said, "Let the Lord, the God of the spirits of all flesh, set a man over the congregation." (Numbers 27:16.)

The Preacher, as recorded in Ecclesiastes, stated: "Then shall the dust return to the earth as it was: and the spirit shall return unto God who gave it." (Ecclesiastes 12:7.)

One of the more specific statements in the Old Testament confirming preexistence is found in the writings of the prophet Jeremiah, who wrote that the word of the Lord came to him, saying: "Before I formed thee in the belly I knew thee; and before thou camest forth out of the womb I sanctified thee, and I ordained thee a prophet unto the nations." (Jeremiah 1:5.)

In reference to this glorious preexistence, Job records an experience he had in a conversation with the Lord when the Lord demanded of him: "Where wast thou when I laid the foundations of the earth? declare, if thou hast understanding. . . . Whereupon are the foundations thereof fastened? or who laid the corner stone thereof; When the morning stars sang together, and all the sons of God shouted for joy?" (Job 38:4, 6-7.)

These sons of God could hardly have shouted for joy when the foundations of the earth were laid unless they had been intelligent, living spirits.

In our spiritual preexistence we must have enjoyed the blessings of freedom of choice. If this were not so, certain individuals, such as Jeremiah, would not have been chosen before their birth for specific assignments upon this earth. The principle of free agency in the preexistence was taught by Paul in his letter to the Ephesians. He indicated that all had been blessed with spiritual blessings in heavenly places and assured the Ephesians that they had been chosen before the foundation of the world to be members of Christ's church, and that because of this holy choice they should live righteously during this life's probation. (See Ephesians 1:3-6.)

This same thought was expressed by the author of the epistle to the Hebrews, who presented the argument that although we have fathers of our flesh who correct and guide us, how much more important it is for us to be subject to the Father of our spirits and thus live righteously and joyfully. (See Hebrews 12:9.)

The fact that certain preexisted spirits, applying their own free agency, were sinful and disobedient is clearly apparent in the general epistle of Jude, where it is recorded: "And the angels which kept not their first estate, but left their own habitation, he hath reserved in everlasting chains under darkness unto the judgment of the great day." (Jude 6.)

That this disobedience among the spirits ultimately developed into violence is specifically recorded in Revelation as follows:

> And there was war in heaven: Michael and his angels fought against the dragon; and the dragon fought and his angels,
> And prevailed not; neither was their place found any more in heaven.
> And the great dragon was cast out, that old serpent, called the Devil, and Satan, which deceiveth the whole world: he was cast out into the earth, and his angels were cast out with him. (Revelation 12:7-9; see also Isaiah 14:12-14.)

THE PREEXISTENCE OF JESUS OF NAZARETH

The preexistent life of Jesus of Nazareth is referred to in many places in the New Testament. For example, John records in his Gospel:

> In the beginning was the Word, and the Word was with God, and the Word was God.
> The same was in the beginning with God.
> All things were made by him; and without him was not anything made that was made. . . .
> And the Word was made flesh, and dwelt among us, (and we beheld his glory, the glory as of the only begotten of the Father,) full of grace and truth. (John 1:1-3, 14.)

Over and over again, during his ministry, Jesus emphasized the fact that he had come from the Father and would return to the Father. Moreover, he declared that he had come into this life for the specific purpose of doing the Father's will. (See John 3:13; 6:38; 8:56-58; 16:27-30.)

The apostle Peter also testified of the preexistence of Jesus in his general epistle written to the church sometime around A.D. 63. In this letter, he was attempting to persuade members of the church that they had not been redeemed with corruptible things such as silver and gold, but had been redeemed with the "precious blood of Christ, as of a lamb without blemish and without spot: Who verily was foreordained before the foundation of the world, but was manifest in these last times for you." (1 Peter 1:19-20.)

CONCEPT OF PREEXISTENCE IN OTHER SCRIPTURES

During and before the ministry of Jesus, a substantial number of other ancient scriptures that did not become a part of the canon of the Bible exercised strong influence on religious thought and teachings. The principle of preexistence is clearly taught in several of the books now known as the Pseudepigrapha. For example, in the ancient book of Enoch, the preexistent choice of Christ as the Redeemer is clearly recorded. Enoch, who saw in a vision the preexistent spirits, declared:

> And their dwellings were with the righteous and holy and elect. And at that hour that Son of Man was named in the presence of the Lord of Spirits. . . . He shall be a staff to the righteous whereon to stay themselves and not fall, and He shall be the light of the Gentiles, and the hope of those who are troubled of heart. All who dwell on earth shall fall down and worship before Him, and will praise and bless and celebrate with songs the Lord of Spirits. And for this reason hath He been chosen and hidden before Him, before the creation of the world and forever more.[1]

In the pseudepigraphic book of the Assumption of Moses the preexistent selection of Moses is recorded: "Accordingly, He designed and devised me, and He prepared me from the foundation of the world that I should be the mediator of His covenant."[2]

In the pseudepigraphic book of the Secrets of Enoch, also known as Second Enoch, an even more specific reference is given to the general principle of the preexistence of all souls. This account states: "For all souls are prepared to eternity, before the formation of the world." In commenting on this passage, Dr. R. H. Charles states:

> The Platonic doctrine of the pre-existence of souls is here taught. We find that it had already made its way into Jewish thought in Egypt as recorded in the Wisdom of Solomon. (Ch. 8:19, 20) This doctrine was accepted and further developed by Philo. According to him the whole atmosphere is filled with

[1]Charles, *op. cit.,* p. 216.
[2]Ibid., p. 415.

souls, (spirits) among these those who are nearer to earth and are attracted by the body descend into mortal bodies.[3]

RESULTS OF THE FALL OF ADAM

The holy scriptures affirm that Adam's fall brought death into the world and opened the door to sin. Adam and Eve were warned against partaking of the forbidden fruit and were told that if they did so, they would surely die. The Bible records that they were tempted by Satan and partook of the forbidden fruit. When they did so, they became mortal beings and, through their disobedience to the Lord's commandment, opened the door to sin and disobedience not only for themselves, but also for their posterity.

This action also gave mankind free agency, which actually was a part of God's original plan for his children. In this sense, Adam's fall constituted an important first step in God's plan of salvation. Without freedom of choice, man could not learn the difference between right and wrong and could not have been in a position to fulfill the real purpose of life, which, through the process of trial and error, enables man to gain the experiences and to develop qualities of character these experiences make possible.

In this process of free choice and trial and error, man, being imperfect, is bound to make mistakes and commit errors, both deliberate and unintentional, some far more serious than others. Since the fall of Adam, Satan has been so clever and has used his wiles and persuasions so effectively that sin has been much more rampant in the world than righteousness. In fact, many of the prophets and religious leaders who have spent their lives in teaching righteousness and in calling people to repentance have concluded that natural man is an enemy to God and has been since Adam's transgression. (See Romans 7:5-25; 8:7; 1 John 3:4.) They believe that man will remain carnal and devilish unless he yields to the promptings of the Holy Spirit, overcomes temptations, and accepts the redeeming power of a Savior.

[3]Ibid., p. 444.

Under these circumstances, the Lord's plan of salvation for his children could not be fulfilled without a divine procedure through which all persons could overcome death, be forgiven of sins, and prepare, in righteousness, to return into the presence of an all-loving and just Creator.

Because sin and death came into the world through the actions of one man, it is logical that the procedure whereby mortality and evil might be overcome should also be inaugurated by one man. This man, of course, would need to be someone specially selected and trained for this purpose. He would need to have a supernatural power over death itself and to surrender his own life voluntarily in order to restore, through the resurrection, life to all others.[4] This remarkable individual would also need to be someone who had power to resist and overcome sin so as to live a perfect life.

No naturally born man could possibly meet these requirements. This divine personage would, of necessity, need to be at least half-God and half-man, and therefore, the actual Son of God.

The apostle Paul, in his first letter to the Corinthians, expressed this need beautifully and succinctly:

> If in this life only we have hope in Christ, we are of all men most miserable.
>
> But now is Christ risen from the dead and become the firstfruits of them that slept.
>
> For since by man came death, by man came also the resurrection of the dead.
>
> For as in Adam all die, even so in Christ shall all be made alive.
>
> But every man in his own order, Christ the firstfruits; afterward they that are Christ's at his coming. (1 Corinthians 15:19-23.)

Jesus of Nazareth, known by Christians as Jesus the Christ, is the only human in recorded history who was born of a mortal mother and an immortal father — even God himself. According to the record, Jesus lived a life without sin. He overcame the severe temptations designed and given to him by Satan. He

---

[4]Note: Jesus claimed this power for himself (see John 10:17-18).

established the gospel, through which all men could be forgiven of their sins and prepare themselves for the blessings of eternal life. Moreover, by willingly and voluntarily surrendering his own life, he introduced the principle of the resurrection and became, himself, the firstfruits of this glorious blessing.

The logic of the plan of redemption as presented in the gospel of Jesus Christ is overwhelming. Jesus taught that if men would have faith in him, would repent of their sins and be baptized as a symbol of this repentance, and would then remain faithful to his righteous teachings, they would, through his atonement, be resurrected and forgiven of all of their sins and transgressions. As the prophet Isaiah proclaimed:

> Wash you, make you clean; put away the evil of your doings from before mine eyes; Cease to do evil;
> Learn to do well. . . .
> Come now, and let us reason together, saith the Lord: though your sins be as scarlet, they shall be as white as snow; though they be red like crimson, they shall be as wool.
> If ye be willing and obedient, ye shall eat the good of the land. (Isaiah 1:16-19.)

The symbolic nature of this divine redemption process might be explained as follows: Through Adam's transgression, actually a part of God's plan of salvation for his children formulated in heaven before the foundation of the world, came the Fall, which brought death and introduced sin into the world. Inasmuch as man is born into the world by water, blood, and the spirit, and in this way becomes of dust a living soul to be redeemed from death and sin, everyone must similarly be born again into the kingdom of heaven. This rebirth must also be through water and spirit and is made authentic through the cleansing power of the blood of the Redeemer. This is why Jesus and his disciples so frequently emphasized the fact that in order for one to be saved, he must be born again. (See John 3:3-5; 1 John 4:7-9.)

Through the gospel and the Savior's personal sacrifice, all men will be resurrected into eternal life in the world to come, and each person who has repented of his sins and has lived righteously will be blessed with eternal life and immortal glory.

This glorious opportunity and blessing is majestically declared in the scriptures: "For God so loved the world, that he gave his only begotten Son, that whosoever believeth in him should not perish, but have everlasting life." (John 3:16.)

The apostle Paul understood this glorious process and taught it with power and clarity when he explained to the church members at Rome: "Know ye not, that so many of us as were baptized into Jesus Christ were baptized into his death? Therefore we are buried with him by baptism into death: that like as Christ was raised up from the dead by the glory of the Father, even so we also should walk in newness of life." (Romans 6:3-4.)

In this sublime plan of salvation, those who follow the Savior's teachings and are baptized by one having authority of God, through Christ himself, will receive the spirit of the Holy Ghost through which they are justified and will be sanctified through the blood of Christ. This is undoubtedly why, in his final instructions to his disciples, Jesus commanded: "Go ye therefore, and teach all nations, baptizing them in the name of the Father, and of the Son, and of the Holy Ghost: Teaching them to observe all things whatsoever I have commanded you: and, lo, I am with you alway, even unto the end of the world. Amen." (Matthew 28:19-20; see also Mark 16:15-16.)

THE MYSTERY OF THE ATONEMENT

In numerous places in the New Testament, the will of God, the kingdom of heaven, and God's plan for his children are referred to as mysteries. (See Mark 4:11; Luke 8:10; 1 Corinthians 2:14; Ephesians 1:9; 5:32; 6:19.) On one occasion when Jesus was addressing the people in parables, his disciples asked him why he spoke in this way. His answer was that it was possible for his disciples to understand the mysteries of the kingdom of heaven, but the people in general did not have this comprehension. (See Matthew 13:11.)

The atonement is surely one of the great mysteries of the scriptures. This glorious blessing cannot be comprehended by finite, human minds. It must be accepted through faith and through the sure knowledge that as man's intelligence is expanded, the natural laws through which this miracle may be performed will be fully understood. The power of the Almighty lies in his infinite knowledge and understanding of all of the laws of nature that he established. As man has advanced in his quest for knowledge, he is discovering that the universe is a universe of absolute law and order. As these laws have been discovered and understood, he has been able to reach out into space, to explore the moon, to soft-land scientific instruments on other planets, and to observe and study them even though they are millions of miles away.

With the Creator's laws being so absolute, precise, and infinite, it is surely not unreasonable to expect that the miraculous process of the atonement is also based on natural but celestial, eternal laws.

The word *atonement* means to restore to "oneness" those who through sin have been estranged from God. The word itself is found but twice in the Bible (Leviticus 17:11; Romans 5:11), but the process of reconciliation to God is discussed extensively, particularly by Paul in his various letters to the branches of the church in Asia. For example, in one of his letters to the Corinthians he states:

> Therefore if any man be in Christ, he is a new creature: old things are passed away; behold, all things are become new.
> And all things are of God, who hath reconciled us to himself by Jesus Christ, and hath given to us the ministry of reconciliation;
> To wit, that God was in Christ, reconciling the world unto himself, not imputing their trespasses unto them; and hath committed unto us the word of reconciliation. (2 Corinthians 5:17-19; see also Ephesians 2:14-21.)

In Hebrews 9, the author describes this process of reconciliation of atonement as practiced during Old Testament days. This account describes the details of blood sacrifices as commanded in Leviticus 17:11, which explains that the life of the flesh is in the blood, "and I have given it to you upon the altar to make an atonement for your souls: for it is the blood that maketh an atonement for the soul." The explanation in Hebrews outlines the ancient reasons for this sacrifice and then explains:

> For if the blood of bulls and of goats, and the ashes of an heifer sprinkling the unclean, sanctifieth to the purifying of the flesh:
>
> How much more shall the blood of Christ, who through the eternal Spirit offered himself without spot to God, purge your conscience from dead works to serve the living God?
>
> And for this cause he is the mediator of the new testament, that by means of death, for the redemption of the transgressions that were under the first testament, they which are called might receive the promise of eternal inheritance. (Hebrews 9:13-15.)

The atonement provided by the Redeemer is the glorious gift of God to all of his children. Through it all mankind is freed from the bonds of death; those who keep the Lord's commandments and repent of their sins are forgiven; and the way is opened for them to enjoy the blessings of eternal life.

4
WHO WAS
JESUS OF
NAZARETH?

A lthough the New Testament is the prime source of information about Jesus, it is not the only proof of the actuality of his existence. And though there are some biased individuals who take delight in attempting to prove he was a myth, no reasonable person today doubts his actual historicity. Even time is now dated from his birth.

It is true that there is little information about Jesus outside of the New Testament, yet enough exists to establish fully his reality. The historian Flavius Josephus, who is recognized as a careful and accurate historian, particularly since the discovery of the Dead Sea Scrolls, wrote:

> Now, there was about this time, Jesus, a wise man, if it be lawful to call him a man, for he was a doer of wonderful works, — a teacher of such men as received the truth with pleasure. He drew over to him both many of the Jews and many of the Gentiles. He was [the] Christ; and when Pilate, at the suggestion of the principal men amongst us, had condemned him to the cross, those that loved him at the first did not forsake him, for he appeared to them alive again the third day, as the divine prophets had foretold these and ten thousand other wonderful things concerning him; and the tribe of Christians, so named from him, are not extinct at this day.[1]

---

[1]Flavius Josephus, *Antiquities of the Jews*, Book 18, chapter 3, verse 3, in Whiston, *op. cit.*

Jesus was also known to the Romans through a letter from Pliny, governor of Bithynia, and also through a reference in the works of the historian Pacitus, who indicated in his writings that Jesus was believed by his followers to be the Messiah of the Jews and the Son of God. Moreover, Jewish tradition, as recorded in the Talmud, depicts Jesus as a rabbi, lists his disciples in the meridian of time, and indicates that his condemnation was due to sorcery and the fact that he led Israel astray. This report indicates that his execution came on the eve of the Feast of the Passover.

UNAUTHENTICATED DESCRIPTIONS OF JESUS

Although the New Testament provides no information on the physical appearance of Jesus, a number of partial descriptions have been preserved. These cannot be authenticated and consequently have not been generally accepted. Although some critics have gone to great lengths to prove that they are spurious, the results of their efforts have not been conclusive.

The authors have studied these descriptions, found on ancient manuscripts in the Cambridge University Library in Cambridge, England. The manuscripts are obviously very old and probably date back to the early part of the Christian era. One of the most interesting of these documents is a description of Jesus that has been published many times. It is the Lentulus description, which was found in Jerusalem by Emperor Theodosius the Great in the public registers of Pontius Pilate. These were translated in the nineteenth year of Tiberius Caesar, emperor of the Romans in the seventeenth year of the government of Herod, the son of Herod, King of Galilee; they are dated on the 8th calendar of April, which is 23 days of the month of March, CCII Olympiad.

On pages 73 and 74 of this manuscript is a handwritten statement attributed to Lentulus, consul of Jerusalem, addressed to the senate and people of Rome:

> There hath appeared in our time and is yet among us, a person of great virtue called Jesus Christ who is said by the people to be a prophet and his disciples call him the Son of God, he raiseth the dead and healeth the diseased; he is a man

of tall stature of comely presence. His looks strike a veneration on those that behold him and there is something that a man sees in him which affects one with an awe and love. His hair is the color of a hazel nut, almost ripe. It lies plain to his ears and then cutteth into rings, it gives a delightful brightness and lies waving upon his shoulders and parts on the top of his head like the Nazarenes. His brow is smooth and looks well, his face without spots of wrinkles, his cheeks adorned with a moderate red, his mouth and nose of comely size, his beard grows thick of the same color with his hair and parts in the midst. His aspect breathes a great deal of innocency and descretion, his eyes are quick and clear.

In his reprehensions he is terrible. In his admonitions he is kind and winning, tempered with a pleasant and charming gravity. He was never seen to laugh but often to weep. The shape of his body is tall and well-made, his arms proportionable and his hands are lovely. He is modest and not overforward in his discourse. In short, you shall hardly imagine a more comely person.

This interesting description of Jesus would not be included here if it were not for one significant and important fact. Professor Charles Anthon, Jay Professor of the Greek and Latin Languages at Columbia University, is believed to have been one of America's greatest Classical scholars. For some twenty-five years, Dr. Anthon worked on his book *Classical Dictionary of Principal and Proper Names Mentioned by Ancient Greek and Roman Authors*. This 1450-page work of extremely small type was published by Harper and Brothers in 1853. On page 731 of this dictionary is the name Gaetulicus Lentulus with this biography: "Gaetulicus Lentulus was Consul A.D. 26, and was put to death by Caligula on a charge of conspiracy. (From Dio Cass., 59, 22-Sueton, Vit, Calud., 9) Gaetulicus was distinguished as an historical and political writer. (Voss., Hist. Lat., 1, 25.-Crus, AD Sueton., Vit. Calig., 8.)"

The fact that Lentulus was a historical and political writer during the lifetime of Jesus and that he was put to death by the tyrannical ruler Caligula for conspiracy, probably for writing something that Caligula did not like, is strong evidence that Lentulus could have written the account reproduced above.[2]

[2]According to Professor Charles Anthon's account, Caligula was born in A.D. 12, probably in Germany. His full name was Caius Caesar Augusta Ger-

Another description purportedly of Jesus and a letter concerning Jesus, claimed to have been sent by Pontius Pilate to the Emperor Tiberius, are in the same file in the Cambridge University Library as the Lentulus description. These other documents are extremely interesting, but because no outside proof has been uncovered to help substantiate their authenticity, they are not reproduced here. Nevertheless, they should, in their support of the New Testament, answer questions of critics who attempt to cast doubt on Jesus' historicity.

TESTIMONIES OF IMMORTAL BEINGS

Before Jesus' birth, at the time of his baptism, and during his ministry on earth, immortal beings, both heavenly angels and spiritual beings who were in the service of Satan, testified of his Godhood.

According to Luke's account, the angel Gabriel was sent from God to visit Mary, Jesus' mother, before Mary was with child, and the angel promised her that she would be the mother of the Son of the Highest and that the Lord God would give her son the throne of David. When Mary expressed astonishment, the angel told her that the power of the Highest would overshadow her and that the child who would be born from her would be called the Son of God.

Luke also tells the beautiful story of the birth of Jesus and of the visitation of the angels of the Lord to the shepherds in the fields, keeping watch over their flocks. His dramatic account describes how, as the angel of the Lord came upon them, the

manicus. At the age of twenty he was brought into the court of his grandfather, Tiberius, where he soon exhibited a vicious temper as well as extreme cruelty toward the unfortunate. Tiberius had appointed his two grandsons, Caligula Caius Caesar and Tiberius Gemellus, as joint heirs of the empire. However, Caligula's lust for power soon eliminated his cousin, and he became the sole potentate. A ruthless, corrupt ruler, he possessed no scruples against murder or assassination of his rivals and thus created deep animosities and many enemies. At the age of twenty-nine, in the fourth year of his tyrannical reign (A.D. 41), he was murdered. It is obvious that this type of ruthless character would not have hesitated to eliminate a consul at Jerusalem, such as Lentulus, who might have offended him.

glory of the Lord shown about them. The shepherds, who were afraid, were assured by the angel that the Savior, even Christ the Lord, would be born that day in Bethlehem. Following this glorious announcement, "suddenly there was with the angel a multitude of the heavenly host praising God and saying, Glory to God in the Highest, and on earth peace, good will toward men." (Luke 2:13-14.)

The third event recorded by Luke of the visitation of heavenly beings occurred when Jesus' parents, according to Jewish custom, brought the child to Jerusalem. A certain man, named Simeon, whose righteousness entitled him to the presence of the Holy Ghost, had been promised that before he died he would see the Christ. When Jesus visited at the temple with his parents, the Spirit led Simeon there, and he took the child in his arms and blessed God and said: "Lord, now lettest thy servant depart in peace, according to thy word: For mine eyes have seen thy salvation, Which thou hast prepared before the face of all people; A light to lighten the gentiles, and the glory of thy people Israel." (Luke 2:29-32.)

The next great event was when a heavenly witness was told that Jesus was the Messiah; this took place when Jesus was baptized by John the Baptist, and is recorded in all four of the Gospels.

On at least two other occasions the New Testament records visits by heavenly representatives who testified of the Messiahship of Jesus. According to Luke, one of these visits was at the time of Jesus' resurrection. Soon after his body had been laid in the sepulchre provided by Joseph of Arimathea, certain women came with ointments to prepare the body and found the stone rolled away from the sepulchre. Upon entering, they saw two men clothed in shining garments standing at each end of the tomb. The women were afraid and bowed their faces to the earth, but one of the angels inquired: "Why seek ye the living among the dead? He is not here but is risen: remember how he spake unto you when he was yet in Galilee, Saying, the Son of Man must be delivered into the hands of sinful men, and be crucified, and the third day rise again." (Luke 25:5-7.)

Another time when heavenly beings visited the earth was at the time of the ascension of Jesus, recorded in the first chapter of Acts. According to this record, after his resurrection Jesus remained some forty days with his followers and disciples, teaching them of things pertaining to the kingdom of God. Then, after promising his chosen disciples that they would be visited by and have the power of the Holy Ghost, he ascended into heaven and a cloud received him out of their sight. While they were standing there in amazement, looking into heaven, "two men stood by them in white apparel; Which also said, ye men of Galilee, why stand ye gazing up into heaven? this same Jesus, which is taken up from you into heaven, shall so come in like manner as ye have seen him go into heaven." (Acts 1:10-11.)

If the record is correct, the action and words of these heavenly beings surely provide additional proof that Jesus was the Christ, the Messiah, the promised Redeemer who would come to save all repentant mankind from their sins.

THE WITNESS OF EVIL SPIRITS

On numerous occasions during his ministry, when Jesus met individuals possessed with evil spirits, these spirits immediately recognized him as the Son of God. The first of these witnesses was Satan himself, during the period of the temptation of Jesus in the wilderness.

Each of the Gospels records other instances when Jesus met persons possessed by evil spirits, and on each occasion the evil spirit immediately recognized Jesus as the Son of God. Matthew records one evil spirit as saying. "What have we to do with thee, Jesus, thou Son of God? Art thou come hither to torment us before the time?" (Matthew 8:29.) Mark records another incident of the man possessed with an unclean spirit. He too cried out, saying: "Let us alone; what have we to do with thee, thou Jesus of Nazareth? art thou come to destroy us? I know thee who thou art, the Holy One of God." (Mark 1:24.)

Luke tells of several individuals possessed with devils who came to Jesus and were healed. As the evil spirits departed they were heard crying out, saying, "Thou art Christ, the Son of God." At this point in his ministry, it is recorded that Jesus rebuked these individuals, admonishing them not to speak of the fact that they knew he was the Christ. Jealousy, hatred, and opposition to him were growing rapidly among religious and government leaders, and he desired to avoid this opposition as much as possible until he had completed the work he had been sent by his Father to do. (See Luke 4.)

This type of recognition from Satan and his legions provides evidence not only of Jesus' divinity and Godhood, but also of the importance of his mission. If the record is correct, the evil spirits knew Jesus in the preexistence and were fully aware of the plan of salvation that he would present during his mortal ministry on earth. They were already acquainted with his power and the kingdom of God that he would establish upon the earth.

5
MESSIANIC PROPHECIES IN THE FOUR GOSPELS

The New Testament, or the New Covenant (the true meaning of the phrase), is a record of the birth, life, teachings, death, and resurrection of a child born in Bethlehem who was known as Jesus of Nazareth, or by the Christians as Jesus the Christ.

The unusual and miraculous birth of Jesus is recorded in simple detail in two of the four Gospels in the New Testament, Matthew and Luke. Although the two accounts differ in some minor details, both describe his birth as miraculous in that he was the son of a living, mortal woman, and his father was not mortal, but was God himself. The Matthew account states: " . . . When as his mother, Mary was espoused to Joseph, before they came together, she was found with child of the Holy Ghost." (Matthew 1:18.)

This account continues with the description of Joseph's surprise and concern until in a dream he was assured that Mary was actually with child from the Holy Ghost, which was in fulfillment of the prophecy: " . . . Behold, a virgin shall conceive, and bear a son, and shall call his name Immanuel." (Isaiah 7:14.)

After this divine assurance, Joseph was comforted and protected Mary during her divine and prophetic confinement.

The account in Luke's Gospel is a bit more detailed. Luke records that an angel came unto Mary and told her that she had been selected as highly favored of the Lord and would be blessed above all other women. He assured her that she would conceive in her womb and bring forth a son whom she should call Jesus, and that he would also be called the son of the Highest. This account continues: " . . . and the Lord God shall give unto him the throne of his father, David: And he shall reign over the house of Jacob forever. . . ." (Luke 1:32-33.)

When Mary responded with astonishment, wondering how such could be, since she had not known any man, "the angel answered and said unto her, The Holy Ghost shall come upon thee, and the power of the Highest shall overshadow thee: therefore also that holy thing which shall be born of thee shall be called the Son of God." (Luke 1:35.)

The account in Luke provides beautiful details of the birth in Bethlehem, the reasons for Joseph and Mary's pilgrimage to that city, and the humble birth of the child in a manger. It also provides dramatic details of the visitation of the angels at the time of the birth, the account of the star that guided the wise men who were seeking the place of the Lord's birth so they might bring gifts, and the glorious experience of the shepherds in the fields, keeping watch over their flocks. (See Luke 2.)

For Christians, this is without doubt the most glorious story ever told and adds mightily to their conviction that this baby, Jesus the Christ, was born in fulfillment of ancient prophecy and truly was the Only Begotten Son of God.

The New Testament gives only scant detail of the events that followed this remarkable birth. Herod was king of Judea at the time, and when he heard of the birth of Jesus, who was to become the King of the Jews, he became violently jealous lest this child be raised up to replace him. Consequently, he requested through attempted deception that the wise men who were journeying to visit the newborn child bring him word so that he, too, might worship him. The wise men, however, were forewarned in a dream of Herod's plot and returned another way so as not to provide him with any information. Moreover, recognizing the danger, an angel appeared to Joseph and Mary and instructed them to take the child into Egypt, where they should remain until after Herod's death. They, of course, followed the angel's instructions.

The New Testament is even more brief in its information about Jesus' childhood and youth. After the family's return from Egypt, the account merely states that "the child grew, and waxed strong in spirit, filled with wisdom; and the grace of God was upon him." (Luke 2:40.)

Only once does any one of the Gospels describe Jesus' growth and development. Luke records that when the child was twelve years old the family went to Jerusalem for a religious feast. Afterwards the family, in company with others, began the return trip. When the group had traveled a day's distance from Jerusalem, they discovered that Jesus was not with them, so they returned to the city and searched for him for three days. They found him in the temple conversing with the rabbis and doctors, listening to them and asking them questions. Luke's account records that these learned teachers were astonished at the young boy's understanding and wisdom. When Mary and Joseph chided him for having caused them such concern, he responded with the question: " . . . wist ye not that I must be about my Father's business?" (Luke 2:49.)

Following this experience Jesus returned to Nazareth with his parents and from then until the time of his meeting with John the Baptist some eighteen years later he "increased in wisdom and stature, and in favour with God and man." (Luke 2:52.)

JOHN THE BAPTIST AND JESUS

John the Baptist, who prepared the way for Jesus and his ministry, also was born under remarkable and unusual circumstances. Elisabeth, a cousin of Mary, the mother of Jesus, and her husband, Zacharias, were elderly and without children. Zacharias was a priest with special responsibilities in the temple. On one occasion, while he was performing his service, he was visited by an angel and was told that his wife would bear him a son and he should call the child John. Due to his and Elisabeth's ages, Zacharias apparently doubted the fulfillment of this promise, and as a result he was struck dumb until after the birth of his son. After the child's birth, Zacharias's relatives and wife were about to give him another name when the father was asked through a written note what name he desired. He wrote, "His name is John," and immediately he regained the power of speech.

John the Baptist was a few months older than Jesus and his period of growth and development is told in only a few short sentences in the New Testament: "And the child grew, and waxed strong in spirit, and was in the desert till the day of his shewing unto Israel." (Luke 1:80.)

The baptism of Jesus by John is another of the classic stories in the New Testament, which states that after John had grown into manhood, "the word of God came unto John the son of Zacharias in the wilderness. And he came into all the country about Jordan, preaching the baptism of repentance for the remission of sins." (Luke 3:2-3.)

John counseled the people to prepare themselves for the coming of the Lord, commanding them to bring forth fruits worthy of repentance and to be baptized by immersion as evidence of their repentance and cleanliness. Multitudes of people followed and were baptized by him, and it was under these circumstances that Jesus came to him to be baptized. When John met Jesus, he recognized him as the promised Messiah and hesitated, claiming that he was not worthy to baptize him, but Jesus insisted, saying: "Suffereth it to be so now: for thus it becometh us to fulfil all righteousness. . . ." (Matthew 3:15.)

Thus Jesus was baptized by John, and, according to the record, when he came up out of the water the heavens were opened unto him and he "saw the Spirit of God descending like a dove, and lighting upon him: And lo, a voice from heaven, saying, This is my beloved Son, in whom I am well pleased." (Matthew 3:16-17.)

This important event is recorded in all four Gospels. The three synoptic Gospels give the impression that the spirit, in the form of a dove, and the voice from heaven were seen and heard only by Jesus. John, however, states in his account that John the Baptist stated: "I saw the Spirit descending from heaven like a dove, and it abode upon him." (John 1:32.)

Both John the Baptist and Jesus were at this time about thirty years of age, and the record in John's Gospel indicates that John the Baptist perhaps did not then fully recognize Jesus, but he had been told that the person upon whom he should see the Spirit descending would be the Messiah. In this account, John the Baptist is recorded as saying: "And I saw, and bear record that this is the Son of God." (John 1:34.)

After his baptism, Jesus went immediately into the wilderness, where he remained for some forty days and nights, fasting and praying in preparation for his ministry. His preparation also included many temptations from Satan, who was determined to divert him from his divine mission. These temptations took the form of three powerful diverting motivators: first, an attempt to appeal to his intense hunger, for Jesus had fasted forty days; second, an attempt to encourage Jesus to astound men by the display of his supernatural powers; and third, an effort to tempt Jesus to make a compromise with the forces of evil through imposing his own personal will in opposition to the purpose for which God had prepared him. Jesus overcame all of these temptations, declaring, "Get thee behind me, Satan." (Luke 4:8.) He also reminded him of the scripture which counsels: "Thou shalt not tempt the Lord thy God." (Luke 4:12.)

After this period of temptation and preparation, it is recorded that Jesus returned in the power of the Spirit and his reputation spread throughout the entire region.

JESUS' OWN CLAIM OF MESSIAHSHIP

The first public appearance of Jesus in which he made at least an indirect claim of his own Messiahship occurred in his hometown of Nazareth, when he quoted Isaiah and claimed that He was fulfilling Isaiah's prophecy. (See Luke 4:13-29.) It was on this occasion that Jesus uttered that renowned statement, "No prophet is accepted in his own country." (Luke 4:24.)

From this experience Jesus must have concluded that any impression he might give that he was the expected Messiah would stand as a serious obstacle to the performance of his mission and would probably make it impossible for him to preach effectively. Consequently, throughout the early part of his ministry he repeatedly warned those who had been healed not to publish it among the people; and, even more emphatically, he admonished those who would call him the Christ, the Son of God, not to employ these identifications lest they obstruct the purpose of his mission.

Moreover, it was from this time on that he referred to himself as the Son of Man, allowing this designation to be accepted in any way that his listeners desired. He applied this identification to himself some forty times during his ministry. Even at the time of Peter's confession, he employed it with his disciples, asking: "Whom do men say that I the Son of Man am?" and Peter responded: "Thou art the Christ, the Son of the living God." (Matthew 16:13, 16.)

JESUS AS THE SON OF MAN

Jesus' use of the identification "Son of Man" was probably based on Daniel 7:13-14, where this prophet states that he saw in a vision "one like the Son of man came with the clouds of heaven, and came to the Ancient of days [Adam], and they brought him near before him. And there was given him [the Son of Man] dominion, and glory, and a kingdom, that all people, nations, and languages, should serve him: his dominion is an everlasting dominion, which shall not pass away, and his kingdom that which shall not be destroyed."

This prophecy most likely referred to the coming of the Messiah and is a direct prediction of Christ's forthcoming advent upon the earth. Yet, the designation "son of man" is also used to identify a prophet, as shown in Ezekiel 2:1-2, when the Lord said to Ezekiel, "Son of man, stand upon thy feet, and I will speak unto thee. And the spirit entered into me when he spake unto me, and set me upon my feet. . . ." In this instance, the identification "son of man" referred to the prophet Ezekiel or to any prophet selected by the Lord, while Daniel's use of the term probably referred to the coming of the Messiah. Using this designation in this way, Jesus may have employed it deliberately as a veil against his ultimate claim of his own Messiahship.

THE WITNESS IN THE GOSPEL OF MARK

It is generally agreed that Mark's account, probably written sometime between A.D. 64 and 67, was the earliest of the Gospels. Matthew was probably written next, followed by Luke, since both of these Gospels show substantial evidence of having been influenced by the writings of Mark. These books form the synoptic Gospels.

The author of Mark was a close associate of Peter, and his work is believed to contain many of the recollections of Peter's close association with Jesus. Written in Greek, possibly at Rome soon after the death of Peter and Paul, it took the form of a biography of the life of Jesus. Mark apparently intended it as a source of support and inspiration to the early Christian community during this period of heavy persecution.

Possibly the first indirect reference by Jesus to the power of his Messiahship, as recorded in Mark, is when he healed the man of palsy and said, "Son, thy sins be forgiven thee." (Mark 2:5.) The account indicates that certain scribes were present who claimed that Jesus was uttering a blasphemy when he assumed the power of forgiving sins. They indicated that only God had this power. It was then that Jesus replied:

> Why reason ye these things in your hearts?
> Whether it is easier to say to the sick of the palsy, Thy sins be forgiven thee; or to say, Arise, and take up thy bed, and walk?
> But that ye may know that *the Son of man hath power on earth to forgive sins*, (he saith to the sick of the palsy),
> I say unto thee, Arise, and take up thy bed, and go thy way into thine house, (Mark 2:8-11; italics added.)

The account then tells how the sick man did take up his bed and went forth healed, glorifying God. Those present who observed this miracle were heard to say that they had never seen this type of thing done before, thus indicating the great power of Jesus.

The next time that Jesus referred to his Messiahship, as recorded in Mark, occurred when he and his disciples were walking through a cornfield on the Sabbath and some of his disciples picked the corn and ate it. Observed by the Pharisees, Jesus and his associates were accused of violating the law of the Sabbath because they performed this small act of labor. Jesus responded by quoting scripture to the Pharisees and then said: "The sabbath was made for man, and not man for the sabbath: Therefore, the Son of man is Lord also of the sabbath." (Mark 2:27-28.) The claim that he was Lord of the Sabbath would be tantamount to a claim of Messiahship.

After Jesus had selected his twelve apostles, he went with them to the coast of Caesarea Philippi and there taught them many of the doctrines and principles they would be required to teach as his representatives. It was there that he asked them who men said he was. Peter responded with his confession that Jesus was the Christ, the Son of the living God. Jesus then charged the disciples that they should tell no man of him. (See Matthew 16:13-17; Mark 8:27-30.)

Although in this statement Jesus does not indicate clear agreement with Peter's confession, the fact that he did not deny it plus his charge to his disciples not to tell anyone of him would seem to indicate indirect approval of Peter's statement and a positive affirmation that he was the Messiah, the Only Begotten of the Father. In fact, this affirmation of his Messiahship appears to be clearly indicated in Mark 8:38, where he declares: "Whosoever therefore shall be ashamed of me and of my words in this adulterous and sinful generation; of him also shall the Son of man be ashamed, when he cometh in the glory of his Father with the holy angels."

It was immediately following this experience that Jesus took three of his disciples, Peter, James, and John, to a high mountain and was transfigured before them, appearing in a shining garment "white as snow." Elias and Moses appeared to the four of them and talked with Jesus. Then a cloud appeared overhead and a voice came from the cloud, saying, "This is my beloved Son: hear him." After this glorious experience, Jesus charged his disciples not to talk about this experience until after his death and resurrection. (Mark 9:2-9.)

It was during the later period of his ministry that Jesus began to speak more frequently about the necessity of his crucifixion and of his resurrection and also to refer to himself more openly as the Christ. As recorded in Mark 9:37, in reference to the sinlessness of small children, he said: "Whosoever shall receive one of such children in my name, receiveth me: and whosoever shall receive me, receiveth not me, but him that sent me."

Also, when his disciples were critical of one who was casting out devils in his name, Jesus told them not to forbid him and then stated: "For whosoever shall give you a cup of water to drink in my name, because ye belong to Christ, verily I say unto you, he shall not lose his reward." (Mark 9:41.)

Possibly the most powerful and impressive self-assertion as the Christ made by Jesus came after his experience in Gethsemane, when he asked the Father three times if the bitter cup of death might pass him by, emphasizing, however, that not his will but the Father's be done. This was after his betrayal by Judas, and when a high priest asked if he was the Christ, Jesus promptly answered and said: "I am; and ye shall see the Son of man sitting on the right hand of power, and coming in the clouds of heaven." (Mark 14:62.)

This was the direct and positive self-claim that probably sealed his doom and set the stage for the crucifixion. It was after this that he was delivered to Pilate and Pilate asked him if he was the King of the Jews. He replied, "Thou sayest it." (Mark 15:2.) Following this statement, he gave no answer to his accusers.

THE WITNESS IN MATTHEW AND LUKE

The other two synoptic Gospels, Matthew and Luke, with few exceptions and in somewhat greater detail duplicate Mark's account of the Savior. Matthew provides more direct claims to the relationship between Jesus and his Father. For example, in Matthew 11:27, Jesus says: "All things are delivered unto me of my Father: and no man knoweth the Son, but the Father. . . ."

Matthew also records an incident when Jesus' disciples told him that his mother and brethren were waiting to speak to him. Jesus responded, "For whosoever shall do the will of my Father which is in heaven, the same is my brother, and sister, and mother." (Matthew 12:50.)

In Matthew 16:27, Jesus, in teaching his disciples, said: "For the Son of man shall come in the glory of his Father with his angels; and then he shall reward every man according to his works." Later he declared: "Verily, I say unto you, that ye which have followed me, in the regeneration when the Son of man shall sit in the throne of his glory, ye also shall sit upon twelve thrones, judging the twelve tribes of Israel." (Matthew 19:28.)

These types of statements, which are reaffirmed in Luke, provide evidence of the claims of Jesus and his apostles of Jesus' direct relationship to his Father in heaven as the Son and also affirm his own personal conviction that he was sent to earth to do the Father's work.

THE WITNESS IN JOHN'S GOSPEL

John's Gospel, written somewhat later than the others, possibly around A.D. 90-100, and apparently for a generation of disciples who had not known Jesus personally, is much more explicit in claiming Jesus as the Christ. John presents the gospel as an eternal plan formulated in the heavens before the world was organized as a basis for the salvation of all of God's children who lived before Jesus' lifetime, during his ministry, and forever to the end of time. Some students and critics of this Gospel advance the theory that John wrote in the style of a Greek tragedy, a form that could be understood by the people of his time. This account differs not only in this way from the synoptic Gospels but also in the fact that John places the major part of the ministry of Jesus in and around Jerusalem and Judea rather than in the Galilean area, the prime area of activity in the other Gospels. In fact, most Bible historians believe that Jesus' ministry was more concentrated in the Jerusalem area, confirming John's account in this respect.

In addition to the four Gospels, at least two others are available in ancient manuscript form but were not accepted as authentic by the compilers of the King James Version. These are the Gospels of James and Thomas, which supply additional details about various aspects of the life of Jesus but do not add materially to that which is found in the four Gospels. No author of the Gospels would claim to have provided a complete and accurate biography of the life of Jesus. Probably Mark's work, being the earliest, gives the most coherent account, while John's account, somewhat in contrast, is a presentation of a series of scenes from the life of the Savior.

In the beginning of his Gospel, John refers to the Word, which, he says, was with God in the beginning, and "All things were made by him; and without him was not any thing made that was made." (John 1:3.) John continues: "And the Word was made flesh, and dwelt among us (and we beheld his glory, the glory of the only begotten of the Father,) full of grace and truth." (John 1:14.) Thus, John's record establishes the fact that Jesus was present in the preexistent council in heaven and was selected by the Father to present his plan of salvation not only to all who would inhabit this earth, but also to all things that were made, under the Father's direction, by Jesus the Christ.

The first direct claim by Jesus himself, as recorded by John, occurred during the Savior's conversation with a Pharisee named Nicodemus, a ruler of the Jews. Based upon what he had heard and seen, Nicodemus was persuaded that Jesus had been sent from God, because he said: " . . . no man can do these miracles that thou doest, except God be with him." (John 3:2.) Nicodemus wanted to know what he should do to earn his own personal salvation, and Jesus declared that he must be born again of water and of the Spirit in order to enter into the kingdom of God. He explained that this meant baptism by water and by the Holy Ghost. During this conversation, Jesus said, in predicting his own death and resurrection:

> And as Moses lifted up the serpent in the wilderness, even so must the Son of man be lifted up:
> That whosoever believeth in him should not perish, but have eternal life.
> For God so loved the world, that he gave his only begotten Son, that whosoever believeth in him should not perish, but have everlasting life.
> For God sent not his Son into the world to condemn the world; but that the world through him might be saved. (John 3:14-17.)

This statement was a direct affirmation that Jesus had been sent from the Father and was his Only Begotten Son.

Following this experience, Jesus left Judea, went through Galilee, and on to Samaria. There, at Jacob's well, a Samarian woman came to draw water, and Jesus engaged her in conversation. He told her about the living water of the gospel, and as he spoke she perceived that he was a prophet. She said to him: "I know that Messias cometh, which is called Christ: when he is come, he will tell us all things." Jesus replied: "I that speak unto thee am he." (John 4:25-26.)

The woman then went and told her neighbors of her experience. A group of them returned with her to the well and when they had talked with Jesus, John records, many believed on his word "and said unto the woman, Now we believe, not because of thy saying: for we have heard him ourselves and know that this is indeed the Christ, the Savior of the world." (John 4:42.)

This impressive witness of Jesus as the Christ came from unbelievers. Moreover, the fact that he so declared himself to the woman at the well who was also an unbeliever adds further evidence to the efficacy of the claim.

The Gospel of John, more so than the other Gospels, records many occasions when Jesus associated himself with his Father, claiming that he and his Father were one, that is, united in purpose. He claimed that he did nothing except that which the Father had instructed him to do and which he had seen the Father also do.

In John 6 are recorded several statements in which Jesus declares that he has been sent by the Father to do the Father's will. After the miracle of feeding the five thousand with loaves and fishes, a multitude followed him to the other side of the Sea of Galilee. There he admonished them not to labor "for the meat which perisheth, but for that meat which endureth unto everlasting life, which the Son of man shall give unto you: for him hath God the Father sealed." (John 6:27.) He then stated that he was the bread of life and that anyone who would believe on him would neither thirst nor hunger. He also emphasized that he had been sent by the Father and that all who believed his teachings would have everlasting life. He declared: "My doctrine is not mine, but his that sent me. If any man will do his will, he shall know of the doctrine, whether it be of God, or whether I speak of myself." (John 7:16-17.)

On another occasion Jesus challenged the Jews and their understanding of God, claiming that they did not know their own God. He said: "Yet ye have not known him; but I know him: and if I should say, I know him not, I shall be a liar like unto you: but I know him, and keep his saying." (John 8:55.) He then made the startling statement that Abraham, whom the Jews worshiped as their father, not only knew of the coming of Jesus, but also rejoiced to see that day. Jesus also claimed that in the preexistence he had existed even before Abraham. This statement so enraged the Jews that they cast stones at him.

During this period, according to John's record, Jesus performed so many miracles and healed so many who were sick, blind, or crippled, and his teachings had such a positive effect upon the people, that many were calling him the Christ. This angered the Jewish leaders to such an extent that they threatened to kill him and denied him entrance to the temple and their synagogues. In fact, they agreed that any man who confessed that Jesus was the Christ would also be put out of the synagogue.

It was under these circumstances that Jesus restored sight to a man who had been blind since birth, and many of the people thus concluded that Jesus was sent from God. The man who was healed declared that this was a fact, and the Jews cast him out. When Jesus heard this, he found the man and asked him if he believed on the Son of God. The man answered, "Who is he, Lord, that I might believe on him?" And Jesus replied, "Thou hast both seen him, and it is he that talketh with thee." John's account declares that the formerly blind man then believed that Jesus was the Christ, and worshiped him. (See John 9:1-38.)

As the anger and resentment of his enemies grew in intensity, the Savior became more outspoken in the purpose of his mission and the fact that he would need to seal his testimony with his blood. John records this statement: "Therefore doth my Father love me, because I lay down my life, that I might take it again. No man taketh it from me, but I lay it down of myself. I have power to lay it down, and I have power to take it again. This commandment have I received of my Father." (John 10:17-18.) Although this statement further angered the Jews, there were also those who were impressed and who inquired of him if he was the Christ. He replied: "I told you, and ye believed not: the works that I do in my Father's name, they bear witness of me." (John 10:25.)

It was soon after this that Lazarus became seriously ill and his sisters, Mary and Martha, sought Jesus to have him come and bless him. Jesus was delayed for four days, and in the meantime Lazarus died. The sisters, deeply sorrowed, told Jesus when he did arrive that had he been there, their brother would have lived. Jesus then made a remarkable statement about death and the resurrection: "I am the resurrection, and the life: he that believeth in me, though he were dead, yet shall he live: And whosoever liveth and believeth in me shall never die. . . ." (John 11:25-26.)

He asked Martha if she really believed this, and she replied, "Yea, Lord: I believe that thou art the Christ, the Son of God, which should come into the world." (John 11:27.) This statement is one of the classic confessions in the New Testament, testifying that Jesus is the Christ, the expected Redeemer, the Son of God.

Realizing that he must soon give his life for his testimony, Jesus began with more emphasis to teach his disciples so that, after his death, they could continue to build upon the work he had started. He instructed them that in his Father's house were many mansions, and that he would go and prepare a place for them. He told them he would send them a comforter, the Holy Ghost, who would teach them all things and bring all things to their remembrance, "whatsoever I have said unto you." He also told them that he would leave his peace with them, not a peace as the world understood it, but a peace of mind, a genuine peace in their hearts and in their souls. (See John 14.)

One of the most direct claims Jesus made of his Messiahship is found in John 17 in his prayer to his Father shortly before his crucifixion. John records that Jesus lifted up his eyes to heaven and said:

> Father, the hour is come; glorify thy Son, that thy Son also may glorify thee. . . .
> And this is life eternal, that they might know thee the only true God, and Jesus Christ, whom thou hast sent.
> I have glorified thee on the earth: I have finished the work which thou gavest me to do.
> And now, O Father, glorify thou me with thine own self with the glory which I had with thee before the world was. (John 17:1, 3-5.)

No more emphatic and direct statement could have been made than this, in which Jesus stated without doubt that he is the Christ, the Son of God, and that he was with the Father in the beginning, before the world was organized. In this prayer he emphasized that he had given to his disciples the glory which his Father had given him. He also emphasized that the unity that existed between him and the Father was the type of unity he wanted for them. He prayed for them to know that he was the chosen Messiah who was, through them, reestablishing his gospel, God's plan of salvation. Thus all of his children could by obedience return to his divine presence. In praying for them, he declared:

> Father, I will that they also, whom thou hast given me, be with me where I am; that they may behold my glory, which thou has given me: for thou lovest me before the foundation of the world.
> O righteous Father, the world hath not known thee: but I

have known thee, and these have known that thou hast sent
me.

And I have declared unto them thy name, and will declare
it: that the love wherewith thou hast loved me may be in them,
and I in them. (John 17:24-26.)

It was following this prayer that Jesus went forth and, according to all four Gospels, willingly gave his life for all mankind.

6
ADDITIONAL WITNESSES OF JESUS' MESSIAHSHIP

I n addition to the four Gospels, as discussed in the previous chapter, the New Testament from beginning to end abounds with testimonies that Jesus is the expected Messiah and that his birth, ministry, and death fulfilled the predictions of the Old Testament prophets of the ultimate advent of a Savior and Redeemer.

To repeat and reemphasize, Jesus' mission was to atone for Adam's disobedience, which had brought death upon mankind and opened the door for individual sin and transgression. This atonement could be effected only by a half-mortal, half-immortal man, the Son of God, who would willingly give his life so that all mankind would be resurrected from death and might be saved from sin through repentance.

It is difficult, if not impossible, for the finite mind to fully comprehend the nature and effect of the atonement. But to God, the Organizer of the universe and the Creator and Author of all things, nothing is impossible. His noble plan of salvation, established before the foundation of the world, is based on natural law and order and ultimately will be comprehensible to the human mind.

There is no doubt that man himself, regardless of his ability and knowledge, could not devise a plan to break the bonds of death. These bonds could be severed only by a supernatural power from God. According to the scriptures, it was the mission of Jesus to break these bonds, to open the way for all human beings to be forgiven of sin and to return ultimately to their Father in heaven. Birth into a resurrected life has been likened symbolically to birth into mortal life. All mortals are born into this life by water, blood, and the spirit. In a like manner, all can be born into eternal life, after this life, only through water, blood, and spirit — the blood provided through the atonement of Christ, the Redeemer; the water, the baptism to which Jesus subjected himself and which he commanded his disciples to teach all mankind to do; and the spirit, the gift of the Holy Ghost.

Another essential part of Jesus' mission was to restore his gospel and plan of salvation with authority upon the earth. This gospel had been given to all the ancient patriarchs and prophets through the ages but had been corrupted and changed to such an extent that it became necessary for one having God's authority to refine it and call it back to God's commandments. This was the essence of the teaching mission in which Jesus was engaged throughout the three years of his ministry. During this time he reestablished his church and the necessary ordinances to enable all who would follow his teachings not only to be blessed with resurrection from death, but also to return into the presence of their Father in heaven through faith, repentance, and obedience to the laws of the gospel.

To accomplish this, it was necessary for Jesus to replace many of the religious procedures that had become a fundamental part of the theology of the day and which were believed to have been established through the laws of Moses. He claimed that he came not to destroy these laws, but to fulfill them and to turn them back into the original truths of the gospel. In so doing, he was forced to take issue with prevailing practices to such an extent that he aroused the wrath of both religious and governmental authorities, with the result that he was crucified. Yet, he gave his life freely and in conformity with the plan established in the councils in heaven long before the world was organized.

After Jesus' crucifixion and resurrection, the Acts of the

Apostles in the New Testament records that he spent forty days with his disciples teaching them and preparing them to continue the teachings of his gospel and the establishment of his church. After this training period, the account records that he was taken into heaven with the promise that he would come again to the earth in power and majesty in the last days.

Having been strengthened by Jesus' presence and teachings, his disciples went forward with power and conviction, taught the gospel, and testified to all who would hear them or read their writings that Jesus was the Christ who had come as promised by the Old Testament prophets. The essence of the message was that he provided the only path to salvation for all mankind. Repeatedly the disciples emphasized that no other path was available to mankind whereby they could be saved. (See Acts 4:12; 10:43; Romans 3:24.)

THE TESTIMONY OF PETER

Among the most dedicated, courageous, and powerful of Jesus' disciples was Simon Peter, who became head of the twelve disciples because of his devotion and leadership ability. Peter, along with the apostles James and John, composed the inner circle of the apostles, and they were exclusively with Jesus on several important occasions, including his transfiguration and the raising of a young girl from the dead. They were also chosen to accompany him when, in the Garden of Gethsemane, he prayed to his Father asking, if possible, that he might be spared the awful cup of the crucifixion; "nevertheless, not what I will, but what thou wilt." (Mark 14:36.)

In spite of the intimate association Peter had with Jesus, at the time of Jesus' condemnation Peter denied three times that he knew him. (See Luke 22:54-62.) It was under these tragic circumstances that Jesus admonished his chief apostle to remain steadfast, saying, "... when thou art converted, strengthen thy brethren." (Luke 22:32.)

After the crucifixion and the resurrection, Peter was converted and became a stalwart, devoted disciple who, along with the apostle Paul, did much to establish and strengthen the foundations of Christianity.

Probably one of the most concise statements of the essence of Jesus' ministry was given by Peter during the conversion of Cornelius and his associates in Jericho. Cornelius was a non-Jew, a centurion of the Roman army, and the Bible records that he was a devout man who, with all his family, feared God. He had been praying for guidance and had received a vision in which he was told to contact Peter, then in Jericho, who would tell him what to do. Up to this point, Peter and the other apostles understood that the gospel was only for the Jews, and so Peter apparently showed some opposition toward teaching a gentile and particularly a centurion, generally hated by the Jews. It was under these circumstances that he received a vision in which a sheet was lowered from heaven on which were all manner of wild beasts, creeping things, and birds that Peter considered unfit to eat. He was commanded to partake of the food and was told that what God had cleansed would be fit for his consumption. He was then told to go to Caesaria, where Cornelius lived, teach him the gospel, and baptize and confirm him a member of the church. (See Acts 10:1-25.)

In this process of teaching and conversion, Peter gave a powerful sermon about the universality of the gospel, stating that God was no respecter of persons and that the gospel Jesus had preached had been proclaimed throughout all Judea and was the way of salvation for everyone. For Cornelius and his people Peter reviewed the life and teachings of Jesus, pointing out how he had been anointed by God with the Holy Spirit and with power and had gone about doing good, healing the sick, and helping those who were oppressed by the devil.

Peter performed many miracles and God was with him always. He related how he had been commanded to preach the gospel and to testify that it was Jesus who was ordained of God to be the judge of the quick and the dead and that through his name, whosoever would believe on him would receive remission of sins. (Acts 10:42-43.)

On one occasion, Peter and John entered the temple at the hour of prayer. There they met a cripple who, lame from birth, was brought every day to the gate of the temple to beg for alms. Upon seeing him, Peter said that neither he nor John had silver or gold, but that they would give freely that which they had. Peter said to the man, "In the name of Jesus Christ of Nazareth, rise up and walk." Then he took him by the hand and raised him up, and the man was healed from that moment.

A large crowd witnessed the miracle and, astonished, asked the apostles how this had been done. Peter responded that the people should not marvel at them nor should they think that by the apostles' own power had they accomplished this miracle. He declared that the God of their fathers had glorified his Son, Jesus Christ, who had been among them, who had been condemned and put to death by them, and who had now been raised from the dead by the Father. Peter said it was through faith in Jesus' name that the lame man had been made strong.

When the people heard these things they demanded of Peter what they should do. Peter replied: "Repent ye therefore, and be converted, that your sins may be blotted out, when the times of refreshing shall come from the presence of the Lord; And he shall send Jesus Christ, which before was preached unto you: Whom the heaven must receive until the times of restitution of all things, which God hath spoken by the mouth of all his holy prophets since the world began." (Acts 3:19-21.)

Then Peter told what Moses had prophesied in Deuteronomy 18:15: "For Moses truly said unto the fathers, A prophet shall the Lord your God raise up unto you of your brethren, like unto me; him shall ye hear in all things whatsoever he shall say unto you. And it shall come to pass, that every soul which will not hear that prophet, shall be destroyed from among the people." (Acts 3:22-23.)

Peter testified to those assembled that this prophet to whom Moses referred was indeed Jesus of Nazareth whom they had crucified. Then he outlined the conviction of all the disciples of Jesus that Jesus was the Redeemer, that he had fulfilled the predictions of the ancient prophets, that he had established his gospel through which men's sins could be blotted out, that he had been crucified to redeem all mankind from death brought through Adam's fall, and that he would come again in the last days to lead all of his followers into eternal life. Peter ended with this powerful statement: "Unto you first God, having raised up his Son Jesus, sent him to bless you, in turning away every one of you from his iniquities." (Acts 3:26.)

THE TESTIMONY OF THE APOSTLE PAUL

Paul, whose name previously had been Saul, was originally one of the most vicious persecutors of the Christians. He was present during the stoning of Stephen, one of the church's great missionaries, and consented to his death. Saul went to the high priest in Jerusalem and obtained the names and addresses of Christians in Damascus so that he might apprehend them and bring them back to Jerusalem. On the road to Damascus, he experienced his remarkable vision when a brilliant light shown around him and he heard a voice saying, "Saul, Saul, why persecutest thou me?" Astonished, Saul replied, "Who art thou, Lord?" And the Lord said, "I am Jesus whom thou persecutest; it is hard for thee to kick against the pricks." (Acts 9:1-5.)

As a result of this vision, Saul was struck both blind and dumb and was instructed to go on to Damascus, where a certain disciple named Ananias would meet him, tell him what he needed to do, and would restore his sight and speech. Saul followed these instructions, and after being taught the gospel he was baptized. Following this miraculous experience, his name was changed to Paul and he became the great missionary who testified mightily of Jesus the Christ, spreading the gospel and organizing churches throughout the area surrounding the Mediterranean Sea. It was in one of these branches, at Antioch, that the disciples of Jesus were first called Christians.

The date of Paul's birth is uncertain, but it is believed to be around the year A.D. 10. He was educated in Tarsus and attended rabbinic school in Jerusalem. A Hellenized Jew, he concentrated particularly on the Hellenist Christians during the period of his vicious persecution of the Christians. As a disciple and later one of the apostles of the church, he completed three long missionary journeys during which he preached and established branches of the church in many important places in Cyprus, Syria, Cilicia, Galatia, Asia, and Greece.

Prior to his martyrdom in Rome in A.D. 67, some thirty-seven years after the crucifixion of Jesus, Paul had laid the foundation for a worldwide Christian church. Courageous, powerful, devoted, and persuasive, he possessed a brilliant mind and was a thorough student of the scriptures and teachings of his Master, Jesus the Christ. He knew, beyond a shadow of a doubt, that Jesus was the Messiah, the Son of God who would come a second time to the earth. He also knew that Jesus was Jehovah of the Old Testament, and that it was Jesus who had taught Adam, Enoch, Noah, Moses, and the ancient prophets.

A few of Paul's statements indicating the depth of his knowledge of the scope and universality of the gospel may be noted in these remarkably perceptive observations:

In Athens on Mars' Hill: "Ye men of Athens, I perceive that in all things ye are too superstitious. For as I passed by, and beheld your devotions, I found an altar with this inscription, To The Unknown God. Whom therefore ye ignorantly worship, him declare I unto you." (Acts 17:22-23.)

To King Agrippa, who had just remarked that Paul had almost persuaded him to be a Christian: "I would to God, that not only thou, but also all that hear me this day, were both almost, and altogether such as I am, except these bonds." (Acts 26:29.)

To the Romans: "For I am not ashamed of the gospel of Christ: for it is the power of God unto salvation to every one that believeth; to the Jew first, and also to the Greek." (Romans 1:16.) "For not the hearers of the law are just before God, but the doers of the law shall be justified." (Romans 2:13.) "For the wages of sin is death; but the gift of God is eternal life through Jesus Christ our Lord." (Romans 6:23.)

Regarding the mode and meaning of baptism: "Know ye not, that so many of us as were baptized into Jesus Christ were baptized into his death? Therefore, we are buried with him by baptism into death: that like as Christ was raised up from the dead by the glory of the Father, even so we also should walk in newness of life." (Romans 6:3-4.)

To the Corinthians, whose dissension had caused the church at Corinth to be divided into three parties: "Now I beseech you, brethren, by the name of our Lord Jesus Christ, that ye all speak the same thing, and that there be no divisions among you; but that ye be perfectly joined together in the same mind and in the same judgment. . . . Now this I say that everyone of you saith, I am of Paul; and I of Apollos; and I of Cephas [Peter]; and I of Christ. Is Christ divided? was Paul crucified for you? or were ye baptized in the name of Paul?" (1 Corinthians 1:10, 12-13.)

To the Christians in Corinth: "Know ye not that ye are the temple of God, and that the Spirit of God dwelleth in you? If any man defile the temple of God, him shall God destroy; for the temple of God is holy, which temple ye are." (1 Corinthians 3:16-17.)

With respect to the antiquity of Christ's gospel: "Moreover, brethren, I would not that ye should be ignorant, how that all our fathers were under the cloud, and all passed through the sea; And were all baptized unto Moses in the cloud and in the sea; And did all eat the same spiritual meat; And did all drink the same spiritual drink; for they drank of the spiritual Rock that followed them: and that Rock was Christ." (1 Corinthians 10:1-4.)

Paul's testimony of Christ: "For I delivered unto you first of all that which I also received, how that Christ died for our sins according to the scriptures; And that he was buried, and that he rose again the third day according to the scriptures: And that he was seen of Cephas, then of the twelve: After that, he was seen of above five hundred brethren at once; of whom the greater part remain unto this present, but some are fallen asleep. After that, he was seen of James; then of all the apostles. And last of all he was seen of me also, as of one born out of due time." (1 Corinthians 15:3-8.)

On our eternal hope in Christ: "If in this life only we have hope in Christ, we are of all men most miserable. But now is

Christ risen from the dead, and become the firstfruits of them that slept. For since by man came death, by man came also the resurrection of the dead. For as in Adam all die, even so in Christ shall all be made alive." (1 Corinthians 15:19-22.)

On baptism as a temporal requirement for all, and those who do not have this opportunity can have it done for them by proxy: "Else what shall they do which are baptized for the dead, if the dead rise not at all? Why are they then baptized for the dead?" (1 Corinthians 15:29.)

To the Galatians who were deviating from Christ's gospel: "I marvel that ye are so soon removed from him that called you into the grace of Christ unto another gospel: Which is not another; but there be some that trouble you, and would pervert the gospel of Christ. But though we, or an angel from heaven, preach any other gospel unto you than that which we have preached unto you, let him be accursed." (Galatians 1:6-8.)

Again, pertaining to the age of Christ's gospel: "And the scripture, foreseeing that God would justify the heathen through faith, preached before the gospel unto Abraham, saying, In thee shall all nations be blessed." (Galatians 3:8.)

On the unity and oneness of the church: "One Lord, one faith, one baptism, One God and Father of all, who is above all, and through all, and in you all." (Ephesians 4:5-6.)

Regarding church organization: "And he gave some, apostles; and some, prophets; and some, evangelists; and some, pastors and teachers: For the perfecting of the saints, for the work of the ministry, for the edifying of the body of Christ: Till we all come in the unity of the faith, and of the knowledge of the Son of God, unto a perfect man, unto the measure of the stature of the fulness of Christ." (Ephesians 4:11-13.)

On Christ also being a God, separate from God the Father: "Let this mind be in you, which was also in Christ Jesus: Who, being in the form of God, thought it not robbery to be equal with God: But made himself of no reputation, and took upon him the form of a servant, and was made in the likeness of men: And being found in fashion as a man, he humbled himself, and became obedient unto death, even the death of the cross." (Philippians 2:5-8.)

On Christ's second coming: "For the Lord himself shall descend from heaven with a shout, with a voice of the archangel, and with the trump of God: and the dead in Christ shall rise first." (1 Thessalonians 4:16.)

On apostasy before Christ's second coming: "Let no man deceive you by any means: for that day shall not come, except there come a falling away first and that man of sin be revealed, the son of perdition." (2 Thessalonians 2:3.)

Regarding the Son, Jesus, who through his Father made the world: "God, who at sundry times and in diverse manners spake in time past unto the fathers by the prophets, Hath in these last days spoken unto us by his Son, whom he hath appointed heir of all things, by whom also he made the worlds." (Hebrews 1:1-2.)

On Jesus as the author of eternal salvation: "Though he were a Son, yet learned he obedience by the things which he suffered; And being made perfect, he became the author of eternal salvation unto all them that obey him." (Hebrews 5:8-9.)

It is apparent from these perceptive gospel statements that Paul possessed a remarkable understanding of the gospel of Jesus Christ. From his miraculous conversion to his violent death in Rome, he was unrelentingly diligent in his missionary efforts and unwavering in his conviction that Jesus is the Christ, the Messiah, the Redeemer.

ADDITIONAL WITNESSES IN THE NEW TESTAMENT

In their general letters to the church, the apostles Peter, James, and John gave additional testimonies of Jesus the Christ. Here are only a few:

On the resurrection of Jesus: "Blessed be the God and Father of our Lord Jesus Christ, which according to his abundant mercy hath begotten us again unto a lively hope by the resurrection of Jesus Christ from the dead." (1 Peter 1:3.)

Jesus teaches his gospel to the spirits who were disobedient at the time of Noah: "For Christ also hath once suffered for sins, the just for the unjust, that he might bring us to God, being put to death in the flesh, but quickened by the Spirit: By which also he went and preached unto the spirits in prison; Which sometime were disobedient, when once the longsuffering of God waited in the days of Noah. . . ." (1 Peter 3:18-20.)

James writes on the importance of example: "James, a servant of God and of the Lord Jesus Christ, to the twelve tribes which are scattered abroad, greeting. . . . Be ye doers of the word, and not hearers only, deceiving your own selves." (James 1:1,22.)

John speaks on the trinity and unity of the Godhead: "For there are three that bear record in heaven, the Father, the Word [Jesus Christ],[1] and the Holy Ghost; and these three are one." (1 John 5:7.)

These few statements are only samples of the testimonies born by Jesus' disciples and apostles. Nearly all of them sealed their testimonies with their blood. According to the records, none of those who were with Jesus after his resurrection and during his special teaching period of forty days ever abandoned their convictions. It was only after their deaths that other teachers arose who brought heresies and false doctrines into the church, as was foreseen by Jesus himself and by many of his closest associates.[2]

[1]With reference to the *Word* as used in this scripture, John, in the first chapter of his Gospel, defines the Word as Jesus Christ. Oneness of the Trinity in the scripture refers to unity in thought and action among the three members of the Godhead. Many times during his ministry Jesus spoke of the importance of this oneness and unity and admonished his disciples to be one, even as he and the Father are one. (See John 17:21-23.)

[2]See Matthew 24:4-5, 23-24; John 16:2-3; Acts 20:29-30; Galatians 1:6-8; 2 Thessalonians 2:1-4, 7-12; 2 Timothy 3:1-9; 4:3-4; 2 Peter 2:1-3; 3:3-4; Revelation 13:4-8.

PART II:
THE WITNESS
FOR CHRIST IN
OTHER ANCIENT
DOCUMENTS

7
THE DEAD SEA SCROLLS AND OTHER PSEUDEPIGRAPHA

The discussion in the foregoing chapters has established these important religious and historical facts:

1. The Old Testament prophets clearly predicted the eventual advent of a Messiah and a Redeemer.

2. Based on the fall of Adam and the turbulent history of the Hebrews, there was a definite need for a Savior.

3. According to the New Testament, Jesus of Nazareth fully and specifically fulfilled all of the conditions of this messianic hope.

4. Also according to the New Testament, this same Redeemer, Jesus the Christ, in the last days, would come a second time to redeem and rescue from their sins all who would accept him as the Christ and would believe and follow his commandments.

5. According to the New Testament scriptures quoted in chapter 2, the gospel of Jesus Christ was taught anciently to and by all of the patriarchs from Adam to Malachi, whose teachings and prophecies are recorded in the Old Testament. These prophets attempted to call the people to repentance, to divert them from their apostate ways, and to persuade them to return to the principles and practices of the original gospel. The fact that their teachings and admonitions are recorded in the Old Testament and in other ancient noncanonical records provides convincing evidence of the antiquity of the gospel. It also explains the appearance of occasional similarities in other

world religions, in the Pseudepigrapha, and, most particularly, in the Dead Sea Scrolls. Certainly, even if part of their writings and warnings were changed, corrupted, or lost by careless and designing false teachers, some of the truth they taught would be found.

Students of religious literature are uniformally agreed that before and during the early Christian era, a significant number of religious records existed that never became a part of the canon of the King James Version of the Bible, which was published in 1611, or of other versions that have been published since. Some of the more important of these ancient noncanonical religious records are the Dead Sea Scrolls; the Pseudepigrapha; the Sheperd of Hermas; the Nag Hammadi Books, discovered in Egypt in 1945; the Chenoboskion Discovery — The Gospel of Thomas; and the Didache.

These religious documents have not been accepted as authentic scriptures. Some of them, including the Dead Sea Scrolls, have been discovered quite recently and others were probably written after the beginning of the Christian era. Some were in existence prior to the lifetime of Jesus, and many are older than any of the manuscripts from which the Old and New Testaments were translated and compiled. All of them, with the possible exception of those more recently discovered, were apparently in existence and available when the King James Version was published.

These ancient records support the story told in the Bible. They reinforce the message that Jesus was the Redeemer prophesied in the Old Testament, and that the gospel he and his disciples taught had been taught by Old Testament prophets long before the Savior's ministry. Thus, they add further testimony to the eternal nature of the gospel and to the fact that God's plan of salvation for his children upon this earth applies to all times. It is the plan presented by Jesus in the council in heaven before this world was organized. Moreover, all of us born into mortality on this earth accepted this plan of salvation in our preexistence.

The very fact that they taught Christianity before the time of Christ provides evidence that the gospel he presented during his mortal life was also presented by him in his preexistent state as the Jehovah of the Old Testament. They add to the testimony that he was the Jehovah of the Old Testament and that it was he who taught Adam, Enoch, Noah, Abraham, and the other prophets. With these facts, it is likely that some of the gospel taught anciently through the Old Testament patriarchs and prophets would have remained upon the earth and would have been available to earnest searchers of the truth, such as the Essenes, prior to the time of the birth of Jesus of Nazareth.

THE DEAD SEA SCROLLS

Probably the most important of the ancient, noncanonical religious records that support the Old and New Testaments are the Dead Sea Scrolls (see Chapter 1), which are still being translated. The original find was of seven relatively intact scrolls which, when translated, contained the following records and scriptures:

The First Isaiah Scroll. This scroll, which contains the full sixty-six chapters of the biblical book of Isaiah, is composed of seventeen parchment sheets sewn together. Written in Hebrew by more than one scribe, it was apparently in use for a long time by the Qumran sect, the historians who kept the records. The scroll shows evidence of considerable wear and much use, and has many notations upon its margins. Scholars have indicated that it is so similar to the Isaiah now in the King James Version that it is doubtful the work involved in its translation would be justified. However, enough of the scroll has been translated to persuade the scholars that this record bears more similarity to the Hebrew Massoretic text than to the Greek Septuagint.

The Second Isaiah Scroll. The second scroll of the Book of Isaiah is less complete and in a more advanced state of deterioration than the first Isaiah scroll. It contains many of the chapters and fragments of most of the other chapters of the book of Isaiah. The Qumran sect obviously had at least two copies of this book for their personal and group discussions and study.

Commentary on the Book of Habakkuk. The Habakkuk commentary sheds interesting light on the concepts of members of the sect and how they interpreted this and possibly other scriptures. This scroll was apparently used in the teaching processes of religious discussions of the group. Habakkuk is one of the shortest books in the Old Testament and was probably written near the end of the seventh century B.C. by a Hebrew prophet who lived in Jerusalem just before its capture by the Babylonians. The Qumran sect seemed to have found their existence under the persecuting Hebrews and Romans as troublesome as the conditions that existed at the time Habakkuk wrote his book. "Yet I will rejoice in the Lord, I will joy in the God of my salvation. The Lord God is my strength and he will make my feet like hinds' feet, and he will make me to walk upon mine high places. . . ." (Habakkuk 3:18-19.)

The Lamech Scroll. When the 1948 Israel-Arab war broke out, this scroll was one of four sent to the United States, where three of the four scrolls were unrolled and microfilmed. While examining this scroll, Dr. John C. Trevor, a fellow of the American School of Oriental Research, accidentally broke off a small piece of the parchment. On one side he found inscriptions in Aramaic, which, when translated, proved to be a first-person statement by Lamech, the father of Noah. Since an ancient Greek list of Aprocrypha books mentions the Book of Lamech, which never has been discovered, Dr. Trevor assumed that this scroll might be it. Consequently, the scroll was given the name the Lamech Scroll. A subsequent translation, however, proved the scroll actually to be an apocryphal Genesis.[1]

The Manual of Discipline. This scroll, called the Manual of Discipline by the translators appears to be a book of rules, regulations and procedures followed by the Dead Sea sect that kept the records. It is particularly important because from it we learn much about the beliefs and practices of the Dead Sea Covenantors together with their similarities to Christians.

The Scroll of the War of the Sons of Light Against the Sons of

[1]Nahman Abigad and Yigael Yadin, *A Genesis Apocryphon* (Jerusalem: Magnes Press, Hebrew University, 1956).

Darkness. This scroll is completely new to religious literature. There is no mention of it nor is there any like it in either Hebrew or Christian records. It describes, in detail, an actual or anticipated war between the Children of Light, the followers of righteousness, and the Children of Darkness, who follow Belial, or the devil. This could be a different or possibly corrupted concept of the second coming of Christ as believed by Christians and taught in the Old and New Testaments.

The Thanksgiving Hymns. This scroll is a record of psalms and hymns of thanksgiving that may have been used in the community in its communal praying and singing and contains many interesting similarities to Christianity.

The Copper Scrolls. Since the original discovery, two additional copper scrolls were discovered in 1952 in nearby caves. These scrolls were so badly corroded and so brittle with age that, for several years, they defied unrolling and translation. More recently, however, the hollow areas inside the scrolls were filled with a cementlike substance and after this hardened, they were sawed into small sheets with a delicate instrument that could be maneuvered around the characters. After translation, these scrolls proved to be some sort of a record of the concealment of the community's treasures, possibly religious and ceremonial artifacts. These artifacts, along with the library of the scrolls, were apparently hidden before the sect was forcibly scattered or destroyed. It has been estimated that if the clues given in the Copper Scrolls, now hidden by some eighteen feet of shifting sands, are accurate and could be followed and discovered, the treasure to be found would be of inestimable value.

The Temple Scroll. This is the latest of the intact, or nearly intact, scrolls to come out of the caves. It was found by Jordanians in the early 1960s and was kept by them under most unfavorable conditions. During the June 1967 Six-Day War, one day after the battle of Jerusalem was over, a group headed by Dr. Yigael Yadin, professor of archaeology at the Hebrew University and former chief of staff of the Israeli Army, obtained this scroll from the Jordanians under conditions that, "when fully told, will seem like a tale from the Arabian nights."[2]

The Temple Scroll is approximately 34 feet long, the longest yet to come from the caves. The outer layers are not well preserved, but Dr. Yadin believes not much is missing. The end of the scroll is complete, as indicated by the blank sheet at the end. The contents of the scroll include numerous religious rules on various subjects, enumeration of the sacrifices and offerings according to the Hebrew festivals, a detailed description of the temple and how it was to be built, and a specific description of how Israel's armies should be organized for protection in the event of an attack from the outside. Because nearly one-half of the scroll deals with matters pertaining to the temple, Dr. Yadin has temporarily named this the Temple Scroll.

The scroll, according to Dr. Yadin, was copied by a skilled scribe of Qumran in the so-called Herodian style. This indicates, he claims, that its composition dates from the second part of the first century B.C. or from the beginning of the first century A.D. In fact, he says, "There are good reasons to believe that the composition took place perhaps even earlier."

In comparing the military instructions contained in the Temple Scroll with those in the scroll of the War of the Sons of Light Against the Sons of Darkness, Dr. Yadin finds a distinct difference. The earlier scroll deals exclusively with an offensive eschatological war, "while here [in the Temple Scroll] we deal with a defensive war against an attacking, unnamed enemy."

Dr. Yadin sees special significance in the discovery of the Dead Sea Scrolls in that the acquisition of the first three scrolls by the late Professor E. L. Sukenik took place on November 29, 1947, the day the United Nations decided on the establishment of a Jewish state in Palestine. This fact, together with the obtaining of the Temple Scroll during the 1967 Six-Day War, at a time when the new State of Israel was militarily organized somewhat along the lines as recommended for the armies of

[2]Yigael Yadin, "The Temple Scroll," a special report published by the Hebrew University in Jerusalem, January 1968.

Israel in the Scroll, seems to him to be in the nature of an interesting coincidence.

OTHER PSEUDEPIGRAPHIC DOCUMENTS

One of the significant aspects of the discovery of the Dead Sea Scrolls is the fact that, along with copies of the Dead Sea Covenantors' own writings and books and fragments of books now contained in the Old Testament, the caves also produced a substantial number of additional fragments of long-lost Hebrew and Aramaic documents. These old records proved to be copies of originals of several already familiar apocryphal and pseudepigraphic books. In fact, in one cave alone, the remains of no less than ninety different manuscripts were discovered.

Among these interesting nonbiblical manuscript discoveries were fragments of two Books of Enoch, fragments of a book known to scholars as the Testaments of the Twelve Partriarchs, and several fragments of the pseudepigraphic record known as the Zadokite text.

These, along with many other old manuscripts long known to students of religious literature, are part of a body of sacred writings known as the Pseudepigrapha. Although these books were available in many languages long before the King James Version was produced, they were excluded from the King James Version because of the uncertainty of their authorship and origin. This happened despite the fact that some of these books were fully accepted as scripture by certain ancient church groups and were highly relied upon by ecclesiastical students and teachers hundreds of years before the production of the King James Version from 1604 to 1611.

THE MEANING OF PSEUDEPIGRAPHA

The word *pseudepigrapha* literally means "uncertain writings." When an author writes under an assumed name or uses the name of some other well-known person, his work is described as having been written under a pseudonym. A pseudepigraphic book, then, is one written pseudonymously.

The pseudepigrapha (*pseude* — uncertain; *pigrapha* — writings) have a most interesting historical background. Apocalyptic works, those writings pertaining to divine revelation or prophecy, were produced extensively by religious writers prior to the third century B.C. Bible scholars believe that Joel is perhaps the latest apocalyptist in the Old Testament whose work was not pseudonymous and pseudepigraphic.

Although there is some question as to whether or not certain chapters in Zechariah and Isaiah were actually written by these authors, it is quite certain that from about the third century B.C. on into the Christian era, all writings claiming to be prophetic or based on divine revelation were written pseudonymously.

In the Hebrew religion after the year 300 B.C., particularly during the post-exilic time, Judaism no longer tolerated additional revelation or prophecy. The law of the first five books of the Old Testament was supreme. Hebrew religious teachers and rabbis could interpret and comment on the law of Moses, but none was allowed to add prophetic revelation to it. This significant, historical fact is described by R. H. Charles as follows:

> Accordingly the first fact we are to recognize is, that from the time of Ezra and Nehemiah the law has not only assumed the functions of the ancient pre-Exilic prophets but it has also, so far as it lay in its power, made the revival of such prophecies an impossibility.
>
> Any one who prophesied under his own name after the time of Ezra and Nehemiah could not expect a hearing unless his prophecy had the authority of the law.[3]

According to a Hebrew interpretation of Zechariah 13:1-5, if any person were to declare himself a prophet, his mother and father were to put him to death. Verse 3 in this scripture specifically declares: "And it shall come to pass, that when any shall yet prophesy, then his father and his mother that begot him shall say unto him, Thou shalt not live; for thou speakest lies in the name of the Lord: and his father and his mother that begot him shall thrust him through when he prophesieth."

[3]Charles, *op. cit.*, viii.

Under these severe circumstances, any prophetic works that were written were usually prepared secretly and certainly pseudonymously, often under the name of a well-known prophet. The works in the Pseudepigrapha are of this nature.

The ban on prophecy and revelation established by the Hebrews during 300 B.C. to A.D. 100 has come to be known among Bible students as the Period of Silence. It is believed that many of the manuscripts known now as the Pseudepigrapha came into existence during these four hundred years.

Some Bible scholars contend that all of these ancient records were written pseudonymously during this period.[4] However, others agree that some of these records, particularly those that carry the names of renowned ancient patriarchs and prophets, could have been copies of earlier scriptures that had been handed down from generation to generation from their original writers.

Certainly, there is no question about whether or not religious records have been kept throughout history. It is entirely possible that some of these accounts were passed by word of mouth from generation to generation, but ultimately they were written down. It is interesting that in the pseudepigraphic book of Adam and Eve, after Adam's death, the following instruction is attributed to Eve:

> But hearken unto me, my children. Make ye then tables of stone and others of clay, and write on them, all my life and your father's [all] that ye have heard and seen from us. If by water the Lord judge our race, the tables of clay will be dissolved and the tables of stone will remain; but if by fire, the tables of stone will be broken up and the tables of clay will be baked [hard].[5]

The Pseudepigrapha are probably composed of some books written during the Period of Silence. Others may actually be copies of earlier manuscripts that could have been copies of still earlier ones written originally by the authors whose names they carry. Moreover, when Moses left Egypt, among the pos-

---

[4]Hastings, *op. cit.*, pp. 39, 609.
[5]See Adam and Eve 50:1-2, in Charles, *op. cit.*, p. 152.

sessions he and his group probably carried with them were records of God's dealings with and commandments to his children given through Adam, Enoch, Noah, and other prophets and patriarchs who lived prior to the time of the exodus. Moses probably carried many of these records in their complete form; he may have condensed and abridged others so as to lighten his load, preserving the essential parts so that the children of Israel would have the instructions of the Lord as they had been given to his ancient prophets. Some of the manuscripts that he took with him were possibly originals, or copies of the originals, that are now books in the Pseudepigrapha.

In making this conjecture, the authors do not intend to infer that Moses did not receive direct communication from the Lord on Mount Sinai. This is recorded and accepted by thoughtful and serious students of the scriptures. As recorded in the Old Testament, Moses received direct instructions from the Lord.

During the time when the British Empire encompassed much of the world, its military conquerors brought back to the British Isles not only priceless paintings and sculpture, but also valuable old manuscripts that were stored primarily in the British Museum in London and at the libraries of Cambridge and Oxford universities. Though other libraries and museums around the world have also been recipients of these manuscripts, more are concentrated in Great Britain than anywhere else.

For hundreds of years most of these valuable records were in storage, untranslated. Possibly one of the earliest and most extensive attempts at translation was made in the thirteenth century by Robert Grosseteste, the Bishop of Lincoln, England. Limiting factors were that Dr. Grosseteste translated the manuscripts from the ancient languages into Latin, and much of his translation work was concentrated on the manuscripts known as the Testaments of the Twelve Patriarchs.[6]

---

[6]Biblical scholars who have worked on these old records agree that the originals now available in Hebrew were written either between 147 and 107 or 109 and 106 B.C. In all probability, these are copies of earlier manuscripts no

In 1773 an English explorer, James Bruce, found some ancient manuscripts in Ethiopia; among them was the Book of Enoch, which he brought back to England. A short time later, possibly early in the nineteenth century, Archbishop Richard Laurence of Cashel made the first English translation of the Book of Enoch, published by Oxford Press in 1821. Subsequent editions were published by Oxford in 1832 and 1838.

Other attempts at the translation of these ancient records, most of which were written in Syriac, Ethiopic, Arabic, Greek, and Latin, were made during the eighteenth and nineteenth centuries. The most complete and authentic translation into English was made in the late 1800s and early 1900s by the English scholar R. H. Charles. Dr. Charles, Archdeacon of Westminster and a renowned biblical scholar, was one of the world's outstanding authorities on ancient languages. His *The Apocrypha and Pseudepigrapha of the Old Testament* was first published by the Clarendon Press at Oxford in 1913 in two volumes but in a rather limited edition. No subsequent editions were published until after the discovery of the Dead Sea Scrolls, which focused renewed attention on certain books in Dr. Charles's work. As a result, Clarendon Press published another edition in 1963.

The following chapters give a brief description of each of the books in Dr. Charles's work, along with some examples of the Christianlike teachings, practices, and doctrines contained therein.

---

longer in existence. Presently there are manuscripts of the Testaments of the Twelve Patriarchs in various libraries around the world. One in Greek is at the Cambridge University Library; one in Armenian is at the Bodleian Library at Oxford. There are two Slavonic versions (recensions, or translations, taken from the Greek) and two Armenian versions (also taken from the Greek). There are also two Greek versions that are recensions from the Hebrew. According to Dr. Charles, these testaments had theological influence on New Testament writers, particularly on the subjects of forgiveness, love of God and neighbor, the universalism of the gospel, the coming of the Messiah and his resurrection, and the writings of anti-Christs. (See Charles, *op. cit.,* pp. 292-94.) Portions of quotations from all pseudepigraphic works that are enclosed in brackets are believed by Dr. Charles to be interpolations by Christian editors.

8
BELIEFS OF THE DEAD SEA COVENANTORS

The ancient records found in the caves around the Dead Sea, authoritatively dated at least two hundred years before the Christian era, have a considerable amount of teachings, doctrines, and organizational details similar to those found in Christianity.

As indicated earlier, the Dead Sea caves have produced fragments or complete scrolls of all but one of the books now included in the King James Version of the Old Testament. In addition, fragments found in the caves include certain pseudepigraphic records as well as scrolls written by Qumran historians.

The religious beliefs and practices of the Qumran sect are found primarily in their Book of Psalms and in the Manual of Discipline, or, as some modern translators have called this document, the Book of the Community Rule.

In the following discussion, quotations are taken primarily from these sources along with the Zadokite Document, the contents of which correspond so closely with the Manual of Discipline that one is obviously a copy of the other or both are from the same original source. The Zadokite Document has been known to scholars of religious literature for many years. It was discovered in 1897 by Solomon Schechter, who found this old manuscript in the Ezra Synagogue in the old city of Cairo. The document was first published in 1910 and received relatively little attention until the discovery of the Dead Sea Scrolls and the translation of the Manual of Discipline. Then it became apparent to scholars that the two documents were virtually identical. In fact, a fragment of an earlier copy of the Zadokite Document was found in one of the Qumran caves. Both of these documents provide insight into the organization of the church or community established by the Qumran Convenantors as well as their rules for membership, their general beliefs and practices, and their religious rituals and ceremonies.

English translations of these old records have been made by a number of linguistic and biblical scholars. This book will focus primarily on the translations of Theodor H. Gaster and Geza Vermes.[1]

THE COVENANTORS' CONCEPT OF GOD

Although the Covenantors did not leave a concise description of the God they worshiped, their writings give a rather clear picture of their general concept of the Almighty.[2] Unlike their Jewish brothers and contemporaries, whose *Jahweh* had come to be endowed with the qualities of vengeance and unbending rigidity, these people believed in a God of kindness and compassion, one who would destroy those who persisted in unrighteousness, but who was forgiving of all, even sinners, if they would repent and turn to lives based on his truths.

Insights into the Covenantors' concept of God is found chiefly in their psalms or hymns and to some extent in the Manual of Discipline in conjunction with the Zadokite Document. For example, the first verse of their Psalm 16 reads:

> [Thou has shed] Thy holy spirit
> On righteous and [wicked alike,]
> [And Thou wilt judge all men]
> [According to their deeds.]

[1]Theodor H. Gaster, *The Dead Sea Scriptures in English Translation* (New York: Doubleday, hardbound ed. 1959); G. Vermes, *The Dead Sea Scrolls in English* (Harmondsworth, Middlesex, England: Penguin Books, Ltd., paperbound ed., 1962).

[2]Much of the material for this section is adapted from the author's book *The Dead Sea Scrolls and Original Christianity* (Salt Lake City: Deseret Book Co., 1958).

In another verse of the same hymn we read:

[For thou art a God gracious] and merciful,
Longsuffering and abounding in lovingkindness and truth,
Forgiving transgression and relenting of [evil]
[Unto them that love Him]
And keep His commandments,
Even unto them that return unto Thee
In faithfulness and wholeness of heart
To serve Thee [and do what is] good in Thy sight.[3]

In the Manual of Discipline we read:

Everyone who wishes to join the community must pledge himself to respect God and man; to live according to the communal rule; to seek God...; to do what is good and upright in His sight, in accordance with what He has commanded through Moses and through His servants the prophets; to love all that He has chosen and to hate all that He has rejected; to keep far from all evil and to cling to all good works; to act truthfully and righteously and justly on earth and to walk no more in the stubbornness of a guilty heart and of lustful eyes. . . .[4]

From these sources, we learn that the Covenantors' God was one who opens the ears of all who will hear, engraves truth on their hearts, schools all who seek after truth, shares his transcendental knowledge with all his children, and is directly accessible to all who desire to approach him by prayer in faith and in humility. He is a God who makes covenants with his children, who is just, and who is the author of all good things. He is the fountain of knowledge, the source of all power, and is filled with mercy and bounteous charity. From him come righteousness, strength, glory, and compassion. He is unchangeable and the judge of all living things.

The hymns tell us that the Covenantors' God has a plan for all of his children that rewards each according to his faithfulness. He is the selector of angels and assigns them to rule over all the universe. His anger toward the wicked is terrible; but toward the just and those who repent, he is full of forgiveness

---

[3]Gaster, *op. cit.*, pp. 194-96.

[4]Ibid., p. 39.

and loving kindness. He teaches his children through the mouths of living prophets and urges all to join with him in everlasting covenants. Through his association in the preexistence with the spirits of all mankind, his spiritual children, he knows in advance of their mortality, their every human act and the purpose and intent of their every thought and speech. He is the father of all who accept his truth and abide by it.

Again, from the psalms:

> Thou art long-suffering in Thy judgements
> and righteous in all Thy deeds.
>
> By Thy wisdom [all things exist] from eternity,
> and before creating them Thou knewest their works
> for ever and ever.
> [Nothing] is done [without Thee]
> and nothing is known unless Thou desire it.
>
> Thou hast created all spirits
> [and hast established a statute] and law
> for all their works. . . .
>
> Thou hast fashioned [all] their [inhabi]tants
> according to Thy wisdom,
> and hast appointed all that is in them
> according to Thy will. . . .
>
> [For Thou hast established their ways]
> for ever and ever, . . .
> In the wisdom of Thy knowledge
> Thou didst establish their destiny before ever they were.[5]

The Dead Sea psalmists wrote of their God as though they understood him and accepted him as a veritable and loving father of their spirits. During the time when the universality of God was generally accepted by the Jews, but when the idea of his fatherhood had not yet firmly taken root, the Covenantors saw their God as their father. Moreover, they apparently thought of him as a glorified human being possessing human, though divine, characteristics and emotions. For example, in Gaster's translation, hymn 11:

[5]Vermes, *op. cit.*, pp. 150-51 (selected verses from hymn no. 1).

> For I know that Thy Mouth is truth,
> And in Thine hand is bounty,
> And in Thy thought all knowledge,
> And in Thy power all might,
> And that all glory is with Thee
>
> In Thine anger comes all judgement of affliction,
> But in Thy goodness pardon abounding;
> And Thy mercies are shed upon all,
> Who do Thy will.[6]

It is a characteristic desire for most of us to think of our Father in heaven as a glorified human being. In the above hymn, the psalmists spoke of their God as having a mouth, a hand, a brain, and a personality with infinite knowledge and power. Moreover, the writer of the hymn attributed to his God the natural human emotions of anger, compassion, mercy, and judgment.

It is interesting that these early searchers after truth should have obtained a concept of the Fatherhood of God, for this was not a dominant idea in the Hebrew religion of the day. It is also significant that their idea of the personality of the Father was similar to that taught by Jesus. The Essene psalmists referred to his mouth and hand and spoke of his thoughts and emotions in human terms that they could understand. This was the way Jesus taught his disciples about his Father. In his prayers, he talked directly with his Father even as we would talk to our earthly fathers; and the Father responded and talked to him and his disciples as one man would talk to another.

In describing the reaction of sinners to God's commandments, the Vermes translation of a portion of Hymn 7 records:

> For [they hearken] not [to] Thy [voice],
>   nor do they give ear to Thy word;
> of the vision of Knowledge they say, 'It is unsure',
>   and of the way of Thy heart, 'It is not [the way]'.
> But Thou, O God, wilt reply to them,
> chastising them in Thy might
>   because of their idols
>   and because of the multitude of their sins.[7]

[6]Gaster, *op. cit.*, pp. 177-78.
[7]Vermes, *op. cit.*, p. 162.

These descriptions of the Covenantors' understanding of their God, together with the sublime picture given by Jesus of the attributes and characteristics of the Almighty, all add substance to the statement given in Genesis that states simply that God created man in his own image. (See Genesis 1:27; 2:7.)

THE GODHEAD

There is no evidence in the Dead Sea Scrolls, as far as they are translated, that the Covenantors had a clear understanding of the three personages in the Godhead. Frequent references are made in their scriptures to God and to the Spirit of God, but there is no reference to God the Father, God the Son, and God the Holy Ghost as separate personages.

It is impressive, however, that an ancient apocryphal scripture known as the Shepherd of Hermas, the original of which is believed to have been written by a son of a member of the Dead Sea sect, has an interesting description of a concept of the nature of the Godhead that might have been among the beliefs of the Dead Sea Covenantors. The discovery and translation of the Dead Sea Scrolls have aroused new interest in certain apocryphal books that once formed a part of the canon of biblical scriptures.[8] The Covenantors apparently used some of these books in their teachings and researches. In any event, their writings have several references to these books.

One of these apocryphal books in which a considerable amount of new interest has been aroused is the Shepherd of Hermas, written in approximately A.D. 139 through A.D. 154 and included in the canon of the scriptures until near the end of the fifth century, when it was changed to noncanonical status by the Council of the Roman Church. This book has been a source of controversy to the scholars because of the way it describes the Godhead. It refers to a Messiah and to a Holy Spirit, who, with God the Father, function as a Holy Trinity. The Father is the dominant God with the Son and Holy Spirit performing in

[8]The Apocrypha, consisting of thirteen books, is the excess of scriptures once contained in the Jewish Massoretic Bible and in the Greek Septuagint, but which never became a part of the King James Version.

special capacities. It also contains another bit of interesting information: the author maintains that the church established by the Son of God already had a long history upon the earth before Christ was sent "to purify it and call it back to God's commandments."[9]

THE CHRISTIAN CONCEPT OF THE TRINITY

The theological concept that the Godhead is composed of three personages — God the Father, God the Son, and God the Holy Ghost — is a fundamental Christian doctrine, though there are considerable differences of opinion among the various Christian churches as to how this Godhead is composed, whether or not the three personages are of one entity or whether they are separate and distinct individuals.

Undoubtedly the most famous and most controversial conclusion regarding the nature of the Godhead was arrived at by the council of the Roman Church called by the Emperor Constantine at Nicea on June 14, 325. After much argument, discussion, and compromise, the council arrived at the conclusion now known as the Nicene Creed, as follows:

> We believe in one God, the Father Almighty, Maker of all things, both visible and invisible: and in one Lord Jesus Christ, the Son [word] of God, begotten of the Father, only begotten, that is of the essence [substance] of the Father. God from God, Light from Light [Life from Life], very God from very God, begotten not made, of one essence [substance] with the Father through whom all things came to be, both things in heaven and things on earth; Who for the sake of us men and for our salvation came down, and was made flesh, and became man, suffered, and rose on the third day, ascended into the heavens [to the Father], is coming to judge living and dead; and in one Holy Spirit.[10]

As one considers this definition, it is difficult to imagine a greater mass of confusion in one single paragraph. No attempt

[9]Edmund Wilson, *The Scrolls from the Dead Sea* (Oxford: Oxford University Press, 1955), pp. 75-76.

[10]Bartlett and Carlyle, *Christianity in History*, as quoted in James L. Barker, *The Divine Church* (Salt Lake City: Deseret News Press), 1951, p. 55.

will be made here to point out and analyze the inconsistencies in the statement. The reader is invited to take his own time to accomplish this. It must be pointed out, however, that this description of the Godhead stands in great contrast to the simple, unconfused information in the New Testament, where Jesus continually and consistently claims that he was the Son of the Father. It is difficult to conceive of a son and a father being the same person. Jesus prayed to the Father and received answers from him. One does not pray to himself and receive answers from himself.

At the time of Jesus' baptism by John the Baptist, Matthew states: " . . . [He] went up straightway out of the water: and, lo, the heavens were opened unto him, and he saw the Spirit of God descending like a dove, and lighting upon him: And lo a voice from heaven, saying, This is my beloved Son, in whom I am well pleased." (Matthew 3:16-17.) Here it can be clearly seen that the three members of the Godhead are separate individuals. Jesus was in the water, the Holy Spirit descended like a dove, and the voice of God was heard, coming from heaven.

Students of theology and leaders of certain churches that contend that God the Father, Christ the Son, and the Holy Ghost are one and the same personage often base their argument on the fact that frequently in the New Testament Jesus refers to the fact that he and his Father are one. With respect to this oneness or unity, it is inconceivable that the three person-ages could act otherwise than in perfect harmony together. In John 17:22-23, Jesus stresses the importance of oneness and unity among his disciples. It is recorded that he said: "And the glory which thou gavest me I have given them; that they may be one, even as we are one: I in them, and thou in me, that they may be made perfect in one; and that the world may know that thou hast sent me, and hast loved them, as thou hast loved me."

Innumerable references are made throughout both the Old and New Testaments to the Spirit of God that can dwell in the whole world or can dwell in the heart of an individual. The scriptures also state that God is love, and we know that love encompasses God's personality, but we need not think of him in the limitless scope of the effects of love. Love is an essential attribute that God showers upon all who believe in him and follow his commandments. It is also a human attribute that can affect immeasurably the lives of all that it touches. The apostle Paul, in 1 Corinthians 13, gives a masterful description of the effects and power of love, indicating that it is the greatest of all human and heavenly attributes.

In describing the nature of spirit and the concept of God and the angels as spirits and as separate beings, Thomas Jefferson wrote in August 1813 to John Adams:

> It is too late in the day for men of sincerity to pretend they believe in the Platonic mysticisms that three are one, and one is three; and yet that the one is not three, and the three are not one. . . . But this constitutes the craft, the power and the profit of the priests. Sweep away their gossamer fabrics of factitious religion, and they would catch no more flies.[11]

In other letters on his religious philosophy, Mr. Jefferson writes that when men speak of immaterial existence, they speak of nothing. When they say that God, angels and the human soul are immaterial, they say that there are no human souls, no angels, no God. He claimed he could not reason otherwise and observed that at what age of the Christian church this doctrine of immaterialism crept in, he did not know, but, he claimed, it is a heresy and that Jesus taught none of it. Although Jesus said that God is a spirit, he did not say what a spirit is nor that it is immaterial. The early Christian Fathers of the first four centuries believed spirit to be matter, pure and ethereal, but nonetheless, matter.[12]

THE HOLY GHOST

Although the Spirit of God is referred to extensively in the Old Testament,[13] the terms Holy Spirit or Holy Ghost are not

[11]*The Writings of Thomas Jefferson* (Philadelphia: J. P. Lippincott, 1871), 6:192.

[12]Ibid., 4:475, 577, 579, 483; 7:61-64, 127-28, 164-69, 185-86, 210-11.

[13]In the scriptures references are both to the Spirit of God and to merely the

found there. From the story recorded in the New Testament, however, it is obvious that the Holy Ghost was a member of the Godhead with a special, important function. It is also obvious from the teachings of Jesus that the Spirit, or the Holy Ghost, is a person distinct from the Father and the Son although he has a close relationship to both. In teaching his twelve disciples, as recorded in John 14, 15, and 16, Jesus indicates that the Spirit proceeds from the Father, is sent by the Son, and comes into the hearts of men to teach them and remind them of the teachings of Jesus. (See John 14:16-17, 26; 15:26; 16:7-14.) The Spirit also reveals the truth to the disciples of Jesus and helps them to bear witness that he is the Christ. (See Matthew 10:20; 16:12-13.)

The New Testament also indicates that although the Holy Ghost was present during the ministry of Jesus for the perfor-mance of special assignments, his continued presence and real function came into being only after the Savior's crucifixion and ascension to heaven. For example, in John 14, Jesus prayed to the Father and promised his disciples that if they kept his commandments the Father would give them another Comfort-er who would abide with them throughout their lives. (See John 14:15-17, 26.) This promise is repeated and amplified in John 15:26, where Jesus says: "But when the Comforter is come, whom I will send unto you from the Father, even the Spirit of truth, which proceedeth from the Father, he shall testify of me."

Jesus also clarifies the fact that the Spirit is separate from himself and the Father in this interesting declaration:

> Howbeit when he, the Spirit of truth, is come, he will guide you into all truth: for he shall not speak of himself; but what-soever he shall hear, that shall he speak: and he will shew you things to come.
> He shall glorify me: for he shall receive of mine, and shall shew it unto you.

Spirit, probably meaning the same. See, for example, Genesis 1:2, 41:38; Exodus 28:3; 31:3, 6; 35:31; Numbers 11:17, 25, 29; Deuteronomy 34:9; Judges 13:25; 14:6; 2 Samuel 23:3; 1 Kings 3:28; 22:24; Ezra 36:26; Nehemiah 9:20; Job 26:13; Psalm 51:11; 104; Isaiah 32:15; 63:10; Daniel 4:8-9; 5:11; Joel 2:28; 12:10; Zechariah 12:10.

> All things that the Father hath are mine: therefore said I, that he [the Holy Ghost] shall take of mine, and shall shew it unto you. (John 16:13-15.)

In the Old Testament, the prophet Joel predicted the time would come when the Lord would pour out his Spirit upon all flesh: " . . . your sons and your daughters shall prophesy, your old men shall dream dreams, your young men shall see visions." (Joel 2:28.) This prophecy was fulfilled, as recorded in Acts 2, on the Day of Pentecost when

> suddenly there came a sound from heaven as of a rushing mighty wind, and it filled all the house where they [the disciples] were sitting.
> And there appeared unto them cloven tongues like as of fire, and it sat upon each of them.
> And they were all filled with the Holy Ghost, and began to speak with other tongues, as the Spirit gave them utterance. (Acts 2:2-4.)

Further evidence in the New Testament that the Holy Ghost is a distinct and separate entity in the Godhead is given by Jesus when he distinguished between his own personality and the personality of the Holy Ghost:

> Wherefore, I say unto you, All manner of sin and blasphemy shall be forgiven unto men: but the blasphemy against the Holy Ghost shall not be forgiven unto men.
> And whosoever speaketh a word against the Son of man, it shall be forgiven him: but whosoever speaketh against the Holy Ghost, it shall not be forgiven him, neither in this world, neither in the world to come. (Matthew 12:31-32.)

Many other references that prove the separate nature of the three personages of the Godhead are found in both the New and Old Testaments.[14] Moreover, from these sources it is evident that God is the Father of our spirits and is the God Almighty. His Son, the Only Begotten of the flesh, Jesus Christ, and the Holy Ghost are separate personages in the Godhead and are one with the Father in purpose and determination to help all men find salvation and exaltation.

[14]See Genesis 1:26-27; Exodus 33:9-12; John 12:28-29; Acts 7:55-56; Hebrews 1:1-3.

It is to be expected that dedicated searchers after truth, such as the Dead Sea Covenantors, who had access not only to the Old Testament scriptures but also to the many other ancient religious records available at the time, could understand the Godhead. Their writings, at least, indicate that they believed they knew their God. In their eleventh hymn, as translated by Gaster, they sang:

> Behold, for mine own part,
> I have reached the intervision
> And through the spirit thou has placed within me,
> Come to know thee, my God.[15]

[15]Gaster, *op. cit.*, pp. 182-83.

9
CHURCH
ORGANIZATION
IN THE
ANCIENT
DOCUMENTS

B oth the Dead Sea Scrolls and the Zadokite Document describe the type of church organization established by pre-Christian searchers after truth. In both documents, the people called themselves by the name of *Edah,* the words used by the early Christians to denote "church." This same name was also used to denote the high council or leading hierarchy of the community. This legislative assembly, or council of "General Authorities," was composed of twelve men of holiness who acted as general guides of the community. According to the Gaster translation, these twelve were supervised by three superiors who were the chief leaders of the community. Supporting them was a regular system of *mebaqqerin* or overseers who were the equivalent of the Greek *episkopoi* or bishop.

From the manual itself this organization structure is described as follows:

> In the formal congregation of the community there shall be twelve laymen and three priests schooled to perfection in all that has been revealed of the entire Law. Their duty shall be to set the standard for the practice of truth, righteousness and justice, and for the exercise of charity and humility in human relations; and to show how, by control of impulse and contrition of spirit, faithfulness may be maintained on earth; how, by active performance of justice and passive submission to the trials of chastisement, iniquity may be cleared, and how one can walk with all men with the quality of truth and in conduct appropriate to every occasion. . . .

> So long as these men exist in Israel, the formal congregation
> of the community will rest securely on a basis of truth.[1]

The Vermes translation of this high leadership in the community is basically similar.[2]

Both of these translations indicate that in the supervision of this church leadership, there is also needed a system of bishops, priests, teachers, and deacons. The objective of the group was to prepare themselves "the way in the desert," which was precisely what John the Baptist said when he quoted from the Old Testament in defining his mission. (See John 1:23.)

A similar type of organization that existed at the time of the ministry of Jesus with which the above descriptions can be compared is in the Didache, the Didascalia, the Apostolorum, and the Apostolic Constitution.

SIMILARITIES TO THE CHURCH JESUS ESTABLISHED

From the above quotation it is apparent that the organization of the church established in the Qumran community was strikingly similar to the organization established by Jesus during the period of his mortal existence. He selected twelve apostles to help him in his work and ordained them with his authority, reminding them that he had selected them rather than that they had selected him. (See John 15:16; Matthew 10:1; Mark 3:14; Luke 6:13.)

After his crucifixion, he appointed Peter, James, and John as the chief leaders of the church and instructed them to select additional apostles, so that the quorum of the twelve would be complete. These too were selected and set apart with authority for the work they were required to do. They then ordained disciples to both the Melchizedek and Aaronic priesthoods and set them apart in the various offices of high priests, seventies, elders, priests, teachers, and deacons.

[1]Gaster, *op. cit.*, pp. 35-55.
[2]Vermes, *op. cit.*, p. 85.

Many references are found in the New Testament that provide proof of the establishment of this type of church organization. For example, Luke describes the selection of the apostles as follows: "And it came to pass in those days, that he went out into a mountain to pray, and continued all night in prayer to God. And when it was day, he called unto him his disciples: and of them he chose twelve, whom also he named apostles." (Luke 6:12-13.)

The office of high priest is described by Paul in his letter to the Hebrews. For example: "For every high priest taken from among men is ordained for men in things pertaining to God. . . ." (Hebrews 5:1.) In another place Paul said, "Thou art a Priest for ever after the order of Melchisedec. . . . Called of God an high priest after the order of Melchisedec." (Hebrews 5:6, 10.)

The calling of the seventy is recorded by Luke as follows: "After these things the Lord appointed other seventy also, and sent them two and two before his face into every city and place, whither he himself would come." (Luke 10:1.)

Elders were ordained in the church, as described in Acts: "And when they had ordained them elders in every church, and had prayed with fasting, they commended them to the Lord, on whom they believed." (Acts 14:23.)

The offices in the Aaronic, or Lesser, Priesthood are described by Paul in his first letter to the Corinthians (1 Corinthians 12:27-31), and he discusses qualifications for bishops and deacons in 1 Timothy (1 Timothy 3:1-13).

It is interesting to note that in the hymns and in the Manual of Discipline as well as in the Zadokite Document, references are made to the "greater" and to the "lesser," probably meaning priesthoods. Although the scholars and translators who have been working on the scrolls seem to have no concept as to the meaning of these terms, other materials in the scrolls indicate that the Covenantors knew a good deal about the Aaronic, or Lesser, Priesthood, and were probably informed about the Melchizedek, or Greater, Priesthood.

Thoughtful students of the scriptures should not be surprised to learn that the Dead Sea Covenantors had this same type of church organization. They had available to them not only the books that later became a part of the Old Testament, but also many other documents that contained truths about the original organization of the church. These manuscripts had been in existence many years before their community was formed. It is not strange that a group of earnest seekers after truth would have found evidence of this type of church organization — after all, Jesus was the Jehovah of the Old Testament, and it was he who taught the ancient patriarchs and prophets and instructed them in church organization. Hence, recognizing the organization as true, they would have put it back into effect.

Since John the Baptist, who came out of the wilderness preaching and baptizing with authority, may have been associated with the Dead Sea Covenantors, it is entirely believable that the Dead Sea sect possessed the Aaronic Priesthood. The authority of John's baptism was not questioned. It was he who baptized the Savior in order to fulfill all righteousness.

Members of the Dead Sea sect practiced a strict order of precedence in their communal meetings and their relationships with each other. Those holding the highest authority were seated and served first, the rest in their proper order. In formal discussions and church teachings each, in order, was to have his opportunity to express his opinions and to present information. No one was to be interrupted, and all who wished had the opportunity to speak.

The Manual of Discipline records:

> This is the rule covering public sessions.
> The priests are to occupy the first place. The elders come second; and the rest of the people are to take their places according to their respective ranks ... everyone is to have an opportunity of rendering his opinion in the common council. No one, however, is to interrupt while his neighbour is speaking or to speak until the latter has finished. Furthermore, no one is to speak in advance of his prescribed rank.[3]

The Manual of Discipline sheds interesting light on the ordinances, doctrines, and beliefs of the Dead Sea Covenantors. It

[3]Gaster, pp. 59-60. See also Vermes, p. 81.

is here that these people show particular evidence of having had access to the teachings of the original gospel. The more significant of these ordinances and practices are discussed in some detail.

THE ORDINANCE OF BAPTISM

It is generally admitted by scholars who have worked on the scrolls that the Qumran Sect practiced baptism by immersion. Dr. Charles T. Fritsch, in his book *The Qumran Community,*[4] points out that following several visits to the caves and to the community ruins he became convinced that the complicated water system that had been excavated "played a larger role in the community than the satisfaction of ordinary, daily needs." He concluded that the only plausible answer is that it was used for "baptismal or lustration rites." In support of this conclusion, he quotes the following from the Manual of Discipline: "He may not enter into the water to touch the purity of the holy men, for they will not be cleansed unless they have turned from their wickedness, for uncleanness is in all the transgressors of his word." And: "The sinner cannot purify himself by atonement nor cleanse himself with water of impurity [i.e., water which takes away impurity], nor sanctify himself with seas or rivers nor cleanse himself with any water of washing."

Many additional quotations might be given from the Manual of Discipline that relate to the practice of baptism by immersion and the accepted belief among the Covenantors that the waters would not wash away an individual's sins unless he thoroughly repented. Dr. Fritsch concludes: "Outward lustrations are no substitute for inward purity of heart. The Holy Spirit and not water, cleanses the man of his iniquities. The outward washing with water is only a symbol of the inward cleansing of the man's heart by the spirit."[5]

The Dead Sea Covenantors must have had considerable

---

[4]Charles T. Fritsch, *The Qumran Community: Its History in Scrolls* (New York: Macmillan, 1956.)

[5]Ibid., p. 69.

scriptural material to guide them in their practice of baptism, since the ordinance predates the ministry of Jesus upon the earth. There is compelling evidence from sources other than the Dead Sea Scrolls that this ordinance originated anciently and even may have been practiced by Adam. Yet, although New Testament writers repeatedly discussed and emphasized the importance of baptism, the Old Testament has no direct reference to it. This has caused some to believe that John the Baptist initiated the ordinance and that Jesus was among the first to be subjected to it. John the Baptist was baptizing throughout Judea before he baptized Jesus. However, if Jesus sought baptism to fulfill all righteousness, and if he instructed his disciples to preach the gospel to everyone, telling them that he who believed and was baptized would be saved, then the gospel, including baptism, must be for everyone — for those who lived before Jesus as well as for those who came after his lifetime. If God is no respecter of persons and if the gospel Jesus taught is eternal, it must be the same yesterday, today, and tomorrow, and baptism, as an essential ordinance, must have existed prior to the birth and baptism of Jesus.

Even though the Old Testament makes no direct reference to baptism, the Hebrew Talmud declares that "proselytes of righteousness" were required to accept baptism prior to admission into the church. Dr. Alfred Edersheim says: "All writers are agreed that three things were required for the admission of such proselytes: circumcision, baptism, and sacrifice." He further states: "The fact that baptism was absolutely necessary to make a proselyte is so frequently stated (in the Talmud) as not to be disputed."[6]

Dr. Edersheim draws an interesting parallel between the missions of John the Baptist and the prophet Elijah. He claims that John's baptism was the counterpart of "Elijah's novel rite on Mt. Carmel."[7] It may be recalled that when Elijah was testing the gods of Baal against the power of Jehovah, he

[6]Alfred Edersheim, *The Life and Times of Jesus the Messiah* (Grand Rapids: W. D. Erdman, 1956), 2:745.

[7]Ibid., 1:255.

covered the sacrifice on the altar with water and then called down fire from heaven to consume it. Dr. Edersheim believes there is a similarity between this rite and the gospel's ordinance of baptism by water and by the Spirit. His conclusion suggests that Elijah was familiar with baptism.

Scholars of the Talmud and the Old Testament see evidence that baptism might have been practiced by Abraham when he and his family left their homeland together with "the souls they had gotten in Haran." (Genesis 12:5.) These souls, according to Dr. Adam Clarke, were actually proselytes, or converts.[8] If they were proselytes, they must have been baptized. Hebrew scholars agree that no proselyte came into the Hebrew religion without baptism.

Dr. Edersheim claims that the Talmud finds a reference to baptism in the Exodus account of Moses when he was instructed by the Lord to "go unto the people and sanctify them . . . and let them wash their clothes." (Exodus 19:10.) He claims that Moses was directed to prepare the Israelites by symbolic baptism of their persons and their garments so that they could enter into the presence of the Lord.[9]

In commenting on the passage "let them wash their clothes," Clarke concludes: "And consequently bathe their bodies for according to the testimony of the Jews, these things always went together."[10]

Apparently the apostle Paul fully understood this baptism during the time of Moses. In his first letter to the Corinthians he states: " . . . all our fathers were . . . baptized unto Moses in the cloud and in the sea." (1 Corinthians 10:1-2.)

With respect to the possibility that Adam and Eve and their family were baptized, the ancient pseudepigraphic book of Adam and Eve provides this interesting insight: "And Adam came to Jordan and he entered into the water and he plunged himself altogether into the flood, even [to] the hairs of his head,

[8]Adam Clarke, *Commentary on the Whole Bible* (New York: Layne and Sanford, 1843), 1:92.

[9]Edersheim, *op. cit.*, 1:274.

[10]Clarke, *op. cit.*, 1:397.

while he made supplication to God and sent [up] prayers to him." It also states: "Therefore the Lord shall repel from Himself the wicked, and the just shall shine like the sun, in the sight of God. And in that time, shall men be purified by water from their sins. But those who are unwilling to be purified by water shall be condemned."[11]

The New Testament is clear and emphatic in establishing baptism as an essential part of original Christianity. Jesus, as noted before, was baptized by John. Further, Jesus always taught that baptism must be performed by immersion. (The word *baptism* means to be immersed.) When Nicodemus, a wealthy man and a ruler of the Jews, came to him for instruction, the Savior said: "Verily, verily, I say unto thee, except a man be born again, he cannot see the kingdom of God." (John 3:3.) Nicodemus was confused by this statement and could not understand how a man could be born again. Jesus explained: "Verily, verily, I say unto thee, Except a man be born of water and of the Spirit, he cannot enter into the kingdom of God." (John 3:5.)

If a man is born of water, it would seem obvious that he would be immersed in the water and then come up out of the water, as did Jesus when he was baptized by John.

The apostle Paul understood and taught the necessity of this type of baptism. In his letter to the Romans he said: "Know ye not, that so many of us as were baptized into Jesus Christ were baptized unto his death? Therefore we are buried with him by baptism into death: that like as Christ was raised up from the dead by the glory of the Father, even so we also should walk in newness of life." (Romans 6:3-4.)

Paul also understood that baptism by immersion had been practiced anciently and had always been a fundamental part of the gospel. In his letter to the Corinthians, he wrote:

> Moreover, brethren, I would not that ye should be ignorant, how that all our fathers were under the cloud, and all passed through the sea;
> And were all baptized unto Moses in the cloud and in the sea;

[11]Charles, *op. cit.*, pp. 135, 141.

> And did all eat the same spiritual meat;
> And did all drink the same spiritual drink: for they drank of
> that spiritual Rock that followed them: and that Rock was [the
> gospel of] Christ. (1 Corinthians 10:1-4.)

In his last instructions to his apostles, Jesus said: "Go ye into all the world, and preach the gospel to every creature. He that believeth and is baptized shall be saved; but he that believeth not shall be damned." (Mark 16:15-16.)

BAPTISM BY PROXY FOR THE DEAD

So much importance was attached to baptism in the gospel of Jesus Christ that a procedure was established whereby those who were not baptized in this life may, if they so desire, accept the ordinance, which may be performed by proxy. It was to this vicarious ordinance that Paul referred when he said: "Else what shall they do which are baptized for the dead, if the dead rise not at all? Why are they then baptized for the dead?" (1 Corinthians 15:29.)

In this statement Paul was actually arguing about the reality of the resurrection. When some of his audience seemed to doubt the resurrection, he asked them about a practice that was well known to the Corinthians — the ordinance of baptism for the dead — and called their attention to the practice to prove his point on the resurrection.

COMMUNAL MEALS

In addition to the ordinance of baptism by immersion, the Dead Sea Covenantors conducted their communal meals as a sort of a sacrament. The Manual of Discipline outlines this procedure as follows: "They shall eat communally, and bless communally, and take counsel communally." In addition: "And it shall be when they arrange the table to eat, or the wine to drink, the priest shall stretch forth his hand first to invoke a blessing on the first portion of the bread and the wine." Then the instructions continued that the individual highest in authority in the congregation was to be served first.[12] Although

[12]Gaster, *op. cit.*, p. 49.

this quotation provides no direct proof that the Covenantors had any concept of the sacrament, still it is interesting that they followed this procedure in the conduct of their communal meals.

The sacrament commemorating the Lord's sacrifice was, of course, instituted by Jesus with his disciples at the time of the feast of the unleavened bread, or the Passover. He took the bread, gave thanks, and broke it; then he gave it to the disciples, saying: "This is my body which is given for you: this do in remembrance of me. Likewise also the cup after supper, saying: This cup is the the new testament in my blood, which is shed for you." (Luke 22:19-20.)

In Old Testament predictions of the coming of a Messiah, his sacrifice was specifically described, and under these circumstances it is possible that the Essene group of truth-seekers could have anticipated the Redeemer's sacrifice and conducted their communal meals as a symbol of this event to come.

The sacrament of the Lord's Supper is mentioned in all three Synoptic Gospels and is referred to in detail by Paul in his first letter to the Corinthians.[13]

KNOWLEDGE

The period of time between approximately 200 B.C. and A.D. 100 is known to Bible scholars as the Period of Silence. During this time the Jews closed the books on apocalyptic witnesses and revelation to such an extent that if any person professed to prophesy or to add to the law of Moses, his parents were instructed to destroy him. Yet, it was during this same period that the Dead Sea Covenantors were searching for the truth, interpreting the scriptures, and making efforts within their own community to bring Judaism back to its original purity and to open the door for revelation.

According to their own writings, the Essenes, or Dead Sea Covenantors, placed heavy emphasis on the importance of individual knowledge, wisdom, and free agency. They be-

[13]See Matthew 26:27-28; Mark 14:22-23; Luke 22:19-20; 1 Corinthians 11:24-29.

lieved that God was the source of all knowledge and that it was the responsibility of every member to gain as much knowledge and wisdom as possible. A man must be judged not on the basis of his material possessions, but rather by his righteousness and the extent of his knowledge and wisdom.

With respect to the importance of knowledge, the Dead Sea Covenantors' scriptures record: "Everyone is to be judged by the standard of his spirituality. Association with him is to be determined by the purity of his deeds, and consort with him by the degree of his intelligence. This alone is to determine the degree to which a man is to be loved or hated."[14]

FREE AGENCY

The Covenantors believed in a doctrine of free agency or, as their concept has since been called, the "Doctrine of the Two Ways." This belief is described in sections 3 and 4 of the Manual of Discipline:

> All that is and ever was comes from a God of Knowledge. . . . now, this God created man to rule the world, and appointed for him two spirits after whose direction he was to walk until the final inquisition. They are the spirits of truth and of perversity. The origin of truth lies in the Fountain of Light, and that of perversity in the Well Spring of Darkness. All who practice righteousness are under the domination of the Prince of Lights, and walk in ways of light; whereas all who practice perversity are under the domination of the Angel of Darkness and walk in the ways of darkness . . . for God has appointed these two things [truth and perversity] to obtain in equal measure until the final age.[15]

Dr. Gaster's translation of the Manual of Discipline continues with the description of the evils that will strike those who follow the ways of darkness and the blessings that will be poured out upon those who seek the ways of light. One of the attributes of those who seek light is a "zeal for righteous government."[16]

[14]Manual of Discipline, in Gaster, *op. cit.*, p. 59.
[15]Ibid., p. 43.
[16]Hymn XIII, in ibid., pp. 185-86.

The belief in the "two ways" is both new and unusual for the time and area; the doctrine was not one held by Judaism or by any of the religions in the area, with the possible exception of a small group in Syria.

The Dead Sea sect believed that man should have his own free choice and choose right or wrong in accordance with his own best judgment. They believed that a just God would reward everyone in accordance with his deeds. This point of view is expressed in many of their scriptures. For example, it is beautifully recorded in one of their hymns:

> On all that keep Thy charge
> Thou bestowest grace abounding
> And mercies never failing;
> But upon all things that defy Thee
> Thou bringest perdition eternal.
>
> So, if mortal men keep faith with Thee,
> Behold, Thou crownest their heads
> With a glory everlasting
> And compassest their works
> With perennial joy.[17]

The concept of free choice was introduced upon the earth in the beginning. When Adam was placed in the Garden of Eden, he was told that of every tree in the garden he could freely eat, but of the tree of the knowledge of good and evil he should not eat, for if he did so, he would surely die. Yet, he was given his choice.

The prophets and teachers in the Old Testament taught this doctrine. The Ten Commandments were given not with compulsion, but through exhortation and with a promise. Moses declared that the Lord had set before his people a blessing and a curse; which of these they received depended upon their own free choice. (See Deuteronomy 7.)

Free agency is a fundamental doctrine of original Christianity. Throughout his ministry, Jesus taught through persuasion and without compulsion. His disciples were instructed to preach the gospel to all who would hear and to show compas-

---

[17]Manual of Discipline, Sect. III, in ibid., pp. 43-45.

sion to those who rejected their teachings. All persons were invited to accept the truth and to allow it to bring peace and joy into their lives, but no one was to be forced. Even those who obstructed the spread of the truth were not to be judged by those who taught it. Rather, Jesus and his disciples taught all to plead with their Father in heaven to forgive the unrighteous and those who unknowingly rejected the light. Even as he was being crucified, Jesus pled to his Father to "forgive them; for they know not what they do." (Luke 23:24.)

THE COVENANTORS' CONCEPT OF SIN

The Dead Sea Covenantors had interesting concepts of sin and the nature of original sin, beliefs that closely paralleled those concepts as taught by Jesus. It is highly probable that these concepts could only have been attained from the original source — the gospel plan of salvation.

The Covenantors believed that the effects of sin are the individual responsibility of each person and not the inherited lot of man. Sin, they believed, is brought upon man by his own acts, and only through his own individual efforts can he remove it from his life. Some direct quotations about individual sin from the Manual of Discipline are interesting. For example, with respect to the "two ways" the manual records:

> This is the way those spirits operate in the world. The enlightenment of man's heart, the making straight before him all the ways of righteousness and truth, the planting in his heart of fear for the judgments of God, of a spirit of humility, of patience, of abundant compassion, of perpetual goodness, of insight, of perception, . . . of a spirit of knowledge . . . of a zeal for righteous government, of a hallowed mind . . . of abounding love . . . of a self-respecting purity, . . . of a modesty of behaviour, . . . a general prudence and an ability to hide within one's self the secrets of what one knows — these are the things that come to men in this world through a communion with the spirit of truth.
>
> But to the spirit of perversity belong greed, remissness in right doing, wickedness and falsehood, pride and presumption, deception and guile, cruelty and abundant insolence, shortness of temper and profusion of folly, arrogant passion, abominable acts in a spirit of lewdness, filthy ways in the

> thraldom of unchasitity, a blasphemous tongue, blindness of eyes, dullness of ears, stiffness of neck and hardness of heart.[18]

All of these characteristics, both good and bad, depend on individual thoughts and actions. Although the good and the bad are constantly present to persuade and tempt, each person makes his own decision.

The Covenantors did not believe that man inherited original sin from his first parents, a sin that he could not himself throw off. Rather, they believed that every man is blessed at birth with a fund of divine knowledge and that evil or wrong-doing is a result of deviation from this great gift. Furthermore, there is no evidence in the Dead Sea scriptures of the belief of some churches in a communion or Eucharist, in which the bread and wine represent the Savior's actual flesh and blood and partaking of them has a redeeming power. Although the Covenantors seemed to practice a form of communion in their communal meals, in doing so they partook of the bread and the wine as symbols and in remembrance of their covenants.

THE ANGEL OF DARKNESS

The Covenantors' concept that Belial or the devil was an angel of darkness is also interesting. Their Manual of Discipline records:

> All who practice righteousness are under the domination of the Prince of Lights, and walk in the way of light: whereas all who practice perversity are under the domination of the *Angel of Darkness* and walk in the ways of darkness. Through the Angel of Darkness, however, even those who practice righteousness are made liable to error.... all of the spirits that attend on him are bent on causing the sons of light to stumble.[19]

The Covenantors' teachings and beliefs indicate that they considered Lucifer to be a fallen angel and an individual being. They believed that he is accompanied by a host of spirits, also

[18]Ibid., p. 44.
[19]Manual of Discipline, in ibid., pp. 39-40.

probably fallen angels, who help in his nefarious work, tempting men's souls and leading them toward iniquity and perdition. Satan and his spirits are ever present to cause the fall of man, and to accomplish this, they employ every possible devious device.

These beliefs of the Covenantors are confirmed in the New Testament. With respect to Christian concepts of these forces of good and evil, the apostle James declared:

> Blessed is the man that endureth temptation: for when he is tried, he shall receive the crown of life, which the Lord hath promised to them that love him.
> Let no man say when he is tempted, I am tempted of God: For God cannot be tempted with evil, neither tempteth he any man:
> But every man is tempted, when he is drawn away of his own lust, and enticed.
> Then when lust hath conceived, it bringeth forth sin: and sin, when it is finished, brings forth death. (James 1:12-15.)

The apostle Peter referred to the angels who, with the devil, sinned and were cast down to hell. (2 Peter 2:4.) In the Epistle of Jude, reference is made to the "angels which kept not their first estate, but left their own habitation." (Jude 6.) Also, John the Revelator described the war in heaven and how Satan was cast out. (Revelation 12:7-12.)

As with Jesus and his disciples, the Covenantors had no misconceptions about the extent to which their individual actions would determine their individual blessings. They had no misunderstanding about the purpose of baptism, which, after repentance, was so important in the remission of sins. They knew that their sins would be forgiven only through sincere repentance and restitution of right for wrong. Baptism was merely a symbol of repentance, and alone it would not remit their sins. Rather, they needed to accept baptism with contriteness of spirit and full repentance in their hearts. Only under these circumstances would their sins be forgiven. These concepts are so similar to Christian doctrines as to leave no doubt that the Dead Sea Covenantors had full access to scriptures that expounded doctrines and principles similar to those taught by Jesus and his disciples. In fact, this similarity is so basic and profound as to lead any sincere and thoughtful person to the conclusion that these concepts must have come from the same source.

THE COMMUNAL RULE

In their community, the Dead Sea Covenantors instituted the communal rule, which meant that everyone who joined brought all of his talents and worldly possessions to the group for the good and benefit of all. In other words, everyone had everything in common.

In the Manual of Discipline this requirement is described as follows:

> All who declare their willingness to serve God's truth must bring all of their mind, all of their strength, and all of their wealth into the community of God, so that their minds may be purified by the truth of His precepts, their strength controlled by His perfect ways, and their wealth disposed in accordance with His just design. They must not deviate by a single step from carrying out the orders of God at the times appointed for them.... They must not turn aside from the ordinances of God's truth, either to the right or to the left.[20]

This practice of "everything in common" was also known to the early Christian church. In Acts we read:

> And all that believed were together, and had all things common:
> And sold their possessions and goods, and parted them to all men, as every man had need.
> And they, continuing daily with one accord in the temple, and breaking bread from house to house, did eat their meat with gladness and singleness of heart. (Acts 2:44-46.)

It would seem more than coincidental that the Dead Sea sect and the early Christian church both followed this communal practice. Surely this type of social and community guidance must have come from the same source.

PARALLELS IN IDEAS AND DOCTRINES

In addition to the aforementioned similarities between the

[20]Ibid., pp. 347-50.

beliefs and practices of the Dead Sea Covenantors and the Christian church established by Jesus, a significant number of impressive parallels in theological ideas and doctrines can be cited. According to the translation of Theodor H. Gaster, there are some 140 of these parallels in the New Testament, including nine in Matthew, five in Mark, four in Luke, and twenty-one in John. The remainder are scattered through the Acts of the Apostles, in Paul's letters, in the general epistles, and in the book of Revelation. A few of these parallels follow.

In the first few verses of John, reference is made to life, which was the light of men: "And the light shineth in darkness; and the darkness comprehended it not." (John 1:5.)

In the Dead Sea Scrolls Manual of Discipline, many references are made to such phrases as "angels of light" and "angels of darkness," the "Spirit of Truth," "Light of Life," "walking in the darkness," "children of Light," all of which also occur frequently in John's Gospel.

In the Dead Sea Scrolls Manual (11:11) is found this statement: "And by his knowledge everything has been brought into being. And everything that is, he established by his purpose; and apart from him, nothing is done." In John's Gospel, there is a similar statement: "[He] was in the beginning with God. All things were made by him; and without him was not anything made that was made." (John 1:2-3.)

John records the experience Jesus had with Nicodemus when he was told that in order for a man to be saved he must be born of the water and the Spirit. Similarly to this, one of the Qumran Psalms tells of God purifying "some of the sons of man to abolish the spirit of perversion from his flesh and to cleanse him by his Holy Spirit from all wicked deeds and sprinkle on him the Spirit of Truth as purifying water."[21]

The authors of most of the books written about the Dead Sea Scrolls refer to these many apparent parallelisms and conclude that Jesus and his disciples must have borrowed many of the

---

[21]For a more detailed analysis of these parallels, see J. M. Allegro, *The Dead Sea Scrolls* (Baltimore: Penguin Books, n.d.), pp. 124-33; also, Wilson, *The Scrolls from the Dead Sea* (Oxford: Oxford University Press), pp. 94-95.

theological concepts from these and other sources. For example, Edmund Wilson asked:

> But what was the relation of Jesus to the ritual and doctrine of the Sect, which the Gospels so persistently echo? Could he have been actually a member of the Sect during those early years of his life where we know nothing about him — where he was or how he occupied himself — or was he in contact with it, as Albright believes, chiefly by way of John the Baptist?... but we know also that the rights and precepts of the Gospels and Epistles both are to be found in every other page of the literature of the Sect.[22]

But what these authors and critics apparently overlook are the facts that the New Testament maintains that Jesus came from the Father with the Father's instructions and with his plan, and that this plan had been formulated in a council in heaven long before the world was organized. Both the Old and the New Testaments affirm that such a council was held. Isaiah alludes to it in his statement about Lucifer being cast out of heaven because he had said in his heart that he would exalt his throne above the stars of God, would ascend above the heights of the clouds, and would be like the Most High. (See Isaiah 14:12-14.) The prophet Job also gives evidence of such a council, as do both Jude, the brother of James, and John the Revelator. (See Job 38:4-7; Jude 6; Revelation 12:7-9.)

If these are the facts, and the biblical records appear to support them as such, then it would seem logical that the plan of salvation presented through Old Testament prophets, even though it was subsequently altered by corrupt and false teachers, would have persisted so that conscientious searchers for the truth, such as the Essenes, would have been able to reestablish a theological foundation with striking similarities to the teachings, doctrines, and church organization reestablished again by Jesus and his followers. A careful reading of the scriptures, both in and out of the Bible, appears to confirm this thesis.

[22]Wilson, op. cit., p. 94.

10
THE BOOK
OF JUBILEES

When the Lord spoke to Moses on Mount Sinai, he instructed him, among other things, to tell the children of Israel that once every fifty years, the year following seven times seven years, should be called a Jubilee and should be a sacred year, a special sabbath when liberty would be proclaimed throughout all the land. It would be a year when all debts would be forgiven, all possessions returned to their original owners, no work performed, and the land itself given a sabbatical rest.

The Book of Jubilees is a rewritten history from Adam's time to the period just prior to when Joshua led the children of Israel across the Jordan into the Promised Land. According to Dr. Charles, this rewriting was done by a learned Pharisee sometime between the years 109 and 105 B.C. The rewriting was done from the point of view of the Law of Moses and was designed to establish the supremacy of that law. The writer incorporated into the story a large body of traditional lore and attempted to overcome some difficulties in the biblical narrative. He also attempted to cover some apparent gaps in the Old Testament story and to eliminate many of the offensive elements found therein. This book, which is considered by scholars to be of tremendous importance to an understanding of the transition in Jewish thought from the time of the prophets Ezra and Nehemiah to the time of the book's composition, reveals how dominant the law had become and how completely it had suppressed apocalyptic prophecy and revelation.

A few of the interesting passages in this rewritten history follow. For example, in predicting the apostasy of the people and their return to the Lord, the author states:

> And I will send witnesses unto them, that I may witness against them, but they will not hear, and will slay the witnesses also, and they will persecute those who seek the law, and they will abrogate and change everything so as to work evil before My eyes. And I will hide My face from them, and I will deliver them into the hand of the Gentiles for captivity, and for a prey, and for devouring, and I will remove them from the midst of the land, and I will scatter them amongst the Gentiles. And they will forget all My law and all My commandments and all My judgments . . . and after this . . . when they seek me with all their heart and with all their soul . . . I will build My sanctuary in their midst, and I will dwell with them, and I will be their God and they shall be my people in truth and righteousness . . . and Zion and Jerusalem shall be holy.[1]

Writing of the time when Adam was driven out of the Garden of Eden, the author records: "And on that day was closed the mouth of all beasts, and of cattle, and of birds and of whatever walks, and of whatever moves, so that they could no longer speak: for they had all spoken one with another with one lip and with one tongue."[2]

In reference to the prophet Enoch, we read:

> And he was the first among men that are born on earth who learnt writing and knowledge and wisdom and who wrote down the signs of heaven according to the order of their months in a book, that men might know the seasons of the years according to the order of their separate months. And he was the first to write a testimony . . . of what he saw in a vision as it will happen to the children of men throughout their generations until the day of judgment; he saw and understood everything, and wrote his testimony, and placed the testimony on earth for all children of men and for their generations.[3]

Abram is born and converted to God, the real Creator. The writer records the following:

> And in this 39th Jubilee, in the second week in the first year, Terah took to himself a wife, and her name was Edna, the

[1]Charles, *op. cit.*, pp. 12-13.
[2]Ibid., p. 17.
[3]Ibid., p. 18. (Enoch kept a written record.)

daughter of Abram, the daughter of his father's sister. And in the seventh year of this week she bear him a son, and he called his name Abram, by the name of the father of his mother; for he had died before his daughter had conceived a son. And the child began to understand the errors of the earth that all went astray after graven images and after uncleanness, and his father taught him writing, and he was two weeks of years old, and he separated himself from his father, that he might not worship idols with him. And he began to pray to the creator of all things that He might save him from the errors of the children of men, and that his portion should not fall into error after uncleanness and vileness . . . and he [Abram] took the books of his fathers, and these were written in Hebrew, and he transcribed them, and he began from henceforth to study them, and I made known to him that which he could not [understand], and he studied them during the six rainy months.[4]

In making his remarkably accurate English translation, Dr. Charles used all of the ancient versions, including the Greek, Ethiopic, Latin, and Syriac.

Since the Book of Jubilees is fundamentally a rewriting of a part of the Old Testament, it does not contain a substantial amount of New Testament-type material. Yet, to the significant extent that the Old Testament influenced the New Testament writers and because Jesus and his disciples so frequently quoted the Old Testament, the book must have significantly influenced New Testament teachings and doctrines. One possible example is found in Hebrews 5 where the author, believed to be Paul, makes reference to the priesthood of Melchisidec, or Melchizedek. (See Hebrews 5:6, 10.) Hebrews 7 continues this reference and applies this priesthood to Jesus himself. The Book of Jubilees makes reference to a "priest of the most high God" in the account of a dream that Levi had at Bethel. The account states: "And he abode that night at Bethel, and Levi dreamed that they had ordained and made him the priest of the Most High God, him and his son forever; and he awoke from his sleep and blessed the Lord."[5]

The priesthood of the Most High God, the greater priest-

[4]Ibid., pp. 30, 32.
[5]Jubilees, in Charles, *op. cit.*, p. 61.

hood, was given the name Melchizedek Priesthood in order to avoid the overuse of the name of God. In other words, the Maccabean high priests applied this title to themselves, based upon the account in Genesis 14.

Concerning angels, there are parallels between the New Testament and the Book of Jubilees. The Jubilee account refers to several types of angels, those of sanctification and those who were set over natural phenomena. These two types of angels are also referred to in the New Testament in Revelation, which describes angels of fire and of waters. (See, for example, Revelation 8 and 9.) Also, guardian angels are referred to in the New Testament in Matthew 18:10 and Acts 12:15.

There are additional New Testament parallels in the Jubilees' discussion of demonology. For example, in Jude 6 reference is made to angels that did not keep their first estate, and 2 Peter 2:4 indicates that "God spared not the angels that sinned, but cast them down to hell, and delivered them into the chains of darkness, to be reserved unto judgment."

In Jubilees, this same idea is recorded about angels who were sent down to instruct mankind, who fell from lusting after the daughters of men, and who were subsequently cast down into hell.[6]

Fallen angels as described in the New Testament — as spirits without bodies whose chief is Satan and who would be punished until the final judgment — are strikingly similar to those described in the Book of Jubilees.[7]

In still another area, that of judgment, the Book of Jubilees and the New Testament bear close resemblance. Throughout Jubilees, reference is frequently made to the fact that men will be judged and punished for their own sins. This same idea is repeated by Paul in Galatians 6:7: " . . . whatsoever a man soweth, that shall he also reap." This same thought is repeated in Colossians 3:25: "But he that doeth wrong shall receive for

[6]Ibid., pp. 18-19.

[7]See Matthew 12:43-45; Luke 11:24-26; Mark 3:22; 1 Corinthians 10:20; Revelation 20:2-3.

the wrong which he hath done: and there is no respect of persons."

The Book of Jubilees and the New Testament are both agreed that the final judgment will take place after the close of the Millennium.

11
THE LETTER
OF ARISTEAS

D r. Charles introduces this interesting book thus:

> The Epistle claims to be a contemporary record, written
> with the personal knowledge of an eye-witness, by Aristeas,
> an officer at the court of Ptolemy Philadelphus (285-247 B.C.),
> to his brother Philocrates, giving an account of the circum-
> stances which led up to the composition of the [Greek] LXX
> [Septuagint] version of the Jewish law.[1]

After the conquest and during the long period of Greek
domination of Palestine, the Greek culture so infiltrated the
Jewish people that a majority of them could no longer speak or
read their native tongue. On the other hand, the Jewish religious concepts and practices were so solidly grounded that
they penetrated Greek thought and philosophy. It was a com-
bination of these two developments that resulted in the necessity of the Jewish scriptures being translated into Greek. The
Letter of Aristeas gives a detailed account of the author's concept of how this translation came about. Dr. Charles believes
that the writer could not have been Greek, and he gives convincing reasons for this conclusion. He believes the author was
probably a Jewish apologist, that the letter was written sometime between 130 and 70 B.C. and that both Philo (? B.C.-A.D. 50)
and Josephus (A.D. 37-95) used the letter in their writings.

Some of the details of the translation of the Hebrew scriptures into Greek, now known as the Septuagint, as translated

---

[1]Charles, *op. cit.*, p. 83.

by Dr. Charles, are most interesting. According to the record, Demetrius of Phaleraum, president of the king's library, had received vast sums of money for purchasing and collecting, insofar as was possible, all the books of the world for the library in Alexandria. After some work on the project, Demetrius reported that he had collected more than 200,000 books but was unable to obtain the Jewish books. The king, upon learning that the problem was primarily one of translation, instructed Demetrius to have this translation accomplished. King Philadelphus then wrote a personal letter to Eleazer, Jewish high priest at Jerusalem, requesting that the work of translation begin. As an incentive to Eleazar, the king offered to free the many Jewish slaves — more than 100,000 at that time — in captivity in various Greek cities.

Arrangements were then made for the Jewish leaders to select six linguistic and religious scholars from each of the twelve tribes and arrange to send them and their families to a special community outside Alexandria, where they could begin translating. Seventy-two scholars were selected for the work; hence the name of the translation, Septuagint, which means seventy. Aristeas's letter gives the names of all of these scholars.

The letter describes the method of translation. Each of the scholars worked separately, comparing results under the direction of Demetrius. This work took seventy-two days, after which a festival was held and many valuable gifts were presented to the translators and their families.

Although the full authenticity of the Aristeas story is questioned by some Bible scholars, references to his work can be found in the writings of Aristobulus, Eusebius, Josephus, and Philo. In fact, as quoted by Charles, Philo states: "Philadelphus, the greatest of the Ptolemies in his anxiety to obtain a translation of the Jewish law, sent ambassadors to the Jewish High Priest, and requested him to select men to carry out his wish. The High Priest, thinking that the King's desire was due to divine inspiration, sent some of his most distinguished men to Alexandria."[2]

---

[2]Aristeas, in Charles, *op. cit.*, p. 91.

The earliest reference to the translation of the Septuagint in patristic literature is found in Justin Martyr in his Apologies 1:31, where he states that Philadelphus, wishing to obtain a copy of the record of the Hebrew prophets, sent to King Herod for the book. When it arrived it was found to be unintelligible, because of the language, and Philadelphus sent a second request to Herod for translators.

Other writers who have referred to Aristeas are Clement of Alexandria, Tertullian (the first writer to mention Aristeas by name), and Eusebius in his epistle Praeparatio Evangelical, which gives a long quotation from the Letter of Aristeas. Epiphanius also has a long account of the translation of the Hebrew Bible and quotes Aristeas as his authority.[3] This reference states that seventy-two translators were placed in thirty-six cells and that their translations were found to be in absolute verbal agreement even in their additions and omissions. Epiphanius claims that it was in about the seventh year of Philadelphus that the translation was made. Other early Christian writers, including Jerome, Draeske, and Augustine, have also referred to the Letter of Aristeas.

One of the interesting passages in the Letter of Aristeas states: "For when men from pure motives plan some action in the interest of righteousness and the performance of noble deeds, Almighty God brings their efforts and purposes to a successful issue."[4]

In reference to the king's request for translators, we read:

> I have determined that your law shall be translated from the Hebrew tongue which is in the use amongst you into the Greek language, that these books may be added to the other royal books in my library. It will be a kindness on your part and a reward for my zeal if you will select six elders from each of your tribes, men of noble life and skilled in your law and able to interpret it, that in questions of dispute we may be able to discover the verdict in which the majority agree, for the investigation is of the highest possible importance.[5]

[3]De Mensuris et Ponderibus, p. 155, as quoted in Charles, op. cit., p. 92.
[4]Aristeas, in Charles, op. cit., p. 96.
[5]Ibid., p. 99.

The letter describes the robe worn by Eleazar, the high priest:

> We were greatly astonished, when we saw Eleazar engaged
> in the ministration, at the mode of his dress, and the majesty
> of his appearance, which was revealed in the robe which he
> wore and the precious stones upon his person. There were
> golden bells upon the garment which reached down to his
> feet, giving forth a peculiar kind of melody, and on both sides
> of them there were pomegranates with variegated flowers of a
> wonderful hue. He was girded with a girdle of conspicuous
> beauty, woven in the most beautiful colours. On his breast he
> wore the oracle of God, as it is called, on which twelve stones,
> of different kinds, were inset, fastened together with gold,
> containing the names of the leaders of the tribes, according to
> their original order, each one flashing forth in an indescribable
> way its own particular colour.

Charles provides a footnote on this quotation as follows:
"The oracle of God (Exodus 28:30) reads: 'Thou shall put in the
breastplate of judgment the Urim and the Thummim.' "
Charles then notes that the Septuagint rendering is in error,
which is mainly responsible for the view that the Urim and
Thummim are identified with jewels in the breastplate.[6]

The Letter of Aristeas, regardless of whether or not its full
accuracy and authority can be established, is without doubt the
most detailed and complete description available of the origin
of the Greek translation of the Septuagint.

The Letter of Aristeas has no specific statement of pre-
Christian doctrines or teachings. However, there are a few
interesting parallels in the New Testament. For example, in
Romans 3:2 and in Hebrews 5:12, the author writes about the
oracles of God being given to the Jews. Aristeas records the
same idea in two places in his letter.[7] In 2 Timothy 4:8, Paul
refers to the "crown of righteousness." This same phrase is
used in Aristeas, verse 28.[8] These ideas do not prove that either
of these accounts was copied from the other. Bible scholars,
however, are convinced that the New Testament writers had
access to these records and were influenced by them.

[6]Ibid., p. 104.
[7]Ibid., pp. 158, 177.
[8]Ibid., p. 92.

12
THE BOOKS
OF
ADAM
AND EVE

I n his introduction to the pseudepigraphic Books of
Adam and Eve, Dr. R. H. Charles observes that they
belong to a cycle of legendary matter of which the Jews were
very fond and which the Christians obtained and developed.

In substance, these books purport to give the history of
Adam and Eve after they were driven from the Garden of
Eden, including brief references to the births of Cain and Abel,
and to Cain's murder of his brother, which resulted in their
parents being overcome with grief until they were promised by
an angel that they would have another son, whom they named
Seth.

The story is chiefly concerned with Adam's ill health and his
aged condition when he and Eve are surrounded by their
sixty-three children whom Adam blesses just before he dies.

For his translation, Dr. Charles used the Greek Apocalypsis
Moses with the aid of the Slavonic Life of Adam. He also
employed the Slavonic, Armenian, Christian, and Gnostic versions of the Adam books. With respect to authorship and date,
Dr. Charles believes that Latin Dita, possibly the earliest
legend concerning Adam and Eve, was written by a Jew of the
Dispersion sometime between A.D. 60 and 300. The exact date,
he concludes, is difficult to pinpoint.

In presenting his materials, he has published the Books of
Adam and Eve in two columns, one under the heading of *Dita
Adae et Evae* (Life of Adam and Eve) and the other column

headed by Slavonic *Dita Adae et Evae* (Slavonic Life of Adam and Eve).

Some interesting passages follow:

The devil speaking to Adam: "Mine are the things of earth, the things of Heaven are God's; but if thou wilt be mine, thou shalt labor on the earth; but if thou wilt be God's [pray] go away to paradise."

Adam's response: "The things of Heaven are the Lord's and the things of earth and Paradise and the whole Universe."[1]

Eve's prayer that she might remain with Adam:

> And Eve prayed [in the hour of her death] that she might be buried in the place where her husband Adam was. And after she had finished her prayer, she sayeth: "Lord, Master, God of all rule, estrange not me thy handmaid from the body of Adam, . . . but deem me worthy, even me unworthy that I am and a sinner, to enter into his tabernacle, even as I was with him in Paradise, . . . just as in our transgression, we were [both] led astray . . . but were not separated. Even so, Lord, do not separate us now."
>
> And Michael came and taught Seth how to prepare Eve for burial. And there came three angels and they buried her [body] where Adam's body was and Abel's. And thereafter Michael spake to Seth and saith: "Lay out in this life every man that dieth till the day of the Resurrection." And after giving him this rule, he saith to him: "Mourn not beyond six days, but on the seventh day, rest and rejoice on it, because on that very day, God rejoiceth [yeah] and we angels [too] with the righteous soul, who has passed away from the earth." Even thus spake the angel, and ascended into heaven, glorifying [God] and saying: "hallelujah."[2]

The Books of Adam and Eve have a significant number of ideas, doctrines, and ordinances similar to those of original Christianity. For example, they include reference to Adam's experience in the Jordan River, which can be interpreted as referring to his own baptism. The account states: "And Adam came to Jordan and he entered into the water and he plunged himself altogether into the flood, even [to] the hairs of his head,

---

[1]Adam and Eve, in Charles, *op. cit.,* p. 135.

[2]Ibid., pp. 153-54.

while he made supplication to God and sent [up] prayers to Him."[3]

Bible scholars are well aware of the fact that baptism as a religious ordinance was practiced long before the time of John the Baptist. As pointed out earlier, baptism by immersion was one of the ordinances practiced by the Dead Sea Covenantors long before the birth of Jesus. This being the case, and the compelling logic that God's plan for his children must be consistent and the same yesterday, today, and tomorrow, the conclusion can be drawn that baptism would have been essential for Adam as well as for all his children and their descendants.

In another statement in the Books of Adam and Eve, baptism is again emphasized as being essential: "... and the just shall shine like the sun, in the sight of God. And in that time, shall men be purified by water from their sins. But those who are unwilling to be purified by water shall be condemned."

Dr. Charles, in his footnote commenting on this statement, testifies that this means baptism, or purification, by water.[4]

Concerning the coming of a Redeemer or Savior, the Books of Adam and Eve state: "And once more iniquity will exceed righteousness. And thereafter God will dwell with men on earth [in visible form] and then, righteousness will begin to shine. And the house of God will be honored in the age and their enemies will no more be able to hurt the men, who are believing in God; and God will stir up for himself a faithful people."[5]

A specific reference to the forthcoming advent of the Christ is given in the Books of Adam and Eve, in Charles's translation, page 144. However, Dr. Charles has put this statement in brackets and indicates in his footnotes that it may have been a later Christian interpolation. It states:

[When 5,500 years have been fulfilled, then will come upon

[3]Ibid., p. 135.
[4]Ibid., p. 141.
[5]Ibid., p. 140.

the earth the most beloved king, Christ, the son of God, to revive the body of Adam and with him to revive the bodies of the dead. He Himself, the Son of God, when He comes will be baptized in the River of Jordan, and when He hath come out of the water of Jordan, then He will anoint from the oil of mercy all that believe in Him. And the oil of mercy shall be for generation to generation for those who are ready to be born again of water and the Holy Spirit to life eternal. Then the most beloved Son of God, Christ, descending on earth shall lead thy father Adam to Paradise to the tree of mercy.]

This quotation is tied so specifically to the story in the New Testament that it becomes difficult not to agree with Dr. Charles that this must have been an addition to the Adam and Eve books by a later Christian editor. Nevertheless, these interesting similarities and parallels, although it cannot be proved that they come directly from the writings of Adam and Eve, take nothing in truthfulness away from the New Testament and certainly add substance and divinity to the instructions of a just Father in heaven to his children and to the eternal nature of his plan for their salvation.

13
THE MARTYRDOM OF ISAIAH

The pseudepigraphic record of the Martyrdom of Isaiah is available for translation only in fragmentary bits of manuscripts. Dr. Charles did his work from three manuscripts titled the Martyrdom of Isaiah, the Vision of Isaiah, and the Testament of Hezekiah.

The first of these three, the Martyrdom of Isaiah, is of Jewish origin and is the one most extensively used by Dr. Charles, who believes it was written by a Jew, probably in the first century A.D. As evidence of this he points out that the details of Isaiah's death at the hands of Manasseh, son of Hezekiah, are found in the Talmud and closely resemble the text Dr. Charles translated.

Briefly, the story is that prior to Hezekiah's death, Isaiah prophesied to him that his son, who would inherit the throne, would turn to evil ways and persecute severely all the prophets and true followers of the Lord, and would cause much lawlessness in Israel, particularly in Jerusalem and in Bethlehem.

When Hezekiah died, Isaiah's prophecy was fulfilled, and through Manasseh's evil prophet Belchira, Isaiah was accused of claiming he had seen God and was still alive, whereas the Hebrew law maintained that no one could see God and live. He was also accused of calling Jerusalem Sodom and its evil prophets and sinful people Gomorrah. With these accusations, the king condemned Isaiah to death by having him sawn asunder. While this cruel execution was taking place, Belchira and his wicked associates stood by, chiding and accusing Isaiah and promising him that if he would admit that he had lied as a prophet, he would be saved. This, of course, Isaiah would not do. In fact, the account indicates that angels protected him so that he suffered no pain during his cruel execution.

One of the sources of Dr. Charles's translation was the long lost Testament of Hezekiah. He states that this manuscript is of great value because of its description of the history of the Christian church at the close of the first century A.D. It describes the worldliness and lawlessness that prevailed among the clergy and the covetousness and growing heresies among the Christians. This seems to agree with prophecies about the apostasy found in both the Old and the New Testaments.

The Martyrdom of Isaiah, as described in this pseudepigraphic work, is considered by Bible scholars as a legend probably based on the account in 2 Kings 21. It is interesting, however, that the author of the New Testament book of Hebrews records a lengthy account of the persecutions and violence perpetrated against the witnesses of the Messiah, in both the Old and the New Testaments. In Hebrews 11:37-38 it is recorded how these "were stoned, they were sawn asunder, were tempted, were slain with the sword: they wandered about in sheepskins and goatskins; being destitute, afflicted, tormented; (Of whom the world was not worthy:) they wandered in deserts, and in mountains, and in dens and caves of the earth." Scripture analysts believe that this statement gives evidence of the accuracy of Isaiah's martyrdom as recorded in the Martyrdom of Isaiah.

Again, it cannot be concluded with certainty that the similarities between the doctrines in these pseudepigraphic books and the New Testament prove absolutely the antiquity of the gospel. Yet it is a reasonable conclusion that if the gospel is eternal and consistent, it would have been given to the ancient prophets. Moreover, records of their teachings would have been preserved, and some portions would probably have filtered down to the writers of the Pseudepigrapha.

14
THE BOOK
OF ENOCH

The ancient patriarch Enoch undoubtedly was one of the greatest of the Old Testament prophets. Yet, the account of his life, his testimony, and his theological contributions are confined to a few lines in Genesis and to four brief references to him in other parts of the Bible. The Genesis account (Genesis 5:18-24) is primarily genealogical. Enoch was the seventh generation from Adam, the son of Jared, and the father of Methuselah. His mortal life on the earth was 365 years, and he was the father of many sons and daughters.

The significant part of this brief account is that Enoch was such a remarkable individual and so righteous that he "walked with God: and he was not; for God took him." (Genesis 5:24.)

Two additional biblical genealogical references about Enoch are given: one in the first chapter of 1 Chronicles and the other in Luke 3, where the ancestry of Jesus is recorded. However, the author of the letter to the Hebrews must have had access to a more detailed record of the life of Enoch, for, in his lecture on faith, he states: "By faith Enoch was translated that he should not see death; and was not found, because God had translated him: but before his translation he had this testimony, that he pleased God." (Hebrews 11:5.)

The account in the general Epistle of Jude also gives evidence of detailed knowledge of Enoch: "And Enoch also, the seventh from Adam, prophesied of these, saying, Behold, the Lord cometh with ten thousand of his saints, to execute judgment upon all, and to convince all that are ungodly among them of all their ungodly deeds which they have ungodly committed, and of all their hard speeches which ungodly sinners have spoken against him." (Jude 14-15.)

There is no doubt among students of religious history that Enoch was a great prophet and patriarch, one highly beloved by God, and that he made a careful and detailed record of his prophecies and teachings. The Book of Jubilees records that Enoch was the first among men who learned writing and who, through revelation, received great knowledge and wisdom, not only about this earth but also the entire universe. According to this record, Enoch wrote his testimony describing a vision he had about what would happen to all the children of men throughout all their generations on the earth until the final day of judgment. This account states that Enoch understood everything, wrote his testimony, and placed it on earth for all children of men and for all their generations.

In still another ancient record, Enoch was commanded by the Lord to journey throughout the land, to prophesy, and to teach the people and call them to repentance. The Spirit of the Lord was upon him and he was so effective that large numbers of people were converted to the Lord's gospel. He also established a city that was so filled with righteousness that it was called the city of holiness, even Zion. The Lord promised him and his people that they would dwell in safety forever, and in time the whole city of Zion was taken up into heaven.

In this account, Enoch was commanded to keep a detailed record, "a book of remembrance," and he was shown in vision all things that would happen upon the earth from the beginning until the time of judgment in the last days.[1]

Bible scholars are now well aware of the fact that long before the Christian era, a Book or Books of Enoch were in existence and were highly thought of by ecclesiastical teachers and writers. Dr. R. H. Charles, in his translation of the Book of Enoch, believes that it was the most important religious literature that

---

[1]See Moses, chapters 6 and 7, in the Pearl of Great Price, published by The Church of Jesus Christ of Latter-day Saints, Salt Lake City, Utah, 1972.

provided reliable information about the advance of high Judaic theology that culminated in Christianity. He believes that this book is by far the most important Pseudepigraph of the first two centuries before the Christian era and that it exerted a tremendous influence on nearly all of the writers of the New Testament. He points out, however, that Bible scholars during the early centuries of the Christian era found much in the book that was questionable. This, coupled with criticism by such authorities as Hilary, Jerome, and Augustine, caused the Book of Enoch to be relegated to the background, finally banned, then lost to the civilized world until the last part of the eighteenth century when three copies were found in Ethiopia.

These manuscripts were found in 1773 by the Abyssinian traveler James Bruce, who took them to France and England. One of the ancient manuscripts, copied by C. G. Woide, is now carefully preserved in the Department of Oriental Books at the Bodleian Library, Oxford, England. The authors have personally examined this priceless manuscript, which is written in Ethiopic on 133 leaves (266 pages), and which contains a handwritten account of how the book was obtained in Ethiopia and brought back to the king of France by Bruce.

This account explains that an Ethiopian monk named Gregonius came to Europe near the end of the seventeenth century and claimed that among the books that his mother country possessed was a copy of the Book of Enoch, which the Abyssinians revered during the time of their paganism, even before they had the books of Moses (brought into Ethiopia during the time of King Solomon, approximately one thousand years before the Christian era). Bruce's letter reports that upon obtaining this information, a Frenchman named DeColbart, who was a collector of ancient manuscripts, commissioned a Dominican monk named Wansteben, who was gathering Arabic manuscripts in Egypt, to try to enter Abyssinia and obtain as many manuscripts as possible, but principally the Book of Enoch. The Dominican monk, however, was unable to enter Ethiopia. After the death of DeColbart, another Frenchman, DuRules, was given a similar commission, but while he was attempting to gain entrance into Ethiopia, he was assassinated at Sonnar in

Nubia, the northern section of what is now Egypt. Following these unsuccessful attempts to obtain the manuscripts, several others tried, but all failed.

Through special arrangements with the king of France, James Bruce was able to enter Abyssinia in 1769. There, after considerable diplomatic maneuvering, he found the Book of Enoch in the Ethiopic Old Testament, placed just in front of the book of Job. The Abyssinians had a great respect for this book, which they considered to be an authoritative scripture of the times before the great flood during Noah's time. At this time the Abyssinians were following the religion of the Sabeans, which, mixed with Judaism, was one of the most ancient religions in the world. When the Abyssinians gave up this religion for Judaism, they still preserved their respect for Enoch, whom they acknowledged to be the patriarch of both nations.

In his letter, James Bruce claims that at the time of his first exposure to the Book of Enoch, the Jews in Abyssinia had preserved it in their own canon of scripture. At the same time, the Christians also considered it to be fully authoritative and had maintained it as a part of their canon. Bruce described it as being much like the book of Revelation. Written in the pure Ethiopian language, or Geez, it was without doubt the most classical book of the Abyssinians and, according to Bruce, was the most valuable and rare treasure he brought back from his travels. Apparently a number of copies of the Book of Enoch were found among various religious groups in Abyssinia, but Bruce was able to bring only three copies of the manuscripts back to Europe.

The first English translation of the Enoch manuscripts was made by Richard Laurence, Archbishop of Cashel, and was published by Oxford University Press in 1821. Other editions were published in 1832 and 1838. Although this translation was widely used by scholars over the next seventy-five years, it never became well known to lay church members. The King James Version, published in 1611, was then in wide circulation and, for the reasons described earlier, the Book of Enoch was not included.

The Charles translation of the Book of Enoch, published in

1913, was included in the second volume of his *Apocrypha and Pseudepigrapha of the Old Testament*. He made his translation from a variety of sources including the ancient versions of the Greek, the Latin, and the Ethiopic. He indicates that the Ethiopic version has been preserved in twenty-nine manuscripts, of which fifteen are in England, eight in France, four in Germany, one in Italy, and one in the United States. He rejects the idea that any of these versions actually date back to Enoch, believing instead that these versions were written by different authors at different times. As with the Book of Daniel, Charles believes the Book of Enoch was originally written partly in Aramaic and partly in Hebrew and was probably composed by authors who belonged to the Hebrew Chasids or to their successors, the Pharisees. He also believes that certain portions of the book were derived from an earlier book of Noah, which exerted considerable influence on certain Enoch chapters.[2]

Regarding when the Book of Enoch was written, Charles points out that since citations from Enoch were found in the Testaments of the Twelve Patriarchs and in the Book of Jubilees, the Book of Enoch was written by the end of the second century B.C. Moreover, the inclusion of Enoch in these important ancient scriptures is strong evidence that certain critics considered it to be inspired. The fact that the Epistle of Jude, written during the first century A.D., quotes from Enoch is proof that it was recognized by Jude as sacred scripture.

The significance of the Book of Enoch in this study lies in the fact that it contains a considerable amount of teachings similar to original Christianity, leading many observers to conclude that Jesus and his disciples borrowed many ideas from this more ancient source. Again, these authorities overlook the basic fact that Jesus and his disciples taught an eternal gospel that had been a plan of salvation from the foundation of the world and had been taught to all of the ancient prophets since the world began. Enoch was one of the greatest of these ancient patriarchs, and surely the gospel he taught would have been consistent with that which Jesus and his disciples taught. Con-

[2]Charles, *op. cit.,* pp. 162-65.

sequently, it is logical that there would be much doctrine similar to that of Christianity in records attributed to Enoch. This would be true even if the Enochan literature had been written by many authors at different times, for these authors would have needed some sources for their materials, and if they had received them by inspiration from the Lord, the materials would be consistent with the teachings received by Enoch from the Lord. Also, if the ancient documents originally based upon Enoch's teachings had been handed down from generation to generation, these too would be consistent with the teachings of Jesus.

A careful study of some of the more important teachings and doctrines in Enoch's document reveals many similarities to early Christianity. In his analysis of the influence of Enoch on the New Testament, Dr. Charles finds four direct similarities in the Gospel of Matthew, five in Luke, and three in John.

For example, in Matthew 26:24 we find this phrase: "... it had been good for that man if he had not been born," and in Enoch 38:2, virtually the same statement: "It had been good for them if they had not been born."

Again, in Matthew 19:28 we find: "... when the Son of man shall sit in the throne of his glory," and in Enoch 62:5, a similar statement: "When they see that Son of Man sitting on the throne of his glory."

Luke 1:52 states: "He hath put down the mighty from their seats," while Enoch 46:5 reads: "... shall put down the Kings ... from their thrones."

In John 5:22 we read: "... the Father ... hath committed all judgment unto the Son," and Enoch 69:27: "The sum of Judgment was given unto the Son of Man."

Four additional similarities are found in the Acts of the Apostles, three in the Epistle to the Hebrews, and at least thirteen in Paul's letters.

In Romans 8:38: "... angels ... principalities ... powers," and in Enoch 61:10: "Angels of power and ... angels of principalities."

In Ephesians 1:9: "... according to his good pleasure," and in Enoch 49:4 the identical phrase.

In Hebrews 4:13, "Neither is there any creature that is not manifest in his sight: but all things are naked and made open before the eyes of him with whom we have to do," and in Enoch 9:6: "All things are naked and open in Thy sight and Thou seest all things and nothing can hide itself from Thee."

These are a few examples of the types of similarities in the Book of Enoch and the New Testament. For a more detailed analysis, the reader is directed to Dr. Charles's translation.[3]

In addition to these similarities, the Book of Enoch has a number of significantly interesting passages for all students of theological literature. For example, in the first paragraph of Enoch is this telling statement: "Enoch a righteous man, whose eyes were opened by God, saw the vision of the Holy One in the heavens, which the angels showed me, and from them I heard everything, and from them I understood as I saw, but not for this generation, but for a remote one which is for to come."

With reference to the second coming of the Messiah, we find these verses:

> The Holy Great One will come forth from His Dwelling,
> And the eternal God will tread upon the earth, [even] on Mt.
> Sinai, . . .
> And appear in the strength of His might from the heaven of heavens.
>
> And all shall be smitten with fear,
> And the Watchers shall quake
> And great fear and trembling shall seize them unto the ends of the
> earth.

The verses then go on to explain what will happen to the righteous:

> But with the righteous He will make peace,
> And will protect the elect,
> And mercy shall be upon them.
>
> And they shall all belong to God,
> And they shall be prospered,
> And they shall be blessed.

[3]Ibid., pp. 180-81.

Enoch's vision of the coming Messiah:

> And there I saw One
> who had a head of days,
> And His head was white like wool,
>
> And with Him was another being whose countenance had the
>   appearance of a man,
> And his face was full of graciousness,
> Like one of the holy angels.

Then Enoch asked the angel who he was and received this reply:

> This is the Son of Man who hath righteousness,
> With whom dwelleth righteousness,
> And who revealeth all the treasures of that which is hidden,
> Because the Lord of Spirits hath chosen him. . . .

Enoch saw the preexistent spirit of the coming Messiah:

> And at that hour the Son of Man was named
> In the presence of the Lord of Spirits,
> Yeah, before the sun and the signs were created,
> Before the stars of the heaven were made,
> His name was named before the Lord of Spirits.

Enoch then saw blessings this Messiah would bring to those who would accept and worship him, and continues: "And for this reason hath he been chosen and hidden before Him. Before the creation of the world and forever more."

Regarding the Christ as the firstfruits of the resurrection, Enoch saw and wrote:

> For in those days the Elect One shall arise,
> And he shall choose the righteous and holy from among them,
> For the day has drawn nigh that they should be saved.

> And the Elect One shall in those days sit on My throne.[4]

Enoch's account of man's responsibility for his own sins:

---

[4]In commenting on these verses, Dr. Charles points out that there are three Jewish doctrines of the resurrection. One is that *all Israelites* are to rise in the resurrection. The second is that *all righteous Israelites* should rise in the resurrection. The third is that *all mankind* are to rise in the resurrection. Each of these doctrines is supported by the Old Testament Pseudepigrapha.

Even so sin hath not been sent upon the earth,
But man of himself has created it,
And under a great curse shall they fall who commit it. . . .

And do not think in your spirit nor say in your heart that ye do
not know and that you do not see that every sin is every day
recorded in heaven in the presence of the Most High.

The righteous to dwell eternally with the Father and with the Son:

> In those days the Lord made to summon and testified to the
> children of earth concerning their wisdom: show unto them;
> for ye are their guides, and the recompense over the whole
> earth. For I and My Son will be united with them forever in the
> paths of uprightness in their lives and ye shall have peace;
> rejoice, ye children of uprightness.[5]

With this beautiful and impressive promise to all who live
righteously and who are obedient to God's commandments,
the ancient Book of Enoch comes to a close.

[5]The quotations on these pages are selected from the Book of Enoch in
Charles, *op. cit.*, pp. 188-218.

15
THE BOOK
OF NOAH
AND THE
LAMECK SCROLL

I n his analysis of the contents and sources of the Book of Enoch, Dr. Charles presents convincing evidence that portions of the Book of Enoch were obtained from an earlier manuscript known as the Book of Noah. The existence of such a book is evident from passages found in the Book of Jubilees, which refers to it and describes instructions given by Noah to his children as well as Noah's descriptions of the evils on the earth that brought about the flood. Certain sections of the Book of Enoch record this same material, indicating a close acquaintance with the Noah document. With respect to the interrelationship of these two books, Dr. Charles observes: "Thus it would appear that the Noah saga is older than the Enoch, and that the latter was built upon the debris of the former."[1]

A portion of one of the scrolls found in the Dead Sea Caves in 1947 is probably derived from or is a copy of fragments of this ancient Book of Noah. This is the Lameck Scroll. (In ancient writings the name of Noah's father is spelled both as "Lamech" and "Lameck.")

The Lameck Scroll and three others of the seven original Dead Sea Scrolls were sent to New York and in 1954 were offered at auction. They were purchased through intermediaries by the Israel government and were subsequently sent to Jerusalem, where, under the expert handling of James

[1]Charles, *op. cit.*, p. 168.

Biberkraut, the Lameck Scroll was opened and deciphered.

As translation of the scroll progressed, it soon became apparent that although it contained some writings purported to have been written by Lameck, it also included writings from other important prophets of the same period. In 1956, this translation was published in English and in Hebrew by two Hebrew scholars, Nahman Abigad and Yigael Yadin, who renamed the scroll "A Genesis Apocryphon" and indicated that the scroll may be divided into four books: the Book of Lameck, the Book of Enoch, the Book of Noah, and the Book of Abraham.[2] Because of the poor condition of the scroll, however, only parts of five of the twenty-two columns of characters were translated and reproduced. This scroll was written in Aramaic, and the five columns that have been partially translated are columns 2, 19, 20, 21, and 22. Briefly, the contents of these columns contained a most interesting story.

An extremely unusual son was born to Lameck. The child's body was as white as snow, with parts as red as a rose. His long hair was white as wool, and his eyes were piercing and brilliant. He was able to talk immediately and, according to Lameck, apparently conversed with the Lord. Lameck, concerned and disturbed, wondered if the boy were his own or possibly had been conceived by one of the "watchers" or "sons of heaven." He discussed the matter with his wife, BatEnosh, who swore that the boy was Lameck's. Lameck took his problem to his father, Methuselah, who in turn sought counsel from his father, Enoch, who previously had been taken (translated) into heaven. Enoch told Methuselah to assure Lameck that his son had been sent from God to do a great work on the earth and that his name should be called Noah.

Although this section of the scroll is incomplete, sufficient of the story was translatable to show that it corresponds almost identically with the fragment of the Book of Noah that Dr. Charles had translated and included as a part of the Book of Enoch. This discovery established beyond a doubt that a Book of Noah was in existence hundreds of years before the Chris-

[2]Abigad and Yadin, *op. cit.*

tian era, and, in all probability, did influence and become a part of the Book of Enoch.

Another column in the Apocryphon is a record of the story of Abram and his sojourn into Egypt as described in Genesis 12. This column, although incomplete, tells about a dream Abram had in which he saw a group of people cutting down two trees, a cedar and a palm. "The palm bursts out crying warns the men that they will be cursed if they cut down the cedar. Thus the cedar is saved for the sake of the palm."[3]

Abram interpreted the dream to his wife, Sarai, and told her he had been instructed by the Lord that if they were to go into Egypt as man and wife, he, Abram, would be killed and Sarai would be taken. Therefore, he said that the Lord instructed him to tell Sarai to tell the Egyptians that she was his sister.

This account of Abram's experience in Egypt is extremely enlightening, since the record in Genesis 12 makes no mention that Abram was instructed by the Lord to tell his wife to deceive the Egyptians with respect to her true identity as his wife. Consequently, Bible scholars and commentators have been seriously critical of Abram's actions in this matter.[4]

Other translatable columns of the Apocryphon describe the beauties of Sarai and how her husband, Abram, grieved when the Egyptians took her from him. They also describe how the plague came upon Pharaoh's house and how Abram was finally called in to heal Pharoah, which he did by laying his hands on Pharoah's head and giving him a blessing. Other details are also presented about Abram's sojourn in Sodom and his experiences with Melchizedek, king of Salem.

This Apocryphon account is also interesting in view of the fact that certain old Midrash documents contain a similar account of how the Lord instructed Abram as he crossed the borders into Egypt, an account that has long puzzled scholars. The Genesis Apocryphon now brings some enlightenment to this question. It also adds proof to the existence of these old

[3]Ibid., p. 23.
[4]See Clarke's *Commentary on the Bible,* 1:93; J. R. Dummelow, *Commentary on the Whole Bible,* p. 21; Robert Jamison, A.R. Fausset, and David Brown, *Commentary on the Whole Bible,* p. 24; John Hastings, *Dictionary of the Bible,* p. 5

records purportedly written by ancient patriarchs and adds substance to the conclusion that they were available to religious students long before the Christian era. It is probably true that the manuscripts from which Dr. Charles and others made their translations might have been written by others, but if so, certainly the authors would have had access to the originals, or copies of the originals, from which they obtained their materials. These facts add further evidence to the eternal nature of the gospel and to the fact that the ancient patriarchs, through divine inspiration, were consistent in their teachings, the same teachings later taught by Jesus and his disciples.

16

THE BOOK OF
THE SECRETS
OF ENOCH
(SECOND ENOCH)

The manuscripts from which the English translations of the Book of the Secrets of Enoch were made were found in Russia and Serbia and first published by the Moscow University Press in 1880.[1] A second, incomplete manuscript of the same book was published in a magazine, *Starine*, in 1884.

When these manuscripts were first published, they were believed by the Russians to be partial copies of, or additions to, the first Book of Enoch. However, when Dr. R. H. Charles studied them, he concluded positively that they were additional and separate Enoch literature and could not possibly be another version of the older, better-known Book of Enoch. Consequently, he designated this later document the Book of the Secrets of Enoch, or Second Enoch. He believed that the manuscripts, which were preserved only in Slavonic, were previously written in Greek in Alexandria, Egypt, probably sometime between 33 B.C. and A.D. 70. He came to this conclusion because the manuscripts contain material from other ancient manuscripts available at that time and because Second Enoch mentions that the temple at Jerusalem was still standing. (The temple was destroyed in approximately A.D. 67 or 70.) Dr. Charles provided a more specific date of the manuscripts' composition, placing them sometime during the first fifty years of the Christian era, or during the lifetime of Jesus.

[1] A. Povov, *Transactions of the Historical and Archaeological Society of the University of Moscow* (Moscow: Moscow University Press, 1880), vol. 3.

Second Enoch contains an account of a dream Enoch had wherein two heavenly beings escorted him through each of the Seven Heavens. There he was able to see the condition of those who had lived righteously or unrighteously during their life on the earth, the tortures and sufferings of perdition, and the glorious blessings of those who had kept the Lord's commandments. He was also given insight into the activities and responsibilities of the heavenly hosts and the happenings upon the earth from the beginning to the end.

After he had been led by his hosts through the Seventh Heaven, he was met by Gabriel, who escorted him on through the other heavens to the Tenth Heaven, where he met and conversed with the Lord himself, who rested on a glorious throne. Here Enoch received the great secrets of God. The Lord showed him everything he had created from the beginning and how this creation had taken place. He then revealed what would come to pass upon the earth during its age of seven thousand years and how, after this period, neither space nor time would be measured. During this experience, Enoch received marvelous instructions from the Lord that, after his return to earth, he communicated to his children.

Significant passages in Second Enoch that reveal the nature of the instructions Enoch received from the Lord include the following:

On the preexistence: "For all souls are prepared to eternity, before the formation of the world."[2]

How Satan and his angels were cast out of heaven: "And one from out the order of angels, having turned away with the order that was under him, conceived an impossible thought, to place his throne higher than the clouds above the earth, that he might become equal in rank to my power. And I threw him out from

---

[2]Charles, *op. cit.*, p. 444. In a footnote commenting on the preexistence, Dr. Charles points out that this is a platonic doctrine and one that was further developed by Philo, who believed that the whole atmosphere is filled with souls and that those who are nearest to earth are the ones who descend and later enter mortal bodies. This doctrine, according to Charles, became a fundamental part of Judaism, which taught that all souls that enter human bodies existed before the creation of the world.

the height with his angels, and he was flying in the air continuously above the bottomless."[3]

How Adam was taught the difference between good and evil: "And I called his name Adam, and showed him the two ways, the light and the darkness, and I told him: 'This is good, and that is bad.' "[4]

On the age of the earth and the period of timelessness: "And I appointed the eighth day also, that the eighth day should be the first-created after my work, and that the first seven revolve in the form of the seventh thousand, and that at the beginning of the eighth thousand there should be a time of not-counting, endless, with neither years nor months nor weeks nor days nor hours."[5]

On the records kept by Enoch: "I know all things, and have written all things into books, the heavens and their end, and their plenitude, and all the armies and their marchings."[6]

On man's relationship to his neighbor: "He who vents anger on any man without injury, the Lord's great anger will cut him down . . . but God demands pure hearts, and with all that only tests the heart of man." And, "He who works the killings of a man's soul, kills his own soul, and kills his own body, and there is no cure for him for all time."[7]

Second Enoch has so many thoughts and language similar to those of Christianity that one minister and author, Dr. Charles S. Potter, has speculated that Jesus himself was the author of it.[8] He makes these interesting observations:

---

[3]Ibid., p. 447.

[4]Ibid., p. 449.

[5]Ibid., p. 451. Dr. Charles's comment on this passage is to the effect that long before the Christian era one thousand years had become regarded as one world day. He further points out that this idea led to a concept of the 6,000-year age of the earth to be followed by a 1,000-year millennium, also to be followed by a period of timelessness.

[6]Ibid., p. 455.

[7]Ibid., pp. 458-65.

[8]Charles F. Potter, *Did Jesus Write This Book?* (Greenwich, Conn.: Fawcett Publications, 1967).

> The more I studied the book and meditated upon it, the more impressed I became by the peculiar similarity of its phrases and thought-forms to those of Jesus, as quoted in the gospels. . . . At any rate, whether or not Jesus was the author, the book was written during his lifetime by someone sympathetic with his ideas and was accepted as Scripture by the early Christian Church. If Jesus was not the author, he quoted from its passages which have always been considered original with it and if it can be proved that Jesus was the author of even a part of this very unusual book, that part should certainly be included in a place of special honor in the New Testament itself.[9]

The important point that Dr. Potter overlooks in his tentative conclusion regarding the possibility of Jesus' authorship of Second Enoch is that Jesus states repeatedly that he came from the Father, that he was in the beginning with the Father, and that the gospel he taught was his Father's plan of salvation, taught from the beginning by his prophets to all his children upon the earth.

In his introduction to Second Enoch, Dr. Charles observes that, in view of the fact that the manuscripts from which he made his translation were written by a Hellenistic Jew in Egypt, the book could not have influenced the New Testament writers. In addition, he believes that Second Enoch was derived from an earlier Hebrew book of Enoch that could have been a recension of the original writings of Enoch.[10] This is a more logical explanation of the source of these pre-Christian similarities. Ancient records were kept and the teachings of prophets were passed down from generation to generation through these records. Unfortunately, they were lost, but they must have influenced the thoughts and writing of later editors and writers who composed the manuscripts from which the English translations were made.

No attempt will be made here to provide a detailed analysis of all the similarities to early Christianity in Second Enoch. Briefly, though, Dr. Charles's translation refers to seven

[9]Ibid., pp. 11, 16.

[10]Charles, *op. cit.*, p. 425.

specific similarities in the Gospel of Matthew, two in John's Gospel, one in the Acts of the Apostles, three in Paul's letters, and three in Revelation. Here are a few examples:

FROM THE NEW TESTAMENT	FROM SECOND ENOCH
Matthew 5:9: Blessed are the peacemakers: for they shall be called the children of God.	2 Enoch 52:11: Blessed is he who implants peace and love.
Matthew 5:34-35, 37: But I say unto you, Swear not at all; neither by heaven; for it is God's throne: Nor by the earth; for it is his footstool: neither by Jerusalem; for it is the city of the great King. . . . But let your communications be, Yea, yea; Nay, nay: for whatsoever is more than these cometh of evil.	2 Enoch 49:1: I swear to you, my children, but I swear not by any oath, neither by heaven nor by earth, nor by any other creature which God created. The Lord said: "There is no oath in me, nor in justice, but truth." If there is no truth in men, let them swear by the words Yea, yea, or else nay, nay.
Matthew 14:27: But straightway Jesus spake unto them, saying, Be of good cheer; it is I; be not afraid.	The phrase "Be of good cheer, be not afraid" is frequently used in 2 Enoch.
John 14:2: In my Father's house are many mansions: If it were not so, I would have told you. I go to prepare a place for you.	2 Enoch 61:2: . . .I know all things, how in the great time [to come] are many mansions prepared for men, good for the good, and bad for the bad, without number many.
Acts 14:15: . . . We also are men of like passions with you, and preach unto you that ye should turn from these vanities unto the living God, which made heaven, and earth, and the sea, and all things that are therein.	In 2 Enoch 24-30, the Lord explains to Enoch how he created the heavens and the earth and all things that are in them.

Ephesians 4:25: Wherefore putting away lying, speak every man truth with his neighbour: for we are members one of another.

2 Enoch 42:12: Blessed is he in whom is truth, that he may speak truth to his neighbour.

Colossians 1:16: For by him were all things created, that are in heaven, and that are in earth, visible and invisible, whether they be thrones, or dominions, or principalities, or powers: all things were created by him, and for him.

In 2 Enoch 20, the Lord tells Enoch about dominions, orders, governments, and thrones. Enoch is told that the Lord created "things non-being and visible from invisible things."

Students of the pseudepigraphic book of Second Enoch also point out much similarity between this book and John's book of Revelation. Both deal extensively with eschatological happenings and both record detailed visions about the nature of the heavens and the inhabitants who dwell therein.

Considering the fundamental truths and necessity that the gospel must be consistent and eternal, it must be concluded that both First and Second Enoch did originally come from Enoch, who received direct instructions and inspiration from the Lord and communicated them to his children and his people. In view of the fact that Jesus and his disciples taught the same doctrine in almost identical terms, this fact can only support the eternal, unchangeable nature of the gospel.

17
THE
TESTAMENTS
OF THE TWELVE
PATRIARCHS

T he ancient documents known as the Testaments of the Twelve Patriarchs were well known to scholars many hundreds of years ago, but it was not until the discovery of the Dead Sea Scrolls that the attention of modern scholars was focused on these old testaments. Fragments of them were found along with the other documents, indicating that the Dead Sea Covenantors not only were acquainted with these ancient documents and used them in their teachings, but also that they considered them scripturally as important as the other fragments of manuscripts that later became part of the Old Testament.

The Testaments of the Twelve Patriarchs contain what is claimed to be the last testimony given by each of the twelve sons of Jacob to their assembled families just prior to their deaths. As in the Books of Enoch, this literature has much information that helps to bridge the gap between the Old and the New Testaments and provides many insights into the origins of Christianity. Dr. Charles tells of another important contribution of these pseudepigraphic testaments:

> The main, the overwhelming value of the book lies not in this province [Messianic expectations of Judaism] but in its ethical teaching, which has achieved a real immortality by influencing the thought and diction of the writers of the New Testament, and even those of our Lord. This ethical teaching, which is very much higher and purer than that of the Old Testament, is yet its true spiritual child, and helps to bridge

the chasm that divides the ethics of the Old and the New Testaments.[1]

Dr. Charles believes that these manuscripts were originally written around the third century B.C. and that the author was a Pharisee who was influenced by his loyalty to his party and his respect for John Hyrcanus.[2]

Copies of the Testaments of the Twelve Patriarchs exist in many libraries and museums around the world. The authors examined a copy of the Testament of Levi, one of the twelve testaments, in the British Museum. This copy was written in Armenian and dated A.D. 824. At the Bodleian Library at Oxford they also examined copies of various of the testaments written in Hebrew and Aramaic. These were of a much earlier date. Dr. Charles believes that the earliest Hebrew copies were written sometime between 137 and 107 B.C. Of course, if these were originally composed at that time by an unknown Hebrew author, they would not be genuine writings of the patriarchs themselves. But there is strong likelihood that these were copies of earlier documents that could have been handed down from the patriarchs. In any event, the facts that the copies were written well before the time of Jesus and that they contain teachings and doctrines similar to those of Christianity provide convincing evidence that the gospel Jesus taught was upon the earth well before the time of his birth.

Possibly one of the closest parallels to Christian teachings and the one that has aroused the most controversy on the part of the critics is found in the instructions by the patriarch Joseph

---

[1]Charles, *op. cit.*, p. 282.

[2]John Hyrcanus was a high priest and prince of the Jewish nation who lived during the second century B.C. and died sometime around 106 B.C. He succeeded his father, Simon Maccabaeus, who had been treacherously slain by orders of his own son-in-law. Hyrcanus commenced his reign by punishing the assassins of his father, but his brother-in-law who had arranged for the assassination appealed for aid to Antiochus, king of Syria, who laid siege to Jerusalem and compelled Hyrcanus to pay him tribute. After the death of Antiochus, Hyrcanus profited by the weakness that pervaded Syria and succeeded in capturing many cities in Judea and in conquering Samaria, thus reestablishing an independent Hebrew nation.

to his children and in similar language used by Jesus in his sermon to his disciples on the Mount of Olives, as recorded in Matthew 24 and 25. This sermon was given near the end of Jesus' ministry, when he departed from the temple and made the frightening statement that the temple would be destroyed. His disciples asked him when this would take place and what would be the signs of his second coming. Matthew 24 has a detailed description of these signs, and Matthew 25 records the judgment that will take place when Jesus "shall come in his glory, and all the holy angels with him" (Matthew 25:31), and will sit in judgment and will separate the sheep from the goats. The account records that the kings will say to the righteous: "Come, ye blessed of my Father, inherit the kingdom prepared for you from the foundation of the world: for I was an hungred, and ye gave me meat: I was thirsty, and ye gave me drink: I was a stranger, and ye took me in: Naked, and ye clothed me: I was sick, and ye visited me: I was in prison, and ye came unto me." (Matthew 25:34-36.)

The phrases "I was an hungred, and ye gave me meat," "I was sick, and ye visited me," "I was in prison, and ye came unto me" are similar to Joseph's statement: "I was beset with hunger, and the Lord Himself nourished me . . .," "I was sick, and the Lord visited me," "I was in prison, and my God showed favour unto me."[3]

Because manuscripts of the Testaments of the Twelve Patriarchs were in existence prior to and probably at the time of Jesus and his ministry, it is possible that he would have been familiar with them. Also, in view of the fact that he was with the Father in the beginning, that through him all things were made, and that the gospel was his and his Father's plan that he, Jesus, as Jehovah of the Old Testament, taught to all of these ancient prophets and patriarchs — these facts prove further that the gospel is the same today, yesterday, and tomorrow. The few similarities in language take nothing away from the sermon that Jesus gave to his disciples on the Mount of Olives;

[3]Joseph, in Charles, *op. cit.*, p. 346.

in fact, they only add to the proof of his divinity as the Son of God, the Redeemer and Savior.

Another impressive similarity, both in thought and in language, is contained in the statement of Jesus when he answered the Pharisee's question about which was the greatest commandment. Jesus responded: "Thou shalt love the Lord thy God with all thy heart, and with all thy soul, and with all thy mind. This is the first and great commandment. And the second is like unto it, Thou shalt love thy neighbour as thyself." (Matthew 22:37-39.)

In the Testament of Issachar, this same thought is expressed when Issachar said to his children: "Keep the law of God and get singleness, and walk in guilelessness, not playing the busy body with the business of your neighbour, but love the Lord and your neighbour, have compassion on the poor and weak." He also declared: "I love the Lord; likewise also every man with all my heart."[4]

The teachings of Paul have many similarities and parallels with the teachings in the Testaments of the Twelve Patriarchs. For example, in his letter to the Thessalonians, Paul uses the phrase "for the wrath is come upon them to the uttermost." (1 Thessalonians 2:16.) The patriarch Levi, in his testament describing the destruction of Shechem, used a similar phrase: "But the wrath of the Lord came upon them to the uttermost."[5]

This too may be judged as only a coincidental repetition. But Paul's letters to the Romans and the Corinthians show other similarities to the Testaments. These parallels in no way prove that Paul borrowed his ideas from these earlier sources, but he was probably acquainted with the ancient scriptures.

Among the interesting theological concepts found in the Testaments of the Twelve Patriarchs are the following:

From Ruben on abstinence: "Wine and strong drink I drank not." And on the same subject from Judah: "But if ye would live soberly do not touch wine at all, lest ye sin in words of outrage and in fightings and slanders, and transgressions of

---

[4]Issachar, in ibid., pp. 326-28.
[5]Levi, in ibid., p. 308.

the commandments of God, and ye perish before your time."[6]

Levi describes three heavens, or degrees of glory, that will exist in the hereafter to segregate the righteous from the unrighteous.[7]

Simeon advises his children: "Do ye also, my children, love each one his brother with a good heart, and the spirit of envy will withdraw from you."[8]

Each of the patriarchs instructs his children to live righteously and thereby receive the blessings of the Lord and the joy these blessings provide. Perhaps these teachings from all of the patriarchs can best be summarized in this instruction of Levi:

> And now, my children, I command you: Fear the Lord, your God with your whole heart, and walk in simplicity according to all His law. Do ye also teach your children letters, that they may have understanding all their life, reading unceasingly the law of God. For everyone that knoweth the law of the Lord shall be honored, and shall not be a stranger whithersoever he goeth. Yea, many friends shall he gain more than his parents, and many men shall desire to serve him, and to hear the law from his mouth. Work righteousness, therefore, my children, upon the earth, that ye may have it as a treasure in Heaven and sow good things in your souls, that ye may find them in your life. . . . Get wisdom in the fear of God with diligence; for though there be a leading into captivity, and cities and lands be destroyed, and gold and silver and every possession perish, the wisdom of the wise nought can take away.[9]

[6]Ruben, in ibid., p. 296; Judah, in ibid., p. 320.

[7]Levi, in ibid., pp. 304-5.

[8]Simeon, in ibid., p. 302.

[9]Levi, in ibid., p. 311.

18
THE SIBYLLINE ORACLES

The ancient pseudepigraphic writings discussed in the previous chapters, from the point of view of their possible influence and relationship to the teachings of Jesus and his disciples, are the most important books in the Charles volumes, *The Apocrypha and Pseudepigrapha of the Old Testament*. Dr. Charles, however, includes in his translation a number of other ancient writings that he presents under the classifications of apocalypsis, psalms and ethics, and wisdom literature. In addition to these ancient writings, other religious documents have been discovered over the centuries that are important to this study of the origin of Christ's gospel.

One of these documents is known as the Sibylline Oracles. The word *sibyl* refers to any of certain women of antiquity reputed to have possessed powers of prophecy. Anciently, it was not uncommon for individuals seeking counsel, either spiritual or temporal, to visit known so-called prophetesses who had a reputation for the ability to give such advice. The Old Testament refers to such oracles, and they existed extensively in mythology, particularly in Greek.

The Delphi Mountains in Greece are famous for their ancient oracles, chiefly women, whose voices of counsel and advice often seemed to come from deep caverns, from subterranean pools, and from other mysterious places. Persons of importance from all over the then-known world visited Delphi in an effort to receive guidance.

According to Greek mythology, the most famous Delphi sibylline oracle was Pythia, Apollo's priestess. Apollo himself was the most important oracle at Delphi. According to legend, countless thousands of individuals seeking counsel and advice, including kings, philosophers, and religious leaders, sought out these mythological sources of purported wisdom. Even Solomon may have sought wisdom from certain of the ancient oracles.[1] In addition to those at Delphi, many other so-called prophets and prophetesses existed historically and in mythology elsewhere throughout the world.

The advice the sibylline oracles gave was often profound and sage. Hebrew historians believed that many of them obtained their wisdom from the Hebrew scriptures, and it is possible that, as did Plato, Aristotle, and others of the ancient Greek philosophers, they had access to ancient scriptures that provided them with the type of wisdom exhibited by David, Solomon, and other biblical prophets.

In any event, the pseudepigraphic Sibylline Oracles have a certain amount of doctrine and teachings similar to Christianity, particularly in the area pertaining to eschatology, or predictions about the last days. These include such familiar Old and New Testament teachings as the belief that in the last days the world will be destroyed by fire, a great darkness will envelop the earth, the sun will be darkened, the moon and stars will fall, and the Lord will appear in the clouds. The signs to precede this destruction include an increase in wickedness and corruption throughout the world and a great increase in the power of the devil. There will be widespread pride and arrogance and, interestingly, the world will fall under the dominion of a wicked woman. After its destruction, the world will be renewed and a blessed kingdom will be established for the righteous. The Messiah will come from heaven to rule over this kingdom, which will be full of peace and prosperity. Jerusalem will be restored in all its glory, and a temple will be constructed

---

[1]Joan Comay, *Who's Who in the Old Testament* (New York: Holt, Rinehart and Winston, 1971), pp. 367-70.

there through the generosity of people from all over the world.[2]

These eschatological signs of the last days are strikingly similar to those given by Jesus to his disciples as recorded in Matthew 24, Mark 13, and Luke 21.

According to Dr. Charles, these old writings were composed around 150 B.C. and were used as scripture as late as the fifth century of the Christian era. When Rome was burned in 82 B.C., the sibylline books were also destroyed. However, a commission was later appointed to find copies of the books that might be preserved for history. These are the ones that now exist in various university and museum libraries and are basically the ones from which Dr. Charles made his translation. They are significant in their description of their writers' understanding of God and particularly in their predictions of the coming of Messiah and the events preceding the last days. Apparently, there were originally some fifteen books or oracles plus many fragments. Many private collections also existed other than the official ones kept in the capital at Rome. In fact, when the commission began its search for copies, so many were found and so many considered spurious that the Emperor Augustus, near the time of the birth of Jesus, ordered destroyed some two thousand volumes of oracles that he considered unreliable.

[2]Charles, *op. cit.*, pp. 374-75.

19
THE
ASSUMPTION
OF MOSES

The pseudepigraphic book the Assumption of Moses is another of the ancient writings that has certain similarities and parallels to New Testament teachings. In fact, some phrases from this book seem to appear in Jude and in the Acts of the Apostles.

For example, in Jude 4, the writer speaks of certain ungodly men turning the grace of God into lasciviousness and denying the only Lord God, Jesus Christ. This same thought appears in the Assumption of Moses in paragraph 7, verses 1-7, where the writer refers to destructive and impious men who, claiming they are just, pervert the way of the Lord. Also, Jude 18 refers to mockers in the last days who will walk after their own ungodly lusts. This same idea is expressed in the Assumption of Moses where the writer speaks of times being ended and says that in these times the mockers and deceivers will conceal themselves so as not to be recognized and will attempt to lead the righteous into evil ways.

The apostle Peter, in his second general epistle, appears to have been acquainted with the writings now known as the Assumption of Moses, for he includes ideas similar to those found in this ancient book. For example, he writes about false prophets and false teachers among the people who bring damnable heresies into the church. He decries and condemns them, calling them brute beasts who speak evil of the things they do not understand, and he warns that many will follow their pernicious ways. However, they shall utterly perish in their own corruption and receive the results of unrighteousness, even though they portray themselves as righteous while they feast with the saints. (See 2 Peter 2:1-2, 12-16.)

The writer of the Assumption of Moses expresses these same thoughts about impious men who shall rule and claim that they are just. These men shall "stir up the poison of their minds, being treacherous men, self-pleasers, dissemblers in all their own affairs and lovers of banquets at every hour of the day, gluttons, gourmands, devourers of the goods of the [poor] saying that they do so on the grounds of their justice."[1]

Similarly, Acts 7 refers to the experiences of Moses when he brought the children of Israel out of the land of Egypt. In verse 36 it is recorded that "he brought them out, after that he had shewed wonders and signs in the land of Egypt and in the Red sea, and in the wilderness forty years."

A parallel reference is recorded in the Assumption of Moses: "Is not this that which Moses did then declare unto us in prophecies, who suffered many things in Egypt and in the Red Sea, and in the wilderness during forty years: and assuredly called heaven and earth to witness against us, that we should not transgress His commandments, in which he was a mediator unto us?"[2]

These few examples provide striking evidence that certain New Testament writers were acquainted with the Assumption of Moses and considered it as sacred scripture.

The Assumption of Moses begins with an account called the "testament of Moses" in which Moses calls Joshua, a man approved of the Lord, to be the minister of the people and to lead them into the Promised Land. In writing of his own mission, Moses records that the Lord "designed and devised me, and He prepared me before the foundation of the world, that I should be the mediator of His covenant." Moses thus establishes his own preexistence and the fact that, because of

[1]Assumption, in Charles, *op. cit.,* p. 419.
[2]Ibid., p. 417.

his righteousness in the preexistence, he had been specifically chosen for the mission to which he was called.

Moses gives further instructions to Joshua in respect to the way his writings should be preserved:

> And receive thou this writing that thou may knowest how to preserve the books which I shall deliver unto thee: and thou shalt set these in order and anoint them with oil of cedar and put them away in earthen vessels in the place which He made from the beginning of the creation of the world, that His name should be called upon until the day of repentance in the visitation wherewith the Lord will visit them in the consummation of the end of the days.[3]

This specific instruction with respect to the preservation of records must have been in the hands of the Essenes, the Dead Sea Covenantors, for this is basically the way in which the Dead Sea Scrolls were prepared and stored for preservation.

With reference to the second coming of the Savior, which is predicted in the New Testament, the writer of the Assumption of Moses stated:

> And then His kingdom shall appear throughout His creation, and then Satan shall be no more, and sorrow shall depart with him . . . for the Heavenly One will arise from His royal throne, and He will go forth from His holy habitation with indignation and wrath on account of His Son. And the earth shall tremble: to its confines shall it be shaken; and the high mountains shall be made low and the hills shall be shaken and fall. And the horns of the sun shall be broken and he shall be turned into darkness; and the moon shall not give her light, and be turned wholly into blood.[4]

Matthew 24, Mark 13, and Luke 21 have similar descriptions of the signs of the last days and of the second coming of Christ, similarities that again help confirm the gospel's consistency.

[3]Ibid., p. 415.
[4]Ibid., pp. 421-22.

20
THE APOCALYPSE OF BARUCH

Dr. Charles characterizes the Apocalypse of Baruch as Second Baruch and believes the manuscript from which his translation was made was written sometime in the latter half of the first century A.D. He describes it as one of the last noble writings about Judaism prior to the dark and oppressive years around 600 B.C. following the destruction of Jerusalem. According to Dr. Charles, the book was written at various times by different authors and covers certain important theological concepts held by the Jews from A.D. 50 to 100. It provides interesting insights into Hebrew beliefs about original sin, the exercise of free agency, the consequences of Adam's fall, the importance of work on the part of the individual in order to earn his own salvation, the hope of the coming of a Messiah, the belief in a general resurrection, and the advent of the kingdom of God on earth.

This book is particularly interesting to students of Christianity's origin because it was written by Hebrew authors of the Pharisees during the time of the rise and consolidation of Christianity. The nature and spirit of the writings indicate that the author or authors were extremely antagonistic toward the Christians and made a concerted attempt to defend Judaism against the rising threat of the Christian faith.

The Apocalypse of Baruch was originally written in Hebrew, and no part of the original text is known to exist except for a few lines that survive in Rabbinic writings. Fortunately, however, the original text was translated into Greek and then from Greek into Syriac, and was preserved in the Syriac Bible. Dr. Charles's chief translation is from the Syriac, which he claims has come down to us in its entirety. His book also contains a translation of the Greek renditions, available in a somewhat fragmentary form, which he includes in a separate chapter entitled Third Baruch.

Referring to the coming destruction of Jerusalem, the prophet Baruch reports that the word of the Lord came to him in approximately 592 B.C., two years before Nebuchadnezzar's siege when the people were warned of the coming destruction of Jerusalem and certain righteous families were instructed to leave the city: "For I have said these things to thee that thou mayest bid Jeremiah and all those that are like you, to retire from this city. For your works are to this city as a firm pillar, and your prayers as a strong wall."[1]

The siege of Jerusalem by Nebuchadnezzar lasted some two years, and when the city fell, King Zedekiah was taken prisoner along with his children, who were killed before his eyes. Later Zedekiah's eyes were put out.

According to this account, certain righteous families escaped the fate of Jerusalem by leaving the city before it was destroyed. "And I went and took Jeremiah, and Adu, and Seriah, and Jabish, and Gedaliah, and all the honourable men of the people, and I led them to the valley of Cedron, and I narrated to them all that had been said to me. And they lifted up their voice, and they all wept. And we sat there and fasted until the evening."[2]

Referring to the preservation of holy things, Baruch tells how angels came into the city before it was destroyed and removed the holy Ark of the Covenant: " . . . the mercy-seat, and the two tables, and the holy raimant of the priest, and the altar of incense, and the forty-eight precious stones, wherewith the priest was adorned and all the holy vessels of the tabernacle." After these holy things were removed and prepared for preser-

[1]Baruch, in Charles, *op. cit.*, p. 481.
[2]Ibid., p. 483.

vation, angels came into the city with torches, went to the four corners of the walls, and destroyed the walls and the city so that the invaders could not claim to have been able to destroy the holy city and its temples.[3]

Baruch makes an interesting reference regarding eternal life: "For if there were this life only, which belongs to all men, nothing could be more bitter than this."[4] A parallel thought on this aspect of life eternal is found in Paul's statement in 1 Corinthians 15:19: "If in this life only we have hope in Christ, we are of all men most miserable."

The authors of Baruch advance the theological concept that a specific number of spirits are appointed to come to this earth before it fulfills its destiny and is cleansed for its eternal glory:

> For as thou hast not forgotten the people who now are and those who have passed away, so I remember those who are appointed to come. Because when Adam sinned and death was decreed against those who should be born, then the multitude of those who should be born was numbered, and for that number a place was prepared where the living might dwell and the dead might be guarded.[5]

With respect to Adam's sin and the nature of man's free agency, the authors of Baruch record:

> For though Adam first sinned and brought untimely death upon all, yet of those who were born from him each one has prepared for his own soul's torment to come, and again each one has chosen for himself glories to come.... Adam is therefore not the cause, save only of his own soul, but each of us has been the Adam of his own soul.... for since when he transgressed, untimely death came into being, grief was named and anguish was prepared, and pain was created, and trouble consummated, and disease began to be established.

This statement continues with a description of the coming of Satan upon the earth and the wicked influence he would exert upon the minds and hearts of those who followed his evil temptations. But after this black picture, Baruch sees blessings that will come from the fount of Abraham and his sons and

[3]Ibid., p. 484.
[4]Ibid., p. 494.
[5]Ibid., p. 495.

those like them who will bring judgment, righteousness, and a life of blessedness. These, Baruch writes, "are the bright waters which thou hast seen."[6]

Concerning the resurrection, Baruch sets forth the concept that the dead will rise with their bodies exactly in the same form in which they were buried in the earth so that they might be recognized by those who knew them. After this, their bodies will be transformed and spiritualized for the eternities.

It is apparent from these references that many of the concepts advanced by and recorded in the Apocalypse of Baruch are similar to those taught by Jesus and his disciples. The concept of original sin and man's responsibility for the results of his own free agency, the hope of the coming of a Messiah, and the belief in a general resurrection, together with the establishment of God's kingdom on the earth, are all found in the New Testament. In fact, Dr. Charles finds at least twenty parallel phrases and ideas that he believes prove the New Testament writers had access to these manuscripts or that both originated from the same source. Of course, if Baruch was composed during the first century of the Christian era, the similarities could easily be explained. But because the authors of Baruch wrote of historical religious happenings around 600 B.C., it is possible that even if the Apocalypse were written during the first century A.D., its original source could well have been from the earlier period of which Baruch wrote.

Dr. Charles believes that the Syriac and Greek versions from which he made his translation were preserved primarily by the Christians. The book, originally a part of the Syriac Bible, was highly thought of by the Greeks. It is believed that the reason why it was taken out of circulation was because similar documents recording the same history is covered in the book of Fourth Ezra.

[6]Ibid., pp. 511-13.

21
FOURTH
EZRA

According to the Charles translation, there are now a number of versions of Fourth Ezra, all of which Dr. Charles believes are from a Greek version no longer in existence. This version apparently came from an original Hebrew manuscript.

With this information, one cannot help but wonder if perhaps Fourth Ezra was one of the many Hebrew books that was translated into Greek at the time the Septuagint came into existence. Presently there are translations of the book in Latin, Syriac, Ethiopic, Arabic, and Armenian, of which there are two independent versions. Anciently, Fourth Ezra was considered important enough to be included in the first Latin Bible (the Vulgate) as an appendix. It was also included in some of the early English translations of the Bible, but later was relegated to an apocryphal state.

Fourth Ezra is supposedly related to the books of Ezra and Nehemiah as they now exist in the King James Version. It covers one of the historic periods in the life of the Hebrew people when Cyrus captured Babylon in 539 B.C. and became master of the Near East. A benevolent ruler, he decreed that the Jews, under Ezra, should return and rebuild Jerusalem and the temple. This was done during the reigns of Cyrus and his successor, Artaxerxes, during which time Ezra also returned to Jerusalem with the scriptures, the life and teachings of Moses, and laid the foundation for the later development of Judaism as a creed and a way of life.

The contents of Fourth Ezra are closely related both in time and in substance to Second Baruch. They consist of a purported conversation Ezra had with an angel regarding the reasons for the severe persecutions suffered by the Israelites. Ezra found it difficult to understand why the Lord's chosen people, even though they had at times drifted away from the Lord's commandments, should be subjugated and overridden by their enemies, men who had completely rejected the Lord's commandments. The angel answered these questions, pointing out that the children of Israel needed to suffer during this life in order to fully enjoy the rich blessings awaiting them in the hereafter.

The question and answer dialogue in the book presents the concepts of the preexistence of all human spirits, the nature of Adam's fall and the introduction of sin, the promised coming of a Messiah who would ultimately save Israel, and the assurance of a general resurrection. Dr. Charles finds a number of resemblances in thought and in wording between Fourth Ezra and the New Testament. Although the similarities are not extensive, the fact that Fourth Ezra could have been available to the New Testament writers makes the similarities important. Dr. Charles also finds several passages, which are not sufficiently exact to suggest interdependence, in the Gospels of Mark and Matthew, in Revelation, and in Paul's epistles to the Corinthians and the Romans.[1]

In reference to the coming of the Messiah, Fourth Ezra provides this specific account: "For my Son the Messiah shall be revealed, together with those who are with him, and shall rejoice four hundred years. And it shall be, after these years, that my Son the Messiah shall die, and all in whom there is human breath. Then shall the world be turned into the primaeval silence seven days, like as at the first beginnings; so that no man is left."

[1]For details of these similarities, see the references in Charles, *op. cit.*, p. 559.

With respect to the resurrection and final judgment, Fourth Ezra records: "And the earth shall restore those that sleep in her, and the dust those that are at rest therein, And the Most High shall be revealed upon the throne of judgement: . . . truth shall stand, and faithfulness triumph."[2]

[2]Ezra, in ibid., pp. 582-83.

22
OTHER PSEUDEPIGRAPHIC BOOKS IN CHARLES' TRANSLATION

With the exception of the Fragments of a Zadokite Work, the other pseudepigraphic books in Charles' translation have no significant materials that resemble pre-Christian teachings. Consequently, only a brief general description of these books is given here. Although they do not have a direct bearing on the objectives of this study, they are of important interest to theological historians.

The Psalms of Solomon were undoubtedly originally written in Hebrew but the Hebrew original is no longer in existence. The versions from which Dr. Charles made his translations are in Greek and in Syriac.

The collection consists of eighteen psalms that the scholars believe were written sometime during the middle of the first century B.C. They consist of poetic writings that attempt to establish firmly the concept of the relative righteousness of Israel over the other nations of the world, and were probably written in an attempt to prove the righteousness of the Pharisees as against the sins of the Sadducees. They have not exerted any significant influence on Christian literature and, as a matter of fact, had passed out of circulation and even memory until the seventeenth century when they were published by John Lewis de la Cerda in 1626. No attempt is made here to discuss the religious philosophy presented in these psalms.

The Fourth Book of Maccabees, translated from the Greek, was probably originally written by a Jew in Hebrew sometime between 63 B.C. and A.D. 38. Dr. Charles believes it was a sermon delivered by a Hebrew intellectual who had a good command of the Greek language. The author presents the stoic definition of the cardinal virtues of judgment, justice, and temperance, and states that these virtues can best be maintained by individuals who know and practice the laws of Moses. In his presentation he exposes the supremacy of reason and bases his conclusions on the application of pure logic. The book is a scholarly presentation and of great interest to students of theological logic.

Pirke Aboth is a book of the sayings of the fathers, a collection of maxims and ethical nonreligious concepts as taught by rabbis, probably from the third century B.C. to the third century A.D. These sayings are of particular interest to students of Jewish religious thought.

The Story of Ahikar is compared by Dr. Charles with the apocryphal book of Tobit. Classed in the region of folklore and legend, this book includes a story of the sins of ingratitude and the final recompense of a just judgment. Briefly, the account is of a man named Ahikar who served as grand vizier to King Sennacherib of Syria and who displayed great wisdom as a politician and friend to the king. A wealthy man, he was extremely sad because, although he had sixty wives, he had no son to whom he could pass on his wealth and his position of honor in the king's court. He was advised to adopt the son of his sister, a young boy named Nadan, and raise him as his son. This he did, providing the boy with the best possible education not only from his own wisdom but also from the teachings of other sages in the kingdom.

Unfortunately, as the boy grew, he began to covet his uncle's wealth and eventually arranged to have him killed. The uncle, however, persuaded his close friend, the appointed executioner, to have another killed in his place, and Ahikar was hidden in a basement, where he remained for many years.

Then King Sennacherib received a special demand from the king of Egypt that neither he nor Nadan could fulfill. The king realized that his only help could have come from the wise

Ahikar. To his astonishment and delight, he learned that Ahikar was still alive, and joyfully he had him brought back to the king's court and restored to his position. Ahikar then took revenge upon his nephew who had been so cruel and so ungrateful to him, but he continued to teach his nephew even until the nephew's death.

These teachings form the basis of the theological teachings to which Dr. Charles finds parallels in other ancient documents, such as the Testaments of the Twelve Patriarchs, as well as the Old and New Testaments and the Koran. Even though the parallels are somewhat vague and inconclusive, they are interesting in view of the fact that the Ahikar papyrus is believed to be the earliest example of either biblical or apocryphal literature.

The discovery of the papyrus fragments from which the Story of Ahikar has been copied into various languages and translated into English was made by Dr. Rubenshon in his excavation in 1906-1908 at Elephantine, near the first cataracts on the Nile some two hundred miles from Cairo.[1] The papyrus has been dated approximately from 500 to 550 B.C., making it one of the oldest religious manuscripts yet discovered.

The first extensive dispersion of Israel took place during the reign of the Syrian king, Tiglath Pileser III. In approximately 734 B.C., after subjugating the eastern cities, he turned his attention to the west, took Damascus, then placed all of Israel under his control. In the process, he took a large number of Israelite leaders captive into Assyria. Though Samaria successfully resisted this invasion, Tiglath Pileser's successor, Shalmaneser, laid siege to the city. The city held out for another three years, but Shalmaneser's successor, Sargon II, overpowered the fortress and led 27,290 prominent Israelites captive into Babylonia. In a final effort to stamp out the Israelite kingdom, Sargon replaced this people with strangers in a land so despised by the Jews at the time of Jesus. It was during this period that the prophets Amos and Hosea, and later Isaiah,

[1]First published by Sachan Publishing Co. in 1911 as part of the Aramaic papyrus from Elephantiné.

preached to the people and tried, without noticeable success, to persuade them to desist from their evil ways.

The fall of Samaria left Judah still independent but uneasy and insecure. But because Uzziah continued to pay tribute to the Assyrians, Judah was left virtually undisturbed until after Sargon's death. In 701 B.C., however, a revolt occurred and the new Assyrian king, Sennacherib, invaded Judah, captured many of the smaller towns, and invaded Jerusalem. If the story of Ahikar is more than legend and folklore, this would have been the period of the lifetime of his grand vizier to King Sennacherib.

Details will not be given here of the parallels in Ahikar and the New Testament. However, Dr. Charles finds such parallels in Matthew 24:48-51, where the account is given of the evil servant who failed to serve the Lord and was surprised at the unexpected return of his Lord who punished him for his evil deeds. He also finds parallels in the story of the unfruitful fig tree in Luke 13; in the Parable of the Prodigal Son; and in certain New Testament passages in 1 Corinthians and 2 Timothy.[2]

Whether the story of Ahikar is fable, legend, or actual history is not of significance. The fact that it contains ideas, thoughts, and expressions similar in context to the teachings of Jesus only further tends to confirm the thesis that all these theological concepts must have originated from the same source. All ancient philosophies of man's relationship to himself, to others, and to his God were solidly founded on religious concepts. Reason and common sense dictate that a wise Creator would be consistent and logical in the plan he would establish for the growth, development, and happiness of mankind upon the earth and that he would teach this plan through his prophets to all people, regardless of who they were and when and under what conditions they lived.

The teachings of Ahikar are simple, sage, and applicable today as they were when they were written some 2500 years ago. Here are a few examples:

[2]For a more detailed discussion of these similarities, see Charles, *op. cit.*, p. 719.

"My son, do not tell all that thou seest, and do not disclose all that thou hearest."

"My son, it is better to remove stones with a wise man than to drink wine with a fool."

"My son, envy not the prosperity of thy enemy; and rejoice not at his adversity."

"My son, sweeten thy tongue and make savory the opening of thy mouth; for the tail of a dog gives him bread and his mouth gets him blows."

"My son, better is a friend that is at hand than a brother who is far away: and better is a good name than much beauty: because a good name standeth forever, but beauty wanes and wastes away."

"My son, let not a word go forth from thy mouth, until thou hast taken counsel within thy heart."[3]

FRAGMENTS OF A ZADOKITE WORK

The text of a Zadokite work is preserved in two manuscripts in the Cambridge University Library.[4] The original manuscript is believed to have been written during the first century B.C. and contains the beliefs and church organization of a group that had separated itself from the Pharisees, probably during the second century B.C. The members of this group became known as the Sons of Zadok, named for Zadok, a prophet referred to in the Old Testament. (See 2 Samuel 8:17.) They were critical of the Pharisees because of the corruptions they had allowed in the temple rituals and ceremonies, and because they had deviated so far from the law of Moses. This group was not just another sect, but a real third party separating itself from both the Pharisees and the Sadducees.

The Sons of Zadok were intensely religious and ethical in character and depended heavily on theology and the prophets who had interpreted the law of Moses. The group's deep dependence on the prophets separated it entirely from the Pharisees. Its members tended to cling fast to the written law

[3]Ibid., pp. 728ff.
[4]See chapter 7.

and discarded much of the oral tradition held so dearly by the Pharisees.

Organization of the Sons of Zodak consisted of four degrees or orders: priests, Levites, Israelites, and proselytes. From the first three, ten men were chosen in each of the congregations to govern the organization. Connected jointly with these ten were two additional authorities known as censors. One of these apparently headed the group and was responsible for admitting new members into the organization and assigning them to their proper places according to their qualifications. He was also responsible for readmitting those who had been expelled from the organization for various purposes but who had repented.

This executive administered the monthly contributions of the congregation and distributed them to the poor, settled disputes and legal suits between members, and in general served as the judge in the case of initial offenses. In all of these responsibilities, he took counsel from his assistant and his ten associate leaders. All of these leaders, in order to be called to these positions, needed to meet certain moral and intellectual qualifications as well as to be generally between the ages of twenty-five and sixty.

The Zadokites believed in the coming of a Messiah in the last days, a future life, repentance, baptism, a form of foreordination, and individual free agency, and were strictly against divorce. They based their teachings on the law and the prophets.

The important current interest in this Zadokite manuscript has been greatly augmented by discovery of the Dead Sea Scrolls. When one of the Dead Sea Scrolls was translated, it was found to be a record of the organization and beliefs of the Essenes, a group known and named by Josephus. This manuscript, now known as the Manual of Discipline, is so similar in organization and substance to the Zadokite fragment that new interest was aroused in it.

Much of what we know about the Essenes' beliefs and church organization is found in the Manual of Discipline and also in their Book of Psalms. The information is so similar to that in the Zadokite fragment that they must be considered to have influenced each other or to have come from the same source.

Many of the teachings and practices of the Essenes and the Sons of Zadok are so similar to those of the Christians that one of two basic conclusions must be drawn: Either Jesus and his followers were deeply influenced by these teachings and religious practices, or Jesus was the original author of these concepts and, in his preexistent spiritual state, taught them to the Old Testament patriarchs and prophets. These men in turn, through their writings and through their descendants, preserved a sufficient quantity of these teachings that a group of sincere searchers for the truth realized that the Jewish sects of their time had deviated so far from the original gospel truths that they needed to be refined and brought back to God's original teachings.

23
THE DIDACHE

A number of ancient documents not included in the R. H. Charles translation of the Pseudepigrapha have a significant bearing upon the question of the origins of Christianity. Among these is the Didache.

The Didache, which literally means "teachings" or "principles to be taught," was first published from ancient sources in 1883. It dates back to the first century of the Christian era and was initially called Teachings of the Lord by the Twelve Apostles to the Gentiles. Presently, this record exists in Latin and Greek, and parts of it are found in Syriac and Ethiopic.

The Didache portrays church life and beliefs soon after the deaths of the early apostles who served with and knew Jesus. In this document, Christian life is grouped in three categories: morality, worship and organization, and hope.

The document's Christian morality consists of instruction taken from the "two ways" — the way of righteousness (the way of light) and the way of sin (the way of darkness or the way of Belial). The essence of the "two ways" is described in detail in the Manual of Discipline. In the "two ways," the Christian is taught to love God and his neighbor, to live uprightly, and to abstain from vices and from the service of idols.

Christian worship and ritual includes repentance, baptism, fasting, prayer (repeating the Lord's Prayer thrice daily), and the sacrament or Eucharist. After giving sacramental blessings to be said over the cup and the bread and after the meal, the

Didache prescribes rules for the reception and treatment of wandering "prophets" and for the maintenance of the regular ministry.

The third section of the Didache covers the second coming of the Lord and, according to this document, the second coming is in the very near future.

In the Didache it is interesting to note that all prayers were to be offered to God through Christ, for life and immortality had been given to man through Christ. The true prophet was to be received as Christ, and Christian conduct was to be what Christ had commanded.

The document, possibly better than any of the other records at this particular time, gives a more complete picture of the work and teachings of Jesus as they affected the life of the average Christian in the first century of the church's existence. In it Jesus was the messenger from God who came to earth with tidings of immortality, who gave his life for his teachings, and who now was waiting until the appointed day when he would reappear in glory in the clouds of heaven. He came not to establish a new gospel, but to restore the original plan of salvation, to refine it, and to call it back to God's commandments. [1]

Before the deaths of the original apostles, corruptions in doctrine and heresies were beginning to take firm hold in the church. The apostle Paul found many divisions in the churches he visited. For example, in Corinth, he found that the members had divided themselves into four parties: (1) some were following what they thought were Paul's teachings; (2) others were patterning their lives on what they thought were the teachings of Peter, or Cephas; (3) still others were following the "teachings" of Apollos, while (4) a few persons were attempting to hold rigidly to the teachings of Christ. Paul chided the saints for these dissensions and attempted to call them back to the unity of the faith, asking them if Christ was divided. (See 1 Corinthians 1:10-13.)

[1]F. Crawford Burkett, *The Gospel History and Its Transmission* (Edinburgh: T. & T. Clarke, 1906), pp. 270-72. (These references are taken from Didache, pp. 9-15.

One of the most serious of these heresies shortly after this time was known as the Docetic Heresy, which was not the name of a party, but rather a philosophy that began to develop in the church. One Docetic author, who wrote in the Acts of John, denied that the Lord had any material existence, that he could be seen and heard but had no materiality. Others, like Marcion, even denied his birth. All who held this theory were united in their belief of Jesus as not having been, in any real sense, a human being. These unfortunate theories exercised a definite influence on the accurate preservation of the history of the church. [2]

[2]Ibid., pp. 273-74.

24
THE
SHEPHERD
OF HERMAS

Another ancient document, apparently written sometime near the middle of the second Christian era, is the book known as the Shepherd of Hermas. For a long, time this book was accepted as part of the canon of scripture of certain Christian churches. However, near the end of the fifth century, by action of a council of the Roman Catholic Church, it was relegated to a noncanonical status.

This book has always been a puzzle to certain Christian scholars. It describes a Son of God, but he is never referred to as Jesus or as Christ. The book also mentions the Holy Spirit, but the work to be performed by the Holy Spirit is not the same as is described in the New Testament.

Since the discovery of the Dead Sea Scrolls, this old book has received renewed attention. In fact, certain authors believe it bears a close relationship to the doctrines and teachings found in the Dead Sea Scrolls and possibly could be closely related to them. In the Shepherd of Hermas, the Father, the Son, and the Holy Spirit constitute a trinity. The book assigns to God, the Father, the dominant role in the Godhead, and the Son and the Spirit function in special assigned responsibilities. This is an interesting parallel with the teachings of the New Testament, where Jesus taught that he and his Father were separate individuals and that he had come to do the Father's will. Jesus also taught that he, the Father, and the Holy Ghost together formed the Trinity of the Godhead, individual members separate and distinct from one another.

One of the interesting statements of this old document is that the church which the author describes was not established by the Son of God. This church already had a long history behind it, and the Son of God, as in the Didache, was sent to purify it and to bring it back into conformity with God's commandments.[1]

In commenting on the Shepherd of Hermas, Pere Jean-Paul Audet in his *La Revue Biblique* writes: "Something has dictated in a positive way the unity of Hermas' theological thought and something must have also determined its quality."[2]

The Shepherd of Hermas is a book of "visions, mandates, and similitudes," and its author mentions the Didache as one of its sources. The book describes baptism as one of the means of atonement and explains the Holy Spirit as a fundamental part of the cleansing process involved in baptism.[3]

The teachings in the Shepherd of Hermas, similar to those in the Didache, provide interesting insight into the beliefs and practices of the early Christians soon after the deaths of Christ's original apostles and provide striking evidence that these early writings had avoided the distortions in doctrine that later appeared in the various Christian churches.

It is interesting that in a recent lecture, an internationally recognized religious authority emphasized his theory that Christianity has developed through a maturation process. He said that to understand the current concept of the Trinity depends "not so much on what ye think of Christ, but what ye think of the council of Nicaea. It was at this council in A.D. 325 that the issue of the Trinity was resolved."[4]

---

[1]Wilson, *op. cit.*, p. 75.

[2]Audet, Pere Jean-Paul, *La Revue Biblique*, as quoted in Wilson, *op. cit.*, p. 76.

[3]Wilson, *op. cit.*, p. 76.

[4]Dr. Jaroslav Pelikan, Sterling Professor and Dean of the Yale Graduate School, in a lecture at the University of Utah as reported in the *Salt Lake Tribune*, April 8, 1975.

25
THE CHENOBOSKIAN DISCOVERIES

In 1945, approximately two years before the discovery of
the Dead Sea Scrolls, a most interesting collection of
Gnostic documents was accidentally found in Egypt, approximately two hundred miles up the Nile River near a village now
known as Mag Hammadi, site of the ancient city of Chenoboskian. This remarkable discovery was made when some villag-
ers, apparently digging a garden, uncovered a large earthen jar
that contained thirteen volumes of papyrus writings, each
volume securely bound with leather. The peasants apparently
did not realize what they had discovered, and it is recorded
that they sold the documents for a few Egyptian pounds, but
the treasure eventually reached Cairo, where twelve of the
thirteen volumes were obtained by the Coptic Museum. Seven
years later the other volume was purchased by the Jung Institute in Zurich, Switzerland.

About ten years after the discovery, the Jung Institute man-
uscript was published by three scholars and given the title
Gospel of Truth. This document is described as a mystical,
meditative gospel theme derived primarily from the four New
Testament Gospels but known and treasured by the early
Christian fathers, particularly the Coptics.

In 1956, one of the volumes in possession of the Coptic
Museum in Cairo was published by Dr. Pahor Labib, the
museum's director. This publication contains a gnostic Apocryphon of John, a document known to early church writers

during the second century of the Christian era. The discovery also included two gospels, one ascribed to the apostle Philip, the other to the apostle Thomas. The Apocryphon of John, which gives a Gnostic description of human history and how the universe originated, and the Gospel of Philip, which contains a body of Gnostic speculations, are not important in this present study.[1]

The Gospel of Thomas, however, provides another insight into the time soon after the deaths of Jesus' original apostles and is considered to be the most important manuscript discovered at the Chenoboskian site.[2]

From the point of view of Christian doctrine, the Gospel of Thomas adds nothing of any substantial importance to the four New Testament Gospels. It was written from a Gnostic point of view and thus reflects the interpretation of this particular group's understanding of Jesus' teachings. Its importance lies not in the addition of any new Christian ideas, but rather that it confirms part of the gospel given by Jesus in the New Testament, particularly the parables and some of the specific teachings.

It should be remembered that when the King James Version of the Bible was compiled, books for the New Testament had to be selected from a large number of books that had accumulated at least since the second century A.D. On the basis of the compilers' combined judgment, Matthew, Mark, Luke, and John were selected and became an accepted part of the canon. The books not selected became apocryphal and were either in-

[1]The religious movement known as Gnosticism developed early in the Christian era. Some authorities believe that the Essenes (the Dead Sea Covenantors), who escaped from Roman destruction and who did not join the Zealots at Masada, relinquished all hope of salvation during this life and centered their hopes and anticipations on the life to come, after the spirit left this world and went into heaven. These people centered their efforts on gaining spiritual knowledge and attempted to gain peace of mind by concentration on the hereafter. These religious groups were known as Gnostics. The *Gnostic* is derived from the Greek word *Gnosis*, meaning mystical knowledge, or seeking to know.

[2]See R. M. Grant and D. N. Freeman, *The Secret Sayings of Jesus* (Garden City, N.Y.: Doubleday, 1960), pp. 7-20.

cluded in the Greek or the Roman versions and later cast out or were never accepted in either version. Although the Gospel of Thomas was discovered only recently, the fact that it was used by the early Coptic Church provides strong evidence that, along with many other versions, it was available to the compilers of the King James Version during 1604 to 1611, but it was not included as a part of that version.

In addition to providing another witness of the authenticity of the Gospels of the New Testament, particularly of the three synoptic Gospels, the Gospel of Thomas provides another testimony of the historicity of Jesus, that he lived, taught, established a religious movement, was crucified, and was resurrected from the dead. The New Testament Gospel writers were not concerned about presenting historical documents, but rather with the life, ministry, and teachings of Jesus. The Gospel of Thomas provides another historical documentary not only of the fact that Jesus lived, but also of the gospel that he taught.

In addition to the Apocryphon of John and the gospels ascribed to Philip and Thomas, the Chenoboskian find included three versions of the Apocryphon of John, three apocalypses of James, an apocalypse of Paul, and one of Peter. These documents, also translated and published, contain Gnostic interpretations of the teachings of these apostles that do not fully coincide with the writings in the New Testament, yet they add further witness to the lives of these apostles and to their teachings.

Only a few of the passages from the Gospel of Thomas, relating the sayings of Jesus, are given here. For example: "If you do not fast to the world, you will not find the kingdom; if you do not truly keep the Sabbath, you will not see the father."[3]

In the New Testament, Jesus and his disciples emphasized the importance and efficacy of fasting. The Gnostics also had a strong belief in this practice. From the Gospel of Thomas: "He who blasphemes the Father will be forgiven, and who blas-

[3]Ibid., p. 147.

phemes the Son will be forgiven, but he who blasphemes the Holy Spirit will not be forgiven, either on earth or in heaven."[4]

This passage is similar to Matthew 12:31-32, which records the same thought but limits the forgiveness and punishment of blasphemy to the Son of Man and to the Holy Ghost. It is interesting that the Gnostic version refers to all three members of the Godhead and implies their separate beings and natures. (See also Mark 3:28-29.)

Many students of the New Testament have been both confused and mystified by this statement attributed to Jesus, recorded in both Matthew and Mark, in which he says that blasphemy, or words spoken against him, will be forgiven but blasphemy against the Holy Ghost will not be forgiven in this world or in worlds to come. This statement appears to make the Holy Ghost more important and more sacred than Jesus the Christ, the Son of God. The statement in the Gnostic Gospel of Thomas that blasphemy against God, the Father, will also be forgiven but that blasphemy against the Holy Spirit will not be forgiven, adds even more substance to this bewilderment. This confusion might be justified except for one basic fact. Jesus told his disciples that after he was gone, the Father would send the Comforter, the Holy Ghost, "whom the Father will send in my name, he shall teach you all things, and bring all things to your remembrance, whatsoever I have said unto you." (John 14:26; see also Acts 2.)

The Holy Ghost, or Holy Spirit, is the testifier sent by the Father to enlighten men's minds and give them an absolute witness that God lives and that Jesus is the Christ. When a person has received this absolute knowledge through the Holy Ghost and then blasphemes or denies it, that person will not be forgiven in this world nor in the world to come.

Countless millions of individuals who call themselves Christians but who repeatedly blaspheme, take the Lord's name in vain, or speak against God or against his Son, but who have not received the witness of the Holy Ghost, will be forgiven if they repent, for they know not what they do. In other words,

[4]Ibid., p. 158.

where much is given — when an individual progresses in his righteousness and in his knowledge to the point where he actually receives a witness from the Holy Ghost that God lives and that Jesus is the Christ — much is expected. One who is blessed with this divine testimony and then denies it commits a blasphemy that will not be forgiven.

From the Gospel of Thomas we read: "His disciples said to him: twenty-four prophets spoke in Israel and all of them spoke concerning you."[5] "Jesus said to them: You have left the one who lives before your eyes and you have spoken concerning the dead."[6] It is interesting that in the Old Testament are twenty-three prophets who testified of the coming of Christ; Thomas must have added to these John the Baptist, making twenty-four in all.

As indicated earlier, the sayings ascribed to Jesus in this document bear close relationship to his teachings in the New Testament. This book and the other records found near Mag Hammadi in Egypt provide additional evidence that Jesus is the Christ.

[5]Ibid., p. 156.
[6]Ibid., p. 161

PART III:
JUDAIC WRITINGS AND CHRISTIANITY

26
JUDAIC
SCRIPTURES

The doctrines, teachings, church organization, rituals, and religious festivals that comprise Judaism are found in the first five books of the Old Testament, known as the Pentateuch, the Law, or the Torah. These books, consisting of Genesis, Exodus, Leviticus, Numbers, and Deuteronomy, are believed to have been written by Moses and to have been received by him directly from Jehovah.

The Torah is the heart and soul of the Jewish religion, and it is supported and amplified by many other books that have been written as commentaries and explanations of the laws of Moses as well as documentaries of both the oral and written traditions that have developed over the ages. The Torah itself, although believed to have been originally written by Moses, was actually rendered into scriptural form and canonized by the prophets Ezra and Nehemiah in Jerusalem sometime near the fifth century B.C.[1] It will be remembered that about one hundred years earlier the benevolent Persian King Cyrus took a friendly attitude toward the Jews who had been in captivity since the Babylonian conquest and issued a decree permitting them to return to Judea. According to the Old Testament, Nehemiah, who had been honored as "cupbearer" by King Artaxerxes I, was serving wine to the king at the time when he,

---

[1]Bible historians are not sure of the exact times when these two prophets lived.

Nehemiah, had just learned of the terrible conditions under which his Jewish brethren were living in Jerusalem. The king observed Nehemiah's sad countenance and inquired as to the cause. When he obtained the facts, the concerned and generous king arranged for Nehemiah, together with a company of soldiers and builders, to return to Jerusalem to rebuild the city and the temple. (See Nehemiah 2.) It was under these circumstances that Nehemiah and Ezra regathered the Torah and formulated the Mosaic Law into canonized scripture. This accomplishment set the stage for the reestablishment of the Jewish community and the formalization of Judaism again as a unified religion.[2]

When revealed scripture is canonized, an attempt is usually made to close the doors and lock them securely against any further revelations or additions. This is what Ezra and Nehemiah hoped to do when they canonized the Torah. In like manner, the King James scholars supposedly locked their doors against all further revelation when they completed their work and canonized the Protestant Bible in 1611. However, by necessity, canonization automatically opens other doors of interpretation and commentary. In the case of the Torah, these interpretations began rather innocently and haphazardly. When Ezra and Nehemiah finished rewriting the Law, they decreed that it should be read aloud in synagogues, which necessitated the presence of teachers, or rabbis, who could interpret the somewhat complex passages. These interpreters, each attempting to become more erudite than another, gradu-

---

[2]There is considerable disagreement among Bible scholars as to whether or not Moses actually wrote the first five books of the Old Testament. Moreover, there is substantial argument as to just what scriptural material was available to Ezra and Nehemiah. Some scholars believe that much of the Torah, Pentateuch, was already in existence long before the compilation made by Ezra and Nehemiah. For example, Immanuel Lewy, in his book *The Growth of the Pentateuch* (New York: Bookman Associates, 1955), states in the preface: "The present writer views the Pentateuch as a pre-exilic book, to a great extent even antedating Amos and Isaiah." He further states, "I have brought to light evidence that justifies identifying this great master [a great teacher who lived during the United Kingdom] with the prophet Nathan, the first teacher and statesman of moral tradition." See Dr. Lewy's entire book for an interesting thesis on how the Pentateuch developed.

ally became increasingly important until they established a new scholastic interpretation, the first step toward the Talmud, known as Midrash, meaning "exposition."[3]

During this time, the Jews were influencing and being influenced by their successive conquerors, the Babylonians, the Persians, the Seleucids, the Parthians, and the Sassanids, each of which imposed their cultures and at the same time absorbed some of the traditions, and particularly the religious concepts, of the Jews. Naturally, under these circumstances, new interpretations needed to be made of the meaning and application of the laws of Moses. For example, Dimont described this transition during the Greek captivity: "The Hellenization of the Jews began inconspicuously. First it infected their language, manners and customs; then it encroached upon their morals, ethics and religion."[4]

This influence was the second unpremeditated step toward the creation of the Talmud, known as Mishna, the Hebrew word for "repetition." This new method of interpretation of the Torah became rather widespread about two hundred years before the Christian era and became a source of bitter controversy between the Sadducees and the Pharisees, who diametrically opposed each other as to whether or not the Mishna should be allowed to exist. The basic argument of the Pharisees, who accepted the Mishna, was that the priests were selected to perform religious and temple rituals and had not been selected by God to give the last word on the scriptures. It was, they believed, a modern and effective way of searching for and finding the real intent of God's teachings.

As these new interpretations of the Torah became more widely accepted, a problem developed in the church. The rabbis, particularly the Sadducees, were worried lest these interpretations become more widely accepted than the Torah itself, and to keep this from happening they decreed that the Mishna could not be written and become confused with the Law, but could only be preserved orally.

---

[3]For a scholarly, detailed discussion of this development, see Max I. Dimont, *Jews, God and History* (New York: Simon and Schuster, 1962), p. 159.

[4]Ibid., p. 83.

Although the Mishna could now no longer be written down and needed to be memorized, it still kept growing and was ultimately divided into two schools, one led by Hillel and the other by Shamai, both of whom interpreted it differently. Shamai held to the legalistic interpretation listing the importance of property rights. Hillel emphasized the more flexible interpretation based on human rights.

The Mishna continued to grow in content and in popularity until Rabbi Judah Hanasi, fearing that Judaism would set its foundation on the interpretations of the law rather than upon the law itself, decreed that no more interpretations could be added to it. From this development, a new commentary evolved. This new interpretation was not, in the judgment of its developers, an addition to the Mishna, but rather a supplement to it, known as the Gemara. This supplement then continued to grow until some way was found to stop it. This occurred during the period of the rise of the Persian religion of Zoroastrianism and the pagan influences that this religious philosophy began to exert upon the interpretations of the Jewish teachings.

With all these additions and developments, the oral law still remained oral and was committed to memory only by the most astute scholars. The danger was always present that when one of these scholars died, his knowledge and memory died with him. Thus it was decided that the traditions must be committed to writing. The compilation and merging of the Mishna and the Gemara was assigned to a group of scholars known as the Saboraim, who, with their knowledge of Hebrew and Aramaic, were able to combine the traditions into a complete text known as the Talmud. The herculean task, which took some two hundred years, until A.D. 700, resulted in fifteen thousand pages bound into some thirty-five volumes.

No attempt will be made here to delve into the intricacies of this monumental literary accomplishment. Suffice it to say that at the outset the Talmud was complex, difficult to understand, and not within the reach of any except the most scholarly and erudite. The result was that three effective attempts were eventually made to codify and index its contents in such a manner as to make it more readable and useful to interested Jews. The first of these, written in Hebrew, was completed in approximately A.D. 1100 by Rabbi Alfasi. The second Hebrew version, approximately one hundred years later, was prepared by Maimonides and was known as the Mishna Torah. The third was accomplished by Joseph Caro (1488-1575) and was named the Schulchan Aruch (Prepared Table). This has become the classic codification of the mysteries of the Talmud, which are not only indexed but are also somewhat clarified for the average person. This work was accomplished at Safed, where Caro established one of the outstanding Hebrew religious Yeshivas, or academies.

The Talmud is both extremely broad and minutely specific in content. For example, a study of it leads into legalistic interpretations, ethics, morality, and such subjects as medicine, hygiene, astronomy, economics, and government. As a result, many Jewish students have found in this work foundations for accomplishments in medicine, mathematics, astronomy, philosophy, poetry, and business. On the other hand, the Talmud covers such intricate details as the arguments of what is permissible on the Sabbath. Should a Jew walk or ride in a car when he visits the synagogue? When one rides in an elevator on the Sabbath, is the fact that it uses electricity, which in turn requires labor, a violation of the Mosaic Law?

The question of what is kosher and what is not, according to Mosaic Law, is covered in the Torah and interpreted in the Talmud. Thus, although Judaism is rooted and founded on the Mosaic Laws in the first five books of the Old Testament, interpretations and application of these laws are discussed in the Talmud.

DEVELOPMENT OF THE HEBREW BIBLE[5]

The foregoing discussion is concerned solely with the first five books of the Old Testament, the Torah, and the development of interpretations and commentaries on the Mosaic Law

[5]Sources of material for this section are from Hastings, *op. cit.*, pp. 909-16; M. H. Goshen-Gottstein, *Text and Language in Bible and Qumran* (Jerusalem:

as found in these first five books. The Jewish Bible, however, not only contains the Torah, but also the historical books, the prophets, both major and minor, and the other miscellaneous writings that are familiar to readers of the Protestant Old Testament.

The Hebrew Bible, as it now stands, is divided into three parts: the Law, the Prophets, and the Writings. It consists only of the Hebrew books of the Old Testament in a slightly different arrangement from that which is found in the King James Version. The development of the text of the Book, as the Bible is known to the Jews, is an interesting and important historical aspect of Judaism.

The earliest known translation of the Old Testament records from the original Hebrew is the Septuagint. The legendary story of how this version came into existence is described in the Letter of Aristeas (see chapter 11). The Septuagint is the most important of the Targums (translations), as they are called in Hebrew, of the translations of Hebrew scriptures into other languages. During the years immediately preceding and following the Christian era, a number of translations were made. Some of these were the free translations of Hebrew into Aramaic. Others were the Peshitta, the main Syriac translation, the original Old Latin Version, the Coptic, and Jerome's Latin Vulgate.

The Septuagint became the authorized Greek version of the scriptures and, during the Christian era, was used widely by Christian leaders in their attempts to prove to the Jews that their crucified Savior was in fact the Messiah for whom, according to prophecy, they were waiting. This process of arguments so irritated and offended the Jews that they intensified searching through their own scriptures for arguments they could use in refuting those of the Christians.

Orient House, 1960), pp. 156-62; C. Rabin, ed., *Textus* (Jerusalem: Magnes Press, Hebrew University, 1960), 2:112-31: William H. Brownlee, *The Meaning of the Qumran Scrolls for the Bible* (Oxford: Oxford University Press, 1964), pp. 3-41.

THE JAMNIA SYNOD

After the destruction of Jerusalem in approximately A.D. 70, the Jews were scattered and their leaders sought for a unifying force to hold their people together. The Hebrew religion at this time consisted chiefly of communal reading of the Torah in homes and in such synagogues as were available. In order to unify themselves and also to meet the challenge of the Christians who were using the Jews' own scriptures against them, a synod (conference) was convened at Jamnia, located approximately at the present site of Tel Aviv, in about A.D. 90. At this synod, specific and rigid rules were established for the preservation of the scriptures. Not only was a study made of existing versions, and one agreed upon, but also such details as the width of columns and the type of script were prescribed. Because of the rigid specifications it generated, this synod therefore became one of the most important conferences in history in preserving the accuracy of the Hebrew scriptures.

In succeeding years a number of additional versions of Hebrew scriptures were prepared. Among these was one prepared in Greek and known as the Aquilla, which appeared during the latter part of the second century A.D. Early in the third century the Theodotian version was completed, and this was followed a short time later by the Symmachus version. A substantial number of other versions of the scriptures also appeared in Latin.

By the middle of the third century A.D., so many versions of the scriptures were in existence that the now well-known Christian Bible Scholar Origen (A.D. 185-253) decided to bring some order from the confusion. He completed his famous Hexapla, a sixfold version that compared in parallel columns the Septuagint with the four other existing major versions. To these five versions Origen added his own, which later became one of those accepted by Christian scholars.

THE MASSORETIC TEXTS

During this same period, the Jews were also creating new versions of the scriptures and, through the influence of the

Jamnia Synod, were attempting to hold their ancient scriptural traditions to as pure a state as possible. Sometime later, possibly as late as the seventh century A.D., a new group of Jewish recordkeepers came into existence. These were the Massoretes, successors to the scribes who were the recordkeepers prior to and during the lifetime of Jesus. They were the preservers of the Massorah (the textual tradition), and from them came the Massoretic Texts, from which final agreement was secured on the one version that has come down through Judaism to the present time.

Since the creation of the Massoretic Texts, a controversy has arisen among the scholars regarding the relative authenticity of this version as compared with the Septuagint. By and large, until the King James Version, the Septuagint remained the favorite among the Protestants, while the Massoretic Texts were used and considered authentic by Judaism. The Catholics favored their Latin versions, mainly Jerome's Latin Vulgate.

During later years, however, a tendency developed among both Christian and Hebrew scholars to favor the Massoretic Texts. One of the arguments supporting this conclusion was the fact that these texts were basically translations from Hebrew to Hebrew, rather than from Hebrew to Greek and then to some other language. It was felt that some accuracy might have been lost in the process of translation.

Discovery of the Dead Sea Scrolls provided some answers to this controversy. One of the important fragments found in the caves was from the Old Testament book of Samuel. Dr. Frank Cross accomplished some important work on this fragment, and as he carefully brushed the old parchment to bring the characters into focus, he observed with surprise that some of the passages were quite different from the Massoretic Texts. Checking further, he found that these passages coincided far more closely with the Septuagint version. With rising excitement, he discovered that the Qumran copy agreed thirteen times with the Septuagint as against the Massoretic Texts and agreed only four times with the Massoretic as against the Septuagint. As significant as this seemed, Dr. Cross was even more impressed by the fact that the Dead Sea Scrolls preserved many quotations that agreed with neither the Septuagint nor the Massoretic Texts. This discovery has led to questions about scribal accuracy and also about the possibility that the Qumran Samuel might have come from an older source than the Septuagint. Undoubtedly there were Hebrew scriptures long before the third century B.C., and the Samuel fragment could have come from one of these ancient records.[6]

THE SAMARITAN VERSION

A discussion of Hebrew scriptures would be incomplete without mention of the Samaritan Pentateuch. These old records, scrolls rolled on sticks, are presently in the possession of a group of people who claim to be descendants of the original Samaritans and who still live near the site of the ancient city of Sebaste and also near ancient Shechem, where Abraham built his first altar when he entered the land of Canaan. Although Bible scholars have accepted the Samaritan Pentateuch with considerable caution, studies of the Dead Sea Scrolls have added substantially more credulity to the authenticity and accuracy of these old Samaritan records.

[6]F. M. Cross, "A New Qumran Biblical Fragment," Basor Supplementary Studies, December 1953, pp. 15-26.

27
THE TEACHINGS
OF JUDAISM

According to the Old Testament record, more than
twenty-five hundred years elapsed from the time of creation until Moses heard the voice of God out of the burning
bush. This long span of history is covered in fifty relatively
short chapters in the book of Genesis in the Torah and in the
King James Version, and in two chapters in Exodus, the second
book of Moses. Unless the pseudepigraphic books of Adam
and Eve, Enoch, and the Testaments of the Twelve Patriarchs
can be accepted as authoritative versions of original records,
the religious account of God's dealings with his people during
these twenty-five hundred years, as found in Genesis and the
first two chapters of Exodus, is scanty indeed.

From the Genesis account, however, a general picture of
important Hebrew religious concepts can be obtained, but the
details of church organization, if any, and the specifics of
church rituals and teachings as they apply to the individual are
found only in the other four books of the Pentateuch. Thus, if
in the beginning, as recorded in Genesis, God did establish his
plan of salvation for Adam and his posterity, unless other
records have been or will be found, only the briefest of information is available to guide man as to the nature and specifics of
such a gospel, or plan of salvation.

The information that is available, however, is significant.
The short account in Genesis and up to the time of the mission
of Moses tells about one God who created this earth and the

universe and who rules and governs it. This monotheistic concept is the first such account in recorded religious history and was declared at a time when all oriental religions and Greek philosophies expounded the theories of multiple gods.

In Judaism today, a declaration given by Moses himself is repeated by every faithful Jew in his daily prayers in Hebrew, *"Sherma Yisroel Adonoi Elohenu Adonoi Achod."* These are the words that Moses, after his first encounter with God, gave to the children of Israel. They mean, "Hear, O Israel, the Lord our God, the Lord is One." This tremendous revelation of the oneness of God, together with the fact that he was the Creator and the Organizer and is the Governor of all that is in and around the earth, constitutes the basic foundation of Judaism. These also are the prime concepts upon which rest the teachings of Christianity and Islam.

The story of the creation has additional important information about the nature of God and about his relationship to man. Genesis 1:26 records the decision to make man and contains two extremely important concepts: "And God said, Let us make man in our own image, after our own likeness; and let him have dominion. . . ."[1]

From this passage, we find that although God was directing the activity, others possibly were assisting him, as is indicated by the words "us" and "our." Also, God said, "Let us make man in our own image, after our own likeness." This indicates that man and God are in the same image and likeness; this, of

---

[1]This translation is from the King James Version. In a modern translation of the Torah the statement "let us make man in our image, after our likeness" also appears. See *The Torah* (Philadelphia: The Jewish Publication Society of America, 1962), p. 4. In commenting on this passage *The Encyclopedia Judaica Jerusalem* (New York: Macmillan Co., 1971) gives interpretations from many Jewish authorities. It rejects polytheism with Exodus 20:3, "You shall have no other gods before me," but contains the statement "Finally, the plural verb Na'aseh, ('Let us make') and plural noun, be-Zolmenu, ('in our image') and ki-demutenu, ('after our likeness', Gen. 1:26) may refer to a divine council with which God consults before the important step of creating man, though other feasible explanations have been advanced." (Page 1061.) According to rabbinic teachings, these "aggadah" were themselves created forms and not co-architects or co-builders. (Ibid., p. 644.)

course, was an entirely new concept among the pagan religions, which had created their gods in many shapes and forms, often in some vague way related to the elements, the sun, glorified beasts and animals, and nature. This concept of man's likeness to God is further confirmed in Genesis in verses that record that Adam walked and talked with God, as did his children and as did other patriarchs, including Enoch, Abraham, and Moses.

Genesis provides another significant Judaic concept, man's free agency. Adam and Eve were placed in the garden and told that they could partake of the fruit of the trees of the garden except "of the fruit of the tree which is in the midst of the garden. . . ." (Genesis 3:3) God commanded that they should neither eat it nor touch it. Nevertheless, they had their free agency, and the choice was theirs. Adam and Eve did partake of this forbidden fruit and thus introduced sin and death into the world.

In Judaism, the concept of free agency has permeated the entire history of the Jewish people. Time and time again, individually and collectively, the Jews, in exercising their free agency, deviated so far from the laws of Moses and their religious teachings that their prophets over and over again called them to repentance and threatened that unless they returned to the Lord's commandments they would be scattered over the face of the earth and destroyed.

Even in the interpretation of the Law and its commandments, the Jews exercise a wide scope of free agency. For example: "The idea [of free agency] is basic to Judaism; the philosophy transcends dogma and ritual. Within the bounds of God's laws, a Jew is free to choose what he believes and to believe what he chooses."[2]

Both the Torah and the King James Version give two accounts of the creation. The first account is in Genesis 1, but the second in Genesis 2 has given rise to much discussion and commentary. The rabbinic conclusion is that the second ac-

[2]Thompson, et al., *The World's Great Religions* (New York: Time, Inc., 1957), p. 148.

count is merely a repetition of the first. One encyclopedia calls the account in Genesis 1 the Elohim (*Yaaraey*) account and the Genesis 2 account the Jehovah (*Yhwh*).

Concerning this question, the *Encyclopedia Judaica* gives this statement:

> Two general statements may be made: (1) the narrative was not generally taken literally as an act of creation in six days, and (2) the rabbis were fully aware of the difficulties which modern Biblical criticism attempts to solve with the documentary theory, such as the different names of God and the double or treble accounts, that they answered them on the basis of the unity of the account of creation. Although the fact of creation remains a prime article of faith, there is no uniform or binding beliefs as to how the world was created.[3]

Another problem connected with the account of the creation is whether or not God created everything out of nothing or out of already existing materials. The *Encyclopedia Judaica* presents both arguments by such authorities as Bet Shammai, Bet Hillel, Simeon B. Yohai, R. Jacob, and R. Elizar, and the medieval philosophy of Saadiah, Maimonides, and Levi Ben Gersham. The rabbinic conclusion in the *Encyclopedia Judaica* seems to be that God did not create the world out of nothing.[4] The modern rabbinic conclusion, as given by Rosenzweig, is that "creation is an endless on-going process and not an event that took place at one particular moment in the past."[5]

Another interesting aspect of the story of the creation is the fact that in Genesis 1 it is God who creates all things. In Genesis 2, beginning with verse 4, the name *Lord God* first appears and from thereon throughout the chapter, reference is consistently made to that name. This also has given rise to much discussion and commentary. Judaism's conclusion is that God (*Elohim*) and Lord God (*Yahveh* or *Jehovah*) are two names for the same

---

[3]*Encyclopedia Judaica, op. cit.,* p. 1066.

[4]Anciently, Plato advanced the concept that an eternal God brought the world into existence out of already existing materials. Philo could not accept the platonic theory and resolved the problem by concluding that God created the preexistent matter, then made the world out of this preexistent material. Ibid., p. 1066.

[5]Ibid., p. 1070.

God. This one God, according to rabbinic teachings, is not to be referred to as spirit, because he is invisible, yet he manifests his strength in the powers of nature.[6] He is omnipotent, irresistible, omnisciently wise, knows no darkness, reveals the future, is the source of all understanding, gives men their skills, is the sole creator, has no likeness, and no image can be made of him.[7] The *Encyclopedia Judaica* states: "God's essential personality is primarily reflected in His attributes which motivate His acts. He is King, Judge, Father, Shepherd, Mentor, Healer and Redeemer, to mention only a few."[8]

With respect to God's character, the *Encyclopedia Judaica* refers to the fact that Amos was conscious of God's justice, and Hosea referred to God's love combined with forgiveness and compassion. The prophet Ezekiel states that God does not desire the destruction of the wicked, but that those who repent shall live. (See Ezekiel 18:23.)

Genesis 2 in the Torah introduces the Sabbath and lays the foundation for the Judaic observation of the sacred nature of this holy day:

> On the seventh day God finished the work which He had been doing, and He ceased [rested] on the seventh day from all the work which He had done.
> And God blessed the seventh day and declared it holy, because on it God ceased from all the work of creation which He had done. (Genesis [Torah] 2:2-3.)

Adherents of Judaism are divided into three groups, Orthodox, Conservative, and Reform. Within each of these are many divisions, each with its own specific interpretation of how to apply the laws of Moses. With respect to the Sabbath, the Orthodox Jew will perform no work on that day and will refuse to travel, to use the telephone, to write letters or any other thing, to touch money, or to engage in any commercial activity. For all devout Jews, the Sabbath is a holy day, the

[6]See, for example, Exodus 19:18; Isaiah 40:13; Habakkuk 3:4-20; Zechariah 4:6.

[7]For example, Job, 28:23; 42:2; Psalm 24:8; 36:9-10; Isaiah 43:9; Daniel 2:22.

[8]*Encyclopedia Judaica, op. cit.,* p. 650.

Lord's day, which begins at sundown on Friday and ends at sundown on Saturday.

When the Sabbath begins, the Jewish wife, with her husband and children surrounding her, traditionally lights the ritual candles and offers this blessing: "Blessed art Thou, O Lord God, King of the universe who hast sanctified us by Thy law and commanded us to kindle the Sabbath light." Following this, the wine is blessed by the father, or the head of the house; then the family sips the wine and the father cuts the Sabbath loaf. In the devout Jewish home, the Sabbath is a time for refreshing the spirit, for peace and rest, and for family reunion.

Originally, and down through the Christian era, any work on the Sabbath was punishable by death. More recently, broader interpretations have been permitted, but to all devout Jews, the Sabbath (*Shabbat*) is a holy, sacred day, one that is celebrated and observed with rest, reading, prayers, and attendance at religious services.

THE PROMISE GIVEN TO ABRAHAM

Another great Judaic concept found in the Torah version of Genesis is the promise given to Abraham and the covenant the Lord made with him. As recorded in chapter 12:

> The Lord said to Abram, "Go forth from your native land
> and from your father's house to the land that I will show you.
> I will make of you a great nation,
> And I will bless you;
> I will make your name great,
> And you shall be a blessing.
> I will bless those who bless you.
> And curse him that curses you;
> And all the families of the earth
> Shall bless themselves by you. (Genesis [Torah] 12:1-3.)

This promise and covenant was continued by the Lord through Abraham's son and grandson, Isaac and Jacob, and has remained a promised blessing among the Hebrews throughout the four thousand years of their history, as vibrant and as much alive in Judaic faith today as it was when it was given to Abraham.

After Abraham and his party had entered the land of Canaan, the Promised Land, the Lord expanded upon his promise:

> Raise your eyes and look out from where you are, to the north and south, to the east and west, for I give all the land that you see to you and your offspring forever. I will make your offspring as the dust of the earth, so that if one can count the dust of the earth, then your offspring too can be counted. But, walk about the land, to its length and its breadth, for I give it to you. (Genesis [Torah] 13:14-17.)

These basic concepts of obedience to the Lord's instruction are the most important in the first book of the Torah and are repeatedly emphasized. The remainder of Genesis is composed chiefly of the story of Adam and Eve and their posterity, a brief mention of Enoch and his righteousness, the account of evil that spread over the land, and the story of Noah and the earth's destruction by floods, together with the covenant that if such a destruction once again became necessary, it would not be done by water.

After these significant events, the story continues with the generations following Noah and the account of the people's attempt to build a tower to heaven, with the resultant curse of the Lord and the confounding of their language. Until that time all the people had spoken one language, but the Lord's curse produced Babel, or "confusion," and the Lord scattered the people over the face of the earth.

The Genesis account in the Torah then turns to Abraham, his promise, his possession of the promised land, and his posterity, which culminated in the Twelve Tribes of Israel. It concludes with the story of how one of Jacob's twelve sons, Joseph, was sold by his brothers to a caravan, which took the lad into Egypt where, over the years, he became a close friend and adviser to the Pharaoh and, because of his wisdom and foresight, was appointed Pharaoh's second in command in all Egypt. Joseph's story of conservation and preparation for the forthcoming famine, together with the beautiful and touching account of his meeting with his brothers and his father when they came to Egypt for provisions because of the famine in Canaan, is told in Genesis. Then, after Joseph's death, a new king arose in Egypt who did not know Joseph, and burdens and afflictions were imposed upon the children of Israel. The prophet-leader Moses rescued the children of Israel from their sorrowful and grievous condition and led them from Egypt back toward their promised land.

MOSES AND THE TEN COMMANDMENTS

The heart, substance, and foundation of the teachings of Judaism lie in the Ten Commandments, which, according to the record in Exodus in the Torah, were given by the Lord to Moses on Mount Sinai. There, amidst fire, smoke, and the violent trembling of the mountain, the Lord spoke to the people through Moses, saying:

> I the Lord am your God who brought you out of the land of Egypt, the house of bondage: You shall have no other gods before Me.
>
> You shall not make for yourself a sculptured image, or any likeness of what is in the heavens above, or on the earth below, or in the waters under the earth.
>
> You shall not bow down to them or serve them.
>
> For I the Lord your God am an impassioned God, visiting the guilt of the fathers upon the children, upon the third and fourth generations of those who reject Me, but showing kindness to the thousandth generation of those who love Me and keep My commandments.
>
> You shall not swear falsely by the name of the Lord your God; for the Lord will not clear one who swears falsely by His name.
>
> Remember the sabbath day and keep it holy. Six days you shall labor and do all your work, but the seventh day is a sabbath of the Lord your God: you shall not do any work — you, your son or daughter, your male or female slave, or your cattle, or the stranger who is within your settlements. For in six days the Lord made heaven and earth and sea, and all that is in them, and He rested on the seventh day; therefore, the Lord blessed the sabbath day and hallowed it.
>
> Honor your father and your mother, that you may long endure on the land which the Lord your God is giving you.
>
> You shall not murder.
>
> You shall not commit adultery.
>
> You shall not steal.
>
> You shall not bear false witness against your neighbor.
>
> You shall not covet your neighbor's house, you shall not

covet your neighbor's wife, nor his male or female slave, or his ox or his ass, or anything that is your neighbor's. (Exodus [Torah] 20:1-14.)

The Torah account states that all the people witnessed the thunder and lightning, saw the fire and smoke, and felt and saw the trembling of the mountain. Thoroughly shaken and humbled by what they had seen, they promised Moses they would follow his instructions as he received them from the Lord.

The detailed instructions received by Moses and transmitted to the people are recorded in the Torah in the books of Exodus, Leviticus, Numbers, and Deuteronomy. The instructions cover their responsibilities to their God, their relationship to each other and to the stranger within their gates, the nature of their sacrifices and rituals, their festivals and dietary restrictions, and all the commandments they should follow in order to be deserving of the Lord's blessings. No attempt will be made here to list or discuss these complex religious instructions, which are discussed, analyzed, interpreted, and commented upon in the Talmud and in the rabbinic writings. But certain general and fundamental Judaic concepts, practices, and festivals important to an understanding of Judaism are here presented and discussed briefly.

1. *The Messianic Expectation.* Since the beginning of their religion, the Jews have looked forward, despite many disappointments, to the ultimate advent of a Messiah, who will come at the climax of history and will usher into the world the kingdom of God, with its peace, tranquillity, and blessedness. When this happens, devout Jews will accept the reality of the resurrection and the immortality of the soul. It will be a time of judgment and recompense for good and evil.

2. *The Importance of the Family.* The sanctity of the marriage covenant is highly honored by devout Jews, and the family and the home, with the assistance of the rabbi and the synagogue, are the centers of Jewish life. The emphasis is on the ethics of individual actions and the importance of the home as a house of God and the foundation of family worship and training. This center emphasizes the importance of the individual who, al-

though he is made of dust and will return to dust, is motivated by that divine spark which marks his spirit as a child of God.

3. *The Importance of Knowledge.* From their earliest years, conscientious Jewish families teach their children that knowledge is important and learning and wisdom a joy that will bring success and happiness into their lives. This motivation for education has been responsible for the fact that a large percentage of Jews, in relationship to their numbers in the population, have achieved eminence in the arts and sciences. In Jewish life, the scholar is the hero.

4. *Jewish Sacred Festivals.* In addition to the observance of the weekly Sabbath, Jews celebrate a number of important festivals that are closely tied into their religious beliefs. These include Rosh Hashanah (The Jewish New Year), which occurs in September or October, and Yom Kippur and the Day of Atonement, which together constitute a ten-day period of repentance and attempts to return to God. Yom Kippur is a day of fast when one is supposed to weigh carefully his past actions, and, through prayer at the synagogue, seek God's forgiveness.

Also important in Jewish religious life is the Passover, which comes in March or April and which celebrates the Israelites' liberation from Egypt. The holiday of Simchas Torah is celebrated to express Jewish thankfulness for the Torah and for the instructions given through it by the Lord. It also marks the end of a suggested annual reading of the Torah.

Certain of the Jewish festivals, although founded on religious history, are festive days. For example, the Purim, observed in March or April, is a time of family fun and masquerade; it celebrates the time when Queen Esther rescued the Jews from the evil subjugation of the tyrant Haman. The Festival of Shabuoth, celebrated in May or June, is a joyous occasion that acknowledges the people's attitude toward the blessings of the first fruits of the season and also commemorates God's giving of the Ten Commandments to Moses. In some segments of Judaism, this is also the time for the confirmation of children who have reached the age of fifteen. The Feast of the Tabernacles is a week-long celebration in autumn marking the gathering of the harvest and also commemorating the escape of the children of Israel from Egypt during which time they built flimsy shelters of boughs and branches to preserve themselves from the occasional rains and cold of the desert.

The Festival of Lights, known as Hanukkah, observed in November or December, commemorates the victory of Judas Maccabaeus in 166 B.C., when he recaptured Judea and vanquished the Syrians. This celebration is near the Christians' Christmas, and many reformed Jewish families enjoy the occasion with hymn singing and gifts for the children. It is on Hanukkah that families traditionally light a candelabra with eight candlesticks, commemorating the rekindling of the lights in the temple after the Maccabean victory.

5. *The Ritual of Circumcision.* One of the most fundamental of Jewish rituals is circumcision, which, according to Mosaic Law, every male child must undergo eight days after birth. This ritual is performed to commemorate the covenant and promise God gave to Abraham, a central Jewish belief. Circumcision is the first step into Judaism for a child and is followed by bar mitzvah at age thirteen, when the young man becomes a son of the commandment and assumes full, adult religious responsibility.

Also important in the family is the marriage ceremony, a sacred ordinance to Jews. The husband and wife are expected to live together in love and to raise their children in righteousness according to Jewish customs and religious commandments. Although divorce is permitted, marriage and family unity are sacred and the Talmud instructs the husband: "Love thy wife as thyself and honor her more than thyself. Be careful not to cause woman to weep, for God counts her tears."

A GOD-CENTERED RELIGION

Judaism is a "one God"-centered religion. From its beginning, its adherents have been taught to love God and keep his commandments. Judaism was teaching this ages before the Pharisee lawyer asked Jesus which was the greatest commandment in the law, and Jesus replied: " . . . thou shalt love the Lord thy God with all thy heart, and with all thy soul, and with all thy mind, and with all thy strength; this is the first commandment. And the second is like, namely this, thou shalt love thy neighbor as thyself. . . ." (Mark 12:30-31.) Jesus taught that one should do unto others as he would desire others to do unto him. The great Jewish rabbi, Hillel, a hundred years before the Savior, stated this commandment negatively when he said: "Do not do unto others what you don't want others to do unto you." In commenting on this statement, Dimont observes: "There is a world of philosophic difference between these two expressions, and the reader is invited to ponder on them and reason out why he would prefer one to the other as applied to himself."[9]

[9]Dimont, *op. cit.*, p. 47.

28
INTERRELATIONSHIPS BETWEEN JUDAISM AND CHRISTIANITY

Of all the great religions and religious philosophies, both living and extinct, no two are so closely interrelated as are Judaism and Christianity. This close interrelationship is most impressively apparent in their history, in many of their doctrines, in the account of the story of the creation, and in the teachings, exhortations, and predictions of the Old Testament prophets.

Both of these theologies basically accept the Old Testament as the word of God, with some differences in interpretation. Both are monotheistic in that they agree that one God is the creator and governor of this world and of the universe that surrounds it. Both accept without question the predictions of the Old Testament prophets of the coming of a Messiah, a Redeemer who would save the world and its people from their sins and troubles and who would provide a plan through which all mankind might return to a state of blessedness. Both accept the story of the creation, the disobedience of Adam and Eve, the brief account of the righteousness of Enoch and his city, the promise and covenant given by the Lord to Abraham, Isaac, and Jacob, and the story of Joseph and his experiences in Egypt. Moses is considered by both religions as one of the greatest prophets and religious leaders of all time, and the Ten Commandments given to him by the Lord are accepted as divine guides for all mankind.

The teachings and exhortations of the Old Testament prophets are accepted by both religions as the word of God.

Both faiths, with all of their divisions and subdivisions, recognize the need, with some differing interpretations, of applying their teachings and accepting their prophecies if the world is to be spared the dire predictions of destruction.

However, despite these agreements, on other certain basic but extremely important theological concepts these two religions are poles apart and are more fundamentally different, even antagonistic, than are any other of the world's religions or religious philosophies.

There are three differences between Judaism and Christianity: (1) the origin of Christianity; (2) the claim of the Messiahship of Jesus; and (3) certain fundamental differences in doctrinal concepts, church organization, and religious rituals and practices.

THE QUESTION OF THE ORIGIN OF CHRISTIANITY

The question of how the Christian church originated has been discussed and argued ever since the time of the ministry of Jesus. Countless critics and observers, both Jewish and non-Jewish, have maintained that Jesus, in his teachings and ministry, had no intention of establishing a new religion. His purpose, they claim, was the same as that of many of the prophets before his time — to call the Jews to repentance and to persuade them to return to the pure and unadulterated teachings of their forefathers who had given them God's true commandments. These critics claim that it was not until long after the crucifixion of Jesus that his followers, particularly Peter and Paul, began the organization of a church that at first was known by many names, including "The Elect," "The Church," "The Assembly," "The Brethren," and "The Disciples," and was not called "Christian" until many years later at Antioch. (See Acts 11:26.)

Jewish scholars and rabbis, almost without exception, conclude that Christianity was just another of the dissident, divisive sects that broke away from the body of the church, including the Zealots and Essenes, that were so numerous at this time. They point out that the Jewish church also was divided into two main branches — the Sadducees and the Pharisees —

as well as another, smaller group, the Scribes, and that for groups to break away from the body of a church was in no way unusual. These rabbis point out that Jesus was a Jew, he taught extensively in the Jewish synagogue, his audiences were primarily Jews, most of his converts were Jews, all of his closest disciples or apostles were Jews, and early in his ministry he confined his teachings to the Jews and instructed his disciples to do likewise. Moreover, Jesus stated plainly: "Think not that I am come to destroy the law [of Moses], or the prophets: I am not come to destroy, but to fulfil." (Matthew 5:17.)

Rabbinic teachings confirm this Jewish origin of Christianity. Although countless Jewish scholars have expressed their conviction with respect to the Jewish origin of Christianity, for our purposes here this concise statement by a contemporary Jewish scholar will suffice:

> Jesus of Nazareth was born during the reign of Augustus and died during that of Tiberius. As a Jew, he fully accepted the Jewish law. The community that he founded, comparable in some ways to a group such as the Essenes, saw itself as a movement of reform and fulfillment with Judaism, not as a secession from it; and it always called itself the "New Israel." Most of Jesus' ethical precepts, and even the forms in which he expressed them, can be paralleled in rabbinical teachings, and the earliest Christians were devout worshippers at the temple. But, as happened in the case of the extremist Jewish religious groups, he and his followers came into conflict with the Roman authorities and he was executed for sedition.[1]

The prevalent conclusion of certain Christian critics is that Christianity originated from the environment and circumstances of the times. According to this view, prior to and during this period of Jewish history tremendous influences had been exerted on Judea by its past conquerors, including the Babylonians, Assyrians, Persians, Egyptians, Greeks, and Romans. During the ministry of Jesus, these influences were mingling with and being altered by Roman and Greek

[1]David Flusser, "The Son of Man," in *The Crucible of Christianity*, ed. Arnold Toynbee (New York: World Publishing Co., 1969), p. 215. See also *Encyclopedia Judaica, op. cit.*, pp. 506-15, for a discussion of the Jewish concept of the origin of Christianity.

philosophies, mainly the latter, with the result that Jewish religious concepts became extensively Hellenized. It was out of this melange of philosophical influences, the critics claim, that Christianity developed.

For example, Eusebius of Caesaria (A.D. 263-340), a Christian theologian and historian wrote:

> ... I learned from writers, that down to the invasion of the Jews under Adrian, there were fifteen successions of bishops in that church, all which, they say, were Hebrews from the first. .... For at that time the whole church under them, consisted of faithful Hebrews who continued from the time of the apostles, until the siege that then took place.[2]

In writing about these same influences, Jean Danielou states:

> The Judaeo-Christian and "pagano-Christian" Churches differ sharply from each other. In the former, the Jewish religious regulations, such as circumcision, were still held to be obligatory, and the faith was expressed less in theological and metaphysical formulae than by a symbolic system of mystic letters and numbers, secret rites and signs and esoteric names and doctrines. In recent years a number of relics of the Judaeo-Christians have been recovered in Palestine which depict these Jewish religious regulations and rites.[3]

According to religious historians at the time of Jesus' ministry, Judaism had been significantly altered by the pagan influences of the Jews' conquerors and, as a result, the people were not particularly receptive to teachings of Jesus and his disciples, who were calling them back to the commandments of their ancient prophets. In fact, Christianity did not gain a significant foothold in Judea; although it became an organized church there, its growth was slow until it went into the surrounding areas, particularly Greece and Phoenecia, where the antagonism of the Judaizers[4] was not so intense. On this point, one author comments:

---

[2]*Eusebius' Ecclesiastical History*, Book 4, Chapter 5.

[3]Jean Danielou, "That the Scriptures Might be Fulfilled," *The Crucible of Christianity, op. cit.*, p. 261.

[4]According to J. R. Dummelow, Judaizers, as they were called, were always hostile to the wider development of Christianity. They found fault with Peter

Here at once the critic encounters the paradox of Christian origins. The new religion grew out of Judaism; it was Jewish in its form of presentation, it was committed to Jewish disciples; yet, it never took root in Jewish soil. . . . thirty years after the Crucifixion, Palestine was already a backwater. The new faith goes, by a sort of homing instinct, to the great industrial centers of population along the trade routes of the imperial world.[5]

In commenting on the philosophical influences with which the originating Christianity was forced to contend, Christian scholar John Alfred Faulkner observed:

Besides the ordinary state of local religions of antiquity, there were so-called mysteries, or mystery religions, which had wide scope and which, it is claimed, entered into our own faith. The Eleusinian mysteries of Greece, the Dionysiac also of Greece, the Isaic of Egypt, the Mithras religion from Persia, penetrated into the Roman empire, and when Christianity was spreading, formed a background or atmosphere which could not be escaped.[6]

With respect to the nature and extent of the views of pseudo-Christian critics who questioned the authenticity of

---

for his liberal views and attitude toward the gentiles (Acts 11:2) at an early period of the church. Paul, however, was the principal object of their aversion. It is possible that the Judaizers had never forgiven his persecution of the Christians before his conversion; and certainly from the date of his return to Antioch, after his first mission to Galatia, they opposed his admission of the uncircumcised heathen to the fellowship of the church. (See Acts 15:1; Galatians 2:4.) They sent emissaries after him to alienate the Jewish converts from allegiance to him and bring the gentiles into bondage to the Mosaic Law. (See Galatians 1:7; 2:12-13; 3:1; 5:2; 6:12; Philippians 3:2.)

[5]F. R. Barry, *The Relevance of Christianity*, (London: Nesbett and Co., Ltd., 1931), p. 48. For further authoritative observations on this concept of the origin of Christianity, see E. F. Scott, *The Kingdom and the Messiah* (Edinburgh: T. & T. Clark, 1911), preface and chapter 2; T. B. Strong, *The Origins of Christianity* (Oxford: Clarendon Press, 1909), chapter 2; Frederick Harrison, *The Positive Evaluation of Religion* (London: Wm. Heinemann, 1913), chapters 1 and 2; George P. Fisher, *The Grounds of Theistic and Christian Beliefs* (London, Hodder and Stoughton, 1907), p. 324; Carl Mickalson, *Wordly Theology* (New York: Charles Scribner's Sons, 1967), chapter 10; Rudolph Steiner, *Christianity as Mystical Fact* (Rudolph Steiner Publishing Co., 1961), 1:174ff.

[6]John Alfred Faulkner, *Burning Questions in Historical Christianity* (New York: Abingdon Press, 1930), chapter 2.

the New Testament account of the origin of Christianity, here are two enlightening quotations:

> There is a school of thought which disputes the originality and distinctive character of Christianity, maintaining that it gives us nothing more than a synthesis of pre-existing elements under the form of a new myth. . . . it is the result of the impact of the Greek with the Jewish mind in an age of universal syncretism.[7]

> These are the established facts, obvious to anyone who had made a careful study of Israel at the period just before the Christian era, which led to the conclusion . . . that Christianity was nothing more than a Hellenized Judaism. In 1860 Michael Nicolas wrote, "Christianity sprang from the bosom of Judaism; if it has any direct and immediate antecedents, it is there that we must seek them [thus alleging his interest in Christianity as his motive for undertaking a study of the religious doctrines of the Jews]. Towards the end of his life Renan still maintained that, "The whole development of Christianity had its roots in the Judaism of the first and second centuries before Christ. The countries which were the first to surrender to primitive Christianity were those which Judaism had already conquered during the two or three centuries before Jesus Christ."[8]

These observations depict not only the Jewish point of view, but also conclusions of a segment of scriptural critics, so-called Christians, who agree with the basic Jewish concept. The conclusions are, of course, in direct conflict with the story told in the New Testament and do not represent the point of view of the majority of Christian churches.

[7]Ernest Havet, *LeChristianisme et ses Origines,* as quoted in E. DePressense, *The Ancient World and Christianity* (New York: A. C. Armstrong & Son, 1890), page ix.

[8]Charles Guignebert, *The Jewish World in the Time of Jesus* (New York: University Books, 1959), p. 2. Ernest Renan, a researcher in Semitic philology, was first banished from his professorship in Hebrew at the College de France but later, in 1862, was installed in the chair of Hebrew. In his first lecture he referred to Jesus Christ as an incomparable'man. This statement so disturbed the powerful priests that he was suspended as a disturber of the public peace and then began his writings of the life of Jesus and the history of the origins of Christianity.

THE CHRISTIAN CONCEPT OF ITS OWN ORIGIN

As with all of the great world religions, Christianity is fragmented into many different churches and sects. The two main divisions are Catholics and Protestants. Many other Christian churches are not affiliated with Catholicism but do not claim to be among those that protested against the changes and alterations they see in the so-called mother church. Not all of these differing church organizations agree with the origins of Christianity. However, the general, orthodox view, the conclusion accepted by most Christian churches, is that Christianity was founded during the ministry of Jesus Christ and was perfected into a worldwide church by his disciples in the years following his crucifixion.

The arguments and evidence that early Christianity was deeply influenced by existing Judaic and paganistic concepts are most impressive and persuasive. The fact that countless Bible scholars, both Jewish and Christian, have come to this conclusion is of such significance that it cannot be ignored. To do so would be an attempt to set aside one of the most impelling questions concerning Christianity's evolution and development, and even the question of its authenticity.

There is no doubt that after the deaths of the original apostles, as Christianity spread throughout the Greco-Roman world, it absorbed many of the pagan concepts and practices that had for so many years been deeply imbedded in the beliefs and traditions of those who accepted the new religion. Even before his crucifixion, Jesus warned his disciples that many would come in his name claiming to be Christ and would be so clever in their teachings that unless the disciples held fast to his teachings and remained steadfast, even the very elect would be deceived. (Matthew 24:4-5, 23-24.) In the Gospel of John, he warned his followers that they would be cast out of the synagogues and that the time would come when his enemies would kill them and believe they were doing justice because they had not known either Jesus or the Father. (John 16:2.)

The process of alteration and change had already become a serious problem even before the deaths of the original apostles.

In his letters to the saints in the various cities surrounding the Mediterranean and throughout Galatia, Paul frequently called the people to repentance and warned them of dangerous heresies that were creeping in among them. He alerted the Thessalonians not to be deceived by those who would tell them that the day of the second coming of Christ was at hand, for that day would not come until there should be a falling away first and that the devil himself would be revealed as a son of perdition. (2 Thessalonians 2:2-4.)

In writing to Timothy, Paul declared: "For the time will come when they will not endure sound doctrine; and after their own lusts shall they heap to themselves teachers, having itching ears; And they shall turn away their ears from the truth, and shall be turned unto fables." (2 Timothy 4:3-4.)

With respect to the extent to which these predictions had already come to pass during the ministry of the apostles, Paul chided the Galatians that they would soon be lured away from the truth of the gospel of Christ to another gospel that was a perversion of Christ's teachings. Then he added: "But though we, or an angel from heaven, preach any other gospel unto you than that which we have preached unto you, let him be accursed." (Galatians 1:8; see also Galatians 1:6-7.)

Many additional evidences of the extent of change and the amount of heresy that was continually being introduced into the church are scattered throughout the New Testament.[9] These references provide some evidence of the challenge faced by the followers of Christ in their efforts to encourage the saints to hold fast to the truths that had been given to them by Jesus and his apostles. Despite these conscientious efforts, fundamental changes did come into the church, and within a relatively short time, surely no longer than two hundred years, it would have been difficult to recognize the similarities between what was then taught and practiced and what actually were the teachings of Jesus and his apostles.

[9]See, for example, John 16:1-4; Acts 20:29-30; 2 Thessalonians 2:7-12; 1 Timothy 4:1-3; Titus 1:10-16; 2 Peter 2:1-3; Jude 3-4 and 17-19.

In commenting on these basic changes, this representative statement from a Bible scholar is pertiment:

> As someone has said, the history of Christianity between the time when the first Christian congregation fled from Jerusalem, just before Titus' triumph in 70 A.D., a century later, is like a plunge into a tunnel. We know it came out at this end with a fully articulated institution — churches, the equivalent of dioceses, bishops, minor clergy, sacraments and all the rest — together with a proliferating and subtle theology. But we really do not know a great deal about what went on in the tunnel. [10]

This battle over heresies and disagreements over concepts, principles, and rituals culminated in the council at Nicaea in A.D. 325. The controversy became so intense that Emperor Constantine, even though he was not an avowed Christian and was not baptized until he was on his deathbed, decided a conference should be called between the quarreling factions in an effort to come to some kind of acceptable agreement. No attempt will be made here to delve into the basic and minute variations in the interpretation of what should be the true teachings of Jesus. One extremely important doctrinal argument, however, deserves special attention — the bitter controversy of whether or not Christ was of the same substance as God the Father or whether he was of a different, but like, substance. The question was discussed and argued to great lengths, and it appeared as though those who favored his substance as being like the Father's, but not the same, would win. Nevertheless, because of a brilliant argument advanced by Athanasius, the Nicene Creed, which described all three members of the Trinity as being of one substance, won.

JUDAIC INFLUENCES ON CHRISTIANITY

Returning to the basic question of the extent to which Judaism influenced early Christianity, the influence was great. Jesus came not to destroy the law but to fulfill it, and the gospel he taught was the gospel of truth. Consequently, the truths

---

[10]Paul Hutchinson, in *The World's Great Religions* (New York: Time, Inc., 1957), p. 196.

that were a part of Judaism remained a part of the teachings of Jesus. There is no argument whatsoever about this. The real question Bible scholars must recognize is that when they discuss and analyze Christianity, they must make a clear distinction between the pristine teachings of Jesus and his immediate disciples and what later evolved as Christianity.

The logical conclusion is that the teachings of Jesus *did not* evolve from Judaism or any of the pagan religions then dominant in the area where Jesus' gospel grew and flourished. In the first place, the original teachings of Jesus are plainly stated in the New Testament, including the four Gospels, the Acts, the Pauline and General Epistles, and John's book of Revelation. From the point of view of the Jewish scholars, this is presumptive because they do not accept the New Testament. True Christians, however, must not only accept the New Testament but must also base their conclusions about the teachings of Jesus upon this sacred scripture.

One of the fundamental principles of the gospel of Jesus Christ is that it encompasses all truth and light from every source. Moreover, truth and light are everlasting and endure forever. As the Psalmist declared: "For the Lord is good; his mercy is everlasting; and his truth endureth to all generations" (Psalm 100:5), and "Thy righteousness is an everlasting righteousness, and thy law is the truth." (Psalm 119:142.)

Isaiah said, concerning accepting the truth, from whatever source, and making it part of the gospel: "Open ye the gates, that the righteous nation which keepeth the truth may enter in." (Isaiah 26:2.) In this statement, no distinction is made as to whether or not the nation is Israelite or pagan. If it has the truth, Isaiah declares, the gates should be opened so that the truth can enter.

Regarding the light that quickens the minds of all men, Jesus said: "I am the light of the world: he that followeth me shall not walk in darkness, but shall have the light of life." (John 8:12.)

The apostle Paul recognized the universality of truth and exhibited his determination to embrace all of it. He said: "For we can do nothing against the truth, but for the truth." (2 Corinthians 13:8.)

The fact that Jesus accepted and taught all truths, regardless of their source, in no way indicates that he borrowed or that his gospel evolved from the sources of the truths, whether a part of Judaism or of any of the world religions that preceded his birth. He came to fulfill the law, meaning he came to replenish it, to make it complete, to restore it to its pristine truth, to make it truly the word of God. Many truths and much light existed, and still exist, in the religions of the world. Honest seekers after truth, such as Confucius, Tao, Brahman, Buddha, Allah, and the Hebrew prophets and leaders, if they asked with unwavering faith, would undoubtedly find truth and transmit it to their followers. Believing as we do in a just, loving, consistent, concerned Creator, it is only logical that we believe also that he would answer these supplications and provide them with the truth, for he is the origin of all truth that is everlasting, eternal, and forever.

In an article on the origin of Christianity, Dr. J. C. Lambert writes:

> But while Christianity was and is related to all the ethnic faiths, it was deeply rooted in the soil of the Old Testament. In the pagan religions we find many anticipations of Christianity, and in Judaism there is a definite and divine preparation for it. . . .
>
> But notwithstanding its historical connections with the past, Christianity was a religion absolutely new . . . and even Judaism no more accounts for Christianity than the soil accounts for the mighty tree which springs out of it. [11]

Dr. Lambert was obviously referring to the gospel of Jesus Christ. He points out that Jesus carefully distinguished between the permanent truths and passing additions that had come into Judaism. He gave a "fresh reading to its ancient law" and did not hesitate to abrogate those that were superficial. He even set himself above certain basic laws, such as the law of the Sabbath, and did not hesitate to hold himself above such great personalities as David, Abraham, and Moses. In his sermons he spoke with such clarity and definiteness that the people were awed and characterized him as one who spoke with

[11]Hastings, *op. cit.,* p. 129.

authority. The fact that he irritated the Jewish leaders to such a degree that they concluded they needed to eliminate him by the cruelest of deaths — crucifixion — is proof in itself that his was a new religion as far as the Jews were concerned, and certainly not a dissident branch of it.

In summarizing his presentation on Christianity, Dr. Lambert writes: "Christianity (the gospel of Christ) was not a mere spiritualized Judaism but a new and universal religion recognizing no distinction between Jew and Greek, circumcision and un-circumcision and seeing in Christ himself the all in all."[12]

[12]Ibid.

CONCLUSION: CHRIST'S ETERNAL GOSPEL

All the material in this book leads directly back to the fundamental questions posed in Chapter 1: Is Jesus the Christ? Is he, under the direction of the Father, the author of his eternal gospel, the plan of salvation for all mankind?

This final chapter presents some of the persuasive, convincing scriptural evidence that the answers to these vital questions must be in the affirmative. Support of the eternal nature of Christ's gospel is abundantly documented in both the Old and New Testaments. A thoughtful consideration of the evidence in these scriptures must lead to the following conclusions:

1. That the spirits of all mankind preexisted before they became mortal, and Jesus enjoyed a particularly important position in the preexistence.[1]

2. That before the foundations of the world were laid, there was a council in heaven in which Jesus participated and during which a plan of salvation was discussed. This plan was established to guide these spirits once they became embodied as mortal beings upon the earth.[2]

3. That Jesus was born upon the earth, the Only Begotten of the Father, with a mission not to establish his gospel for the first time upon the earth, but rather to call the people to repentance, to refine the gospel, and to bring it back to God's original

[1]See Numbers 16:22; 27:16; Ecclesiastes 12:7; Jeremiah 1:5; Hebrews 12:9.
[2]See Job 1:6; 38:4-7; Jude 6; Revelation 12:7-12.

commandments as established in the primitive plan given to Adam and Eve.

When Jesus began his ministry, after his baptism by John and after his forty days of fasting and prayer in the wilderness, one of his first official acts was to select twelve disciples, who were later ordained and set apart as apostles.[3] He thus opened the door for the reestablishment of his gospel with the ordained power of the higher priesthood and the reorganization of his church. Then he sent his apostles out to preach the gospel, to heal the sick, and to perform miracles. The missionary work of these twelve, together with the powerful preaching and ministry of Jesus, converted many to the gospel who, according to the record, were properly baptized by authority and became members of the church. During this first period of the spreading of the gospel, many congregations of converts were established. The four Gospels do not tell us, however, by what names these congregations, or churches, were known.

At the outset of his ministry, Jesus instructed his disciples to teach the gospel only to the Jews and not to the gentiles. Consequently, the congregations, if they were organized, must have been centered around areas of the Galilee and Judea. According to the account in Acts 11, the disciples, or followers of Jesus, were first called Christians in Antioch. (See Acts 11:26.) This was approximately in the year A.D. 43, some ten years after Jesus' crucifixion. During this period other churches had probably been established by his disciples in certain cities in the Mediterranean area, with one or more located in Jerusalem itself.

The term *church* is found nowhere in the Old Testament and only twice in the Gospels in the New Testament. The first of these, translated from the Greek word *ecclesia*, is recorded in Matthew 16:16, when the Lord asked Peter who he thought that he, Jesus, was. Peter replied: "Thou art the Christ, the Son of the living God." Jesus then told Peter that he had received

---

[3]See John 15:16; Acts 8:14-17; 9:17; 13:1-3; 19:1-6; 2 Timothy 1:6; Hebrews 1:3.

this witness through revelation and that upon this rock of revelation he, Jesus, would establish his church.[4]

The second reference to the word *church* is found in Matthew 18:15-17. Here the Lord is telling his disciples what they should do if one of their brothers should trespass against them. First, they should talk to the person who committed the trespass. If that fails, they should try again with witnesses. Only if this fails should they take the problem to the church. This would seem to imply that a church had already been established.

In the Acts of the Apostles and in the Pauline epistles, after congregations had been organized in the Mediterranean area, the designation *church* is frequently employed. Probably the first time the term was used as a corporate or congregational assembly is recorded in Acts 5, where the story is told of two disciples who attempted deliberately to cheat the Lord in their offerings. Peter admonished them and both of them were

---

[4]Peter's confession has been extensively analyzed and discussed by Bible scholars. Some interpret the statement "and upon this rock I will build my church" (Matthew 16:18) as meaning that Christ's church would be built on Peter. This is a far-fetched conclusion. In the first place, the word *rock* is not capitalized. If this word referred to Peter it would have been. Second, Christ called the church "my church" and not Peter's church. Moreover, Jesus had just stated that Peter had received his testimony through direct revelation from his Father. Therefore, it is much more logical that the reference to "rock" was the rock of revelation, upon which Christ's church was to be built. Peter himself declared that "there is none other name [than Christ's] under heaven given among men, whereby we must be saved." (Acts 4:12.)

Paul understood that the church would be Christ's church and would be guided by revelation. In his first epistle to the Corinthians he refers to the fact that divisions had occurred in the church. Some of the members were calling themselves "of Paul," others "of Apollos," still others "of Cephas" (Peter), and some "of Christ." Paul criticized the members, asking: "Is Christ divided? Was Paul crucified for you? Or were you baptized in the name of Paul?" (or Peter?)

In his letter to the Galatians, Paul wrote: "For as many of you as have been baptized unto Christ have put on Christ." (Galatians 3:27.) And to the Ephesians he wrote: "For the husband is the head of the wife, even as Christ is the head of the church...." (Ephesians 5:23.)

It was upon the rock of *revelation* that Peter and the other apostles received their witness that Jesus is the Christ, and upon this sure rock that Jesus established his church.

struck dead. As a consequence, it is recorded that "great fear came upon all the *church*, and upon as many as heard these things." (Acts 5:11; italics added.)

In the Old Testament, particularly after the Babylonian exile, the Hebrew word *edhah* was translated as "synagogue" and was the name regularly applied to gatherings of the Jewish congregations for the purpose of worship. In the New Testament, in Acts 7, Stephen, just before he was martyred by stoning, was giving his defense at one of the local synagogues. In his impassioned sermon, he reviewed the history of the Israelites from the time of Abraham down to Moses, quoting Moses' prophecy in Deuteronomy 18:15, wherein he declared that God would raise up a prophet whose teachings the Jews should follow. Stephen testified that this prophet was Jesus Christ. In his testimony he also referred to the fact that Moses "was in the *church* in the wilderness with the angel which spake to him in the mount Sinai, and with our fathers: who received the lively oracles to give unto us." (Acts 7:38; italics added.)

There is only one other indirect clue to what the church might have been called anciently. This is found in Genesis 4:26, where the account is given that a son was born to Seth, and then men began to call upon the name of the Lord. According to the ancient Greek, as recorded in a footnote in the King James Version, this phrase could also be translated "or called themselves by the name of the Lord." Although we have no further proof of this possibility, it does seem logical that the Lord's church that Jesus referred to as "my church" should have been called by his name or by "the name of the Lord."

The apostle Paul apparently had a clear understanding of the eternal nature and antiquity of the gospel taught by Jesus. In his letter to the Ephesians, he declared that there was only one gospel, "One Lord, one faith, one baptism, One God the Father of all, who is above all, and through all, in you all." (Ephesians 4:5-6.) Paul also understood that this one gospel had been taught to and preached by Abraham and Moses. In his letter to the Galatians, he declared: "And the scripture, foreseeing that God would justify the heathen through faith, preached before the gospel unto Abraham, saying, In thee shall all nations be blessed." (Galatians 3:7-8.)[5] Bible scholars interpret the words "in thee" as meaning that in Abraham's posterity, through which the predicted Messiah would come, all nations would be blessed.

With reference to Christ's gospel at the time of Moses, Paul records the following in his first epistle to the Corinthians:

> Moreover, brethren, I would not that ye should be ignorant, how that all our fathers were under the cloud, and all passed through the sea;
> And were all baptized unto Moses in the cloud and in the sea;
> And did all eat the same spiritual meat;
> And did all drink the same spiritual drink: for they drank of that spiritual Rock that followed them: and that Rock was Christ. (1 Corinthians 10:1-4.)

Speaking of the children of Israel who came out of Egypt with Moses, the author of the epistle to the Hebrews wrote: "For unto us was the gospel preached, as well as unto them [the children of Israel]: but the word preached did not profit them, not being mixed with faith in them that heard it." (Hebrews 4:2.)

These statements should leave no doubt about Paul's understanding of the antiquity of Christ's gospel and the fact that it was the gospel that was taught originally to the early fathers of the Old Testament. The fact that the children of Israel ate and drank the same spiritual meat and drink that was taught by Christ to his disciples would appear to prove the everlasting nature of the gospel.

Though Paul's statements have motivated considerable discussion by Bible students, they seem to be clear in their meaning and should require no interpretation. For example, Dummelow says, concerning Paul's statement in First Corinthians:

> Their passage through the sea was a break with their old life in Egypt; it definitely committed them to Moses' guidance, was in effect a profession of discipleship to him; they were thus *baptized unto Moses.* This typified our baptism, which is,

---

[5]J. R. Dummelow states: "proclaimed long in advance the central principle of the Christian gospel." (Dummelow, *op. cit.*, p. 951.)

> (1) deliverance from the bondage of sin and entrance upon a
> new life; (2) discipleship to Christ and union with Him. So the
> *spiritual meat* (the 'manna,' Ex. 16) and *spiritual drink* (water
> from the rock, Ex. 17, Nu. 20) by which their life was sus-
> tained, were types of the Body and Blood of Christ, by which
> our souls are nourished.[6]

Dummelow then compares this experience with the present
sacrament of the Lord's Supper where Christians partake of
the bread and the wine as symbols of Christ's body and blood.

In reference to the "spiritual Rock that followed them: and
that Rock was Christ," Dummelow makes this interesting
comment: "We see St. Paul's recognition of Christ's preexistence; the divine power which sustained the Israelites was
the power of Christ working on earth before" his birth upon
the earth.[7]

In addition to Paul, the apostle Peter appears to have had a
clear understanding of the fact that Christ's gospel had been
preached and taught from the beginning, certainly during the
days of Noah. In his general epistle to the church, Peter describes how Christ suffered for sins in order that all his followers might be brought back into God's presence. He describes
also how Christ was put to death in the flesh:

> . . . but quickened by the Spirit: by which also he went and
> preached unto the spirits in prison;
> Which sometime were disobedient, when once the longsuf-
> fering of God waited in the days of Noah, while the Ark was a
> preparing, wherein few, that is, eight souls were saved by
> water. (1 Peter 3:18-20.)

If Christ, after his crucifixion, was quickened by the Spirit
and preached his gospel to those disobedient spirits who had
been in prison since the days of Noah, surely the gospel that he
preached to them was the same gospel that he taught to his
followers during his ministry in mortality here upon the earth.
Any other conclusion would be inconsistent.

Many other evidences of the antiquity of Christ's gospel exist
in the testimonies of his disciples as recorded in the New

[6]Ibid., p. 907.
[7]Ibid.

Testament. Perhaps one of the most specific is the one given by John in the first chapter of his Gospel:

> In the beginning was the Word, and the Word was with God, and the Word was God. . . .
> All things were made by him; and without him was not any thing made that was made.
> In him was life; and the life was the light of men. . . .
> And the Word was made flesh, and dwelt among us, (and we beheld his glory, the glory as of the only begotten of the Father,) full of grace and truth. (John 1:1, 3-5, 14.)

A thoughtful understanding of the meaning of this statement is pertinent to our thesis that, according to the New Testament, Jesus the Christ was with the Father in the council in heaven, where the gospel was presented and accepted as the plan of salvation for all of mankind, and that it was Jesus, as the Jehovah (Lord God) of the Old Testament, who under the direction of the Father, actually created (organized) this physical world and all that surrounds and is in it.

This statement by John, without interpretation, establishes these facts:

1. "In the beginning," the Word existed and was with God.

2. The Word was God.

3. All things that were made were made by him (the Word) and without him was not anything made that was made.

4. In him (the Word) was life (eternal).

5. This life was the light of (all) men.

6. This Word became flesh and dwelt on the earth among mankind.

7. This flesh (Jesus Christ) was the Only Begotten of the Father and was full of grace and truth.

These are significant statements and, if accepted as fact, establish beyond a doubt the preexistence of Jesus Christ, his presence and association with the Father, and his role under the direction of the Father in the creation of the world.

Naturally, such conclusions have been and are the subjects of critical analysis and interpretation. Many Bible critics claim that John's entire gospel is spurious and unbelievable, and was written so long after the facts that it constitutes merely an account by one of Jesus' followers who attempted to invent and subvert a ficticious historical account to fit his own distorted convictions.

However, questions about John's authorship of this Gospel were not raised until the close of the eighteenth century, and these questions were not organized into formal criticisms until the appearance of Bretschneider's treatise, known as *Probabilia,* in 1820. Although this critic's arguments were satisfactorily answered, many other textural analysts continued to advance their doubts about John's authorship. One outstanding Bible commentary disposes of these arguments and then asks:

> Is there one mind of the least elevation of spiritual dissern-
> ment that does not see in this gospel marks of historical truth
> and a surpassing glory such as none of the other gospels
> possess, brightly as they too attest their own verity; and who
> will not be ready to say that if not historically true and true *just*
> *as it stands,* it never could have been by mortal man composed
> or conceived?[8]

Dummelow also meets the arguments of the doubters. As to the quality of the Gospel of John, he maintains that "few books have exercised so wide an influence as this," and "there was nothing like it in literature except the three Epistles attributed to the same source." With respect to its authenticity he quotes such authorities as St. Ignatius (A.D. 110), who reproduced it almost in its entirety; and St. Polycarp (A.D. 110) who quotes John's first epistle, which is a work most closely connected with the gospel. Basilides, the Gnostic (A.D. 120), in referring to John's Gospel, said: "And this is what is meant in the gospel, there was the true light which lighteth every man coming into the world." Dummelow also quotes from Aristides (circa A.D. 130), Papias (A.D. 130), Valentinus (A.D. 140), St. Justin Martyr (A.D. 150), Tatian (A.D. 160), Theophilus of Antioch (A.D. 180), Clement of Alexandria and Tertullian (both A.D. 200), Origen (A.D. 220), and Eusebius (A.D. 330), all of whom testified of the authenticity of John's Gospel.[9]

[8]Jamieson, Faussett, Brown, *op. cit.,* p. 127.

[9]Dummelow, *op. cit.,* pp. 770-71.

Dummelow answers each of the objections or arguments of the doubters as follows:

Objection 1. The Synoptic Gospels, which mention only one Passover, obviously limit the ministry to one year, while the Fourth Gospel . . . extends it to three or four. *Reply.* The Synoptists nowhere state or even hint . . . that the ministry was confined to a single year.

Objection 2. The Synoptists confine the ministry to Galilee and Peraea, but the Fourth Gospel locates a large portion of it in Judaea. *Reply.* The Synoptic Gospels . . . are written from an exclusively Galilean point of view, but even they hint at a ministry in Judaea. (Matthew 23:37; Luke 13:34; 4:44.)

Objection 3. The Synoptists date the last Passover on Thursday evening, but the Fourth Gospel on Friday evening. *Reply.* The discrepancy is perhaps only apparent, but if it is real, the account of the Fourth Evangelist is the more creditable.

Objection 4. The style of the Gospel differs in such a marked degree from the style of the Revelation, that the same writer cannot have written both. *Reply.* If this is so, the Johannine authorship of the Revelation, which is a much more disputable book than the Gospel, may require to be given up. We may suppose, however, that the Revelation was written in the reign of Nero, and the Gospel a quarter of a century later, in which case the difference of style can be sufficiently accounted for.

Objection 5. Our Lord's discourses in the Fourth Gospel differ altogether in style and subject-matter from those in the Synoptics, and therefore cannot be authentic. *Reply.* The Fourth Gospel does not profess to represent the general tenure and style of Christ's teaching. It is a didactic work, intended mainly to produce and enhance faith in our Lord's divine Sonship. the author, therefore, purposely collects and records mainly those sayings of Christ which illustrate the Divinity of His Person.[10]

Most authorities agree that John's Gospel was written sometime late in the first century or possibly early in the second century A.D. John was the younger of the two sons of Zebedee and is believed to have been the youngest of the apostles. As the Gospels proclaim, he, together with Peter and James, was one of the leaders of the Twelve and knew Jesus intimately. He would have been elderly, possibly over ninety, when he wrote his Gospel.

[10]Ibid., p. 772.

The authenticity of his authorship of his Gospel has been presented here in such detail because so much proof is given therein not only that Jesus is the Son of God, but also that he was with the Father before the world was organized. He came from the Father to do the Father's will, as John records, and near the close of his ministry he declared: "I have glorified thee on the earth: I have finished the work which thou gavest me to do. And now, O Father, glorify thou me with thine own self with the glory which I had with thee before the world was." (John 17:4-5.)

FULFILLMENT OF OLD TESTAMENT PROPHECIES

Some of the Old Testament prophecies of the coming of a Messiah and the specific extent and nature in which these prophecies were fulfilled as recorded in the New Testament are summarized as follows:

OLD TESTAMENT

NEW TESTAMENT

"In the beginning God created the heaven and the earth." (Genesis 1:1.)

"In the beginning was the Word, and the Word was with God, and the Word was God. The same was in the beginning with God. All things were made by him; and without him was not any thing made that was made." (John 1:1-3)

"And the Word was made flesh, and dwelt among us, (and we behold his glory, the glory as of the only begotten of the Father,) full of grace and truth." (John 1:14.)

"Hath in these last days spoken unto us by His Son, whom he hath appointed heir of all things, by whom also he made the worlds." (Hebrews 1:2.)

"The Lord thy God will raise up unto thee a Prophet from the midst of thee, of thy brethren, like unto me; unto him ye shall hearken." (Deuteronomy 18:15)

"And he shall send Jesus Christ, which before was preached unto you: Whom the heaven must receive until the times of restitution of all things, which God has spoken by the mouth of all his holy prophets since the world began. For Moses truly said unto the fathers, A prophet shall the Lord your God raise up unto you of your brethren, like unto me; him shall ye hear in all things whatsoever he shall say unto you." (Acts 3:20-22.)

"They part my garments among them, and cast lots upon my vesture." (Psalm 22:18.)

"And they crucified him, and parted his garments, casting lots: that it might be fulfilled which was spoken by the prophet, They parted my garments among them, and upon my [his] vesture did they cast lots." (Matthew 27:35.)

"He keepeth all his bones: not one of them is broken." (Psalm 34:20.)

"For these things were done, that the scripture should be fulfilled, A bone of him shall not be broken." (John 19:36.)

"Therefore the Lord Himself shall give you a sign; Behold, a virgin shall conceive, and bear a son, and shall call his name Immanuel." (Isaiah 7:14.)

"Now all this was done, that it might be fulfilled which was spoken of the Lord by the prophet, saying, Behold, a virgin will be with child, and shall bring forth a son, and they shall call his name Emmanuel, which being interpreted is, God with us." (Matthew 1:22-23.)

"He is despised and rejected of men; a man of sorrows, and acquainted with grief: and we hid as it were our faces from him; he was despised, and we esteemed him not." (Isaiah 53:3.)

"Then opened he their understanding, that they might understand the scriptures, And said unto them, Thus it is written, and thus it behooved Christ to suffer, and to rise from the dead the third day." (Luke 24:45-46.)

"That it might be fulfilled which was spoken by Esaias the prophet, saying, Himself took our infirmities, and bare our sicknesses." (Matthew 8:17.)

To repeat, these are only a few of the numerous Old Testament predictions concerning a Messiah. The important point is that these Old Testament prophets made these specific predictions, and the record of Jesus' birth, life, ministry, and death fulfilled in such minute detail these prophecies.

AUTHENTICITY OF THE GOSPEL ACCOUNTS

As indicated above, another basic argument advanced by the rabbis and by non-Jewish New Testament criticis is aimed specifically at the authenticity of the New Testament gospel accounts. They claim that these accounts were written long after the occurrence of the actual events and that their authors deliberately perverted the facts so that the story of the birth, life, and ministry of Jesus would fit specifically the Old Testament prophecies. In other words, they maintain that the gospel accounts were contrived and distorted in such a way as to provide a false account of what actually occurred.[11]

A thoughtful look at the facts of how the Gospel came into existence provides an adequate and convincing answer to the utter falsity of the validity of this criticism.

The Gospel of Mark, generally agreed to be the first written, was composed, most scholars agree, sometime during the

[11]Michael Grant, *The Jews in the Roman World* (London: Weidenfeld and Nicolson, 1973), chap. 13.

years A.D. 64-67. John Mark was a close personal associate and friend of the apostles Peter and Paul, and his Gospel was written soon after their martyrdom in Rome. This Gospel is believed to reflect the mind and memory of Peter and is considered to be the one that most influenced the other two Synoptic Gospels. According to one authority, "Of the six hundred and sixty verses in Mark's gospel, six hundred are to be found in Matthew's gospel, and three hundred and fifty in Luke's gospel and only sixty in neither."[12]

Accepting the generally agreed-upon dates of the birth of Jesus, with the Christian era beginning with his birth, we know that he began his ministry approximately in the year A.D. 30 and taught for three years before he was crucified. This means that only about thirty years elapsed from the time of Christ's death until Mark's Gospel was written. Thus, at the time Mark's Gospel was written and became the basis of the other Gospel accounts of the life of Jesus, scores of persons, both members and nonmembers of the Church, would have lived in their adult years during the ministry of Jesus and many would have known him intimately, would have heard his sermons, and would have been witnesses to miracles performed by him. If, as his critics contend, the contrived false account of his birth, life, and ministry were composed and circulated among the people, would not countless numbers of these eye witnesses immediately recognize the spuriousness of this account and would not they have raised their voices in opposition to such a fraud?

Reason, and reason alone, dictates without qualification that if this account had been false, a veritable furor of opposition would have been raised among those who knew the facts. The enemies of Jesus would have been quick to grasp this opportunity to discredit and destroy any image of him that might have been established that he was the expected Messiah.

Yet, what are the historical facts? According to the records, both Judaic and non-Jewish, Christian and non-Christian, no

---

[12]Ronald Brownrigg, *Who's Who in the New Testament* (New York: Holt, Rinehart and Winston, 1971), p. 276.

such criticism was raised against the authenticity of Mark's Gospel nor of the other Synoptic Gospels of Matthew and Luke, which were so extensively based on Mark's account. Moreover, there is no evidence whatsoever in the churches that had been established upon the gospel of Jesus Christ that any revolt or apostasies resulted from these accounts.

Although during Jesus' ministry many believed and followed him, there were obviously many others who did not believe. Only one incident is recorded in the Gospels when, after hearing one of his sermons, a substantial number of disbelievers "followed him no more." This is recorded in the sixth chapter of John, where Jesus is describing the symbolic drinking of his blood and eating of his flesh, after his crucifixion. This ritual became the sacrament, during which baptized members partake of the bread and the wine in remembrance of Jesus and his atoning sacrifice, and also in the form of a covenant to remember him always and to keep his commandments.

In this sermon some of his listeners may have misunderstood and believed that he was suggesting that they actually partake of his blood and of his flesh. This to them was "hard doctrine," and "from that time many of his disciples went back and walked no more with him." (John 6:53-66.)

Mark's Gospel minces no words with respect to his declaration of the Messiahship of Jesus. The very first sentence in his account is: "The beginning of the gospel of Jesus Christ, the Son of God." (Mark 1:1.) Mark then continues to declare that a voice came from heaven saying: "Thou art my beloved Son in whom I am well pleased." (Mark 1:12.) He declares: "The time is fulfilled, and the kingdom of God is at hand: repent ye, and believe the gospel." (Mark 1:15.) Mark even records the statement of the man who had been relieved by Jesus of an unclean spirit, who said: " . . . I know thee who thou art, the Holy One of God." (Mark 1:24.) If, at this time, there had been critics who believed that Mark's account was distorted and not based on facts, surely they would have come forth with their statements of criticism.

The only existing accounts of non-Christian contemporaries who wrote of the events of these times and whose records are still available are those of Josephus, Philo, the historian Pacitus, and Pliny the Younger. The letter from Pliny the Younger, then governor of Bithynia, which was written to the Emperor Trajan in A.D. 112, is pertinent to this discussion. All of the Gospels, including John's would have been written by the time Pliny sent his letter to the emperor. Yet no reference to the Gospels or their authenticity is made by Pliny, whose letter is as follows:

> It is my rule, Sire, to refer to you in matters where I am uncertain. For who can better direct my hesitation or instruct my ignorance? I was never present at any trial of Christians; therefore I do not know what are the customary penalties . . . I have hesitated a great deal on the question whether there should be any distinction of ages; whether the weak should have the same treatment as the more robust; whether those who recant should be pardoned or whether a man who has ever been a Christian should gain nothing by ceasing to be such; whether the name itself, even if innocent of crime, should be punished or only the crimes attaching to that name.

Pliny then goes on to explain the procedure he has been following:

> I ask them if they are Christians. If they admit it, I repeat the question a second and third time, threatening capital punishment; if they persist, I sentence them to death. For I do not doubt whatever kind of crime it may be to which they have confessed, their pertinacity and inflexible obstinacy should certainly be punished. . . .
>
> The matter seems to me to justify my consulting you . . . for many persons of all ages and classes and of both sexes are being put in peril by accusations. . . .

According to the record, the Emperor Trajan replied:

> You have taken the right line, my dear Pliny, in examining the cases of those denounced to you as Christians, for no hard and fast rule can be laid down of universal application. They are not to be sought out; if they are informed against, and the charges proved, they are to be punished, with this reservation — that if anyone denies that he is a Christian, and actually proves it, that is by worshipping our gods, he shall be pardoned as a result of this recantation, however, suspect he may have been with respect to the past. Pamphlets published

> anonymously should carry no weight in any charge what-
> soever, they constitute a very bad precedent and are also out
> of keeping with this age. [13]

It is interesting that this report to Trajan, attributed to Pliny the Younger, makes no reference to any of the literature about the Christian church that would have been written by the year A.D. 112. Criticism and persecution against the Christians by the Romans and the Jews were prevalent long before this time, and the Christian church was completely outlawed by the government in Rome.

Textual criticism of the New Testament is of relatively recent origin. During the past several hundred years, particularly during the nineteenth century, this type of criticism has been popular among Bible scholars, both so-called and genuine. They seem to feel that their authority can be established through pointing out seeming inconsistencies regarding authorship, accuracy, dates of authorship, and other aspects of the scriptures.

In his preface to his commentary on the Bible, Bible scholar Dr. John Eadie wrote this about Bible critics:

> Rationalism, engaged in by these critics, makes no preten-
> tions to superior piety. It only boasts of superior reason. It will
> not bow its stubborn heart to the truth of inspiration — it will
> not take the Bible to be the word of God, and cast aside
> evangelical Christianity as slavery and a lie. Not that it as-
> sumes the language of open and unblushing infidelity or
> declares Scripture to be a fable; but it takes away from the
> Bible its divine authority, and deals with it as with any ancient
> book of human origin, subjecting it to ruthless and destructive
> criticism, and confining it within the limits of a narrow and
> deceptive philosophy. It admits the genius of the various
> writers of the Bible, but denies their special and divine com-
> mission, and therefore holds itself at liberty to question any
> statement, deny any conclusion, modify any argument, or
> resist any opinion which may be found in the writings of
> prophets and apostles. In so doing, it seduces the unwary,
> and makes sad havoc among many of our young men, espe-
> cially such of them as feel the pride of mental culture and have

[13]From documents of the Christian Church, Oxford University Press, Oxford, England, 1947.

had little exercise in philosophical speculations. How shall we be preserved from these suicidal errors? Plainly, by taking the Bible for what it professes to be — the pure word of God. There is as much folly in attempting to reduce or modify this claim, as there is in openly denying it. To give the writers of the Bible the credit of genius, but to deny them the gift of inspiration, is a libel on their honesty — is to assign them a place among imposters; for they unanimously maintain that they were under the supernatural control and impulse of the Holy Spirit.[14]

As so beautifully expressed in this statement, and despite the broad and continuously growing array of biblical textual criticism of the Old and the New Testaments, these scriptures still stand as the bona fide records of God's dealings with his people through his prophets. They have stood up solidly against this criticism for hundreds of years and will continue to do so in the future.

In fact, archaeological discoveries made during the past hundred years and particularly the discovery of the Dead Sea Scrolls, continue to confirm the accuracy of the scriptures and the eternal nature of Christ's gospel. These discoveries are also helping to establish the fact that through inspiration and revelation, God is protecting the scriptures. He has preserved them as witnesses, not only of his existence, but also of his love for his children and his guidance for them through his Only Begotten Son, Jesus the Christ, whose coming was predicted by all of the Old Testament prophets since the world began.

[14]John Eadie, *The 1862 Holy Bible* (London: W. R. M'Phun, 1862), p. iv.

APPENDIX

According to the biblical account, Abraham and his ancestors came from the area of the city of Ur in the land of the
Chaldees. Ur, the most famous of the city-states in the land of
the Sumerians, was located in the lower reaches of the Tigres-
Euphrates Valley before the two rivers converged and emptied
into the Persian Gulf. The territory, from the northern mountains in Turkey and the eastern hills in Iran, is a broad, flat
valley, and between the two rivers, a highly fertile land. The
Greeks had given the name Mesopotamia to the land between
the rivers. In this area were centered the kingdoms of
Babylonia and Assyria, but the earliest settlers were from
Sumeria. All of these people were of the Semitic race, and
undoubtedly Abraham's ancestry originated in this genealogy.

According to Genesis 10, Noah's sons settled in this area and
established a kingdom at Babel Erech, Accad, and Calneh, in
the land of Shinar. Noah's son Shem, through nine generations, was a direct ancestor of Abraham.

The earliest historical people who settled in this area, outside
the biblical record, were the Sumerians, who, according to
relatively recent archaeological discoveries, established a
Neolithic civilization in this area thousands of years before
Christ. Long before the Classic Age of Greece and the civic
developments in Egypt, the Sumerians developed a remarkable civilization based on agriculture, a system of loosely knit
city-states ruled by religious leaders who based their worship

on a system of gods strictly connected with nature and the elements. On the foundation of this ancient civilization were built Assyrian and Babylonian empires.

Ziggurat, still standing near the ancient site of Ur, provides silent testimony of the existence of this once great city. In 1923, Leonard Woolley uncovered the death pits of Ur and, although the cemetery had been severely plundered, found nearly two thousand graves, some of which were in sepulchres of stone. In each of these were found bodies, both male and female, clothed in gold, silver, and semiprecious stones. Next to these bodies were golden drinking cups and other interesting artifacts. Stone-built rooms were at the bottom of deep pits, and within these pits, or on the ramps leading to them, were scores of bodies of men, women, and animals. The women had been clothed in red woolen robes, and remnants of musical instruments lay by their sides. These bodies were arranged in such an orderly fashion as to give evidence of peaceful deaths probably made in sacrifice at the time of deaths of their leaders. (See *Horizon Book of Lost Worlds* [New York: American Heritage Publishing Company, 1962], pp. 121-51.)

BIBLIOGRAPHY

ARCHAEOLOGY AND THE BIBLE

Bamm, Peter. *Early Sites in Christianity*. New York: Pantheon Books, 1957.

Basor Supplementary Studies. Unpublished report of Hebrew University, 1951.

Cerem, C. W. *God, Graves and Scholars*. New York: Bantam Books, 1967.

Clark, Sir Kenneth. "The Mystery of Ancient Egypt." *Reader's Digest*, June 1975, p. 86.

Marshall B. Davidson and Leonard Cottrell, eds. *The Horizon Book of Lost Worlds*. New York: American Heritage, 1962.

Debenham, Frank. *Discovery and Exploration*. Garden City, N.Y.: Doubleday, 1960.

Israel Exploration Journal, various issues, 1969-74.

Mazar, B. "The Excavations in the Old City of Jerusalem." Discoveries and studies in Jerusalem of the Israel Exploration Society, 1969-70.

___. "Finds from the Archaeological Excavations near the Temple Mount." 1974.

___. Bulletins of the American Schools of Oriental Research, Jerusalem, 1948-53.

Owen G. Fredrick. *Archaeology of the Bible*. London: Fleming H. Revell Co., 1961.

Politeyan, J. *Bible Discoveries in Egypt, Palestine and Mesapotamia*. London: Elliot Stock, 1915.

Povov, A. *Transactions of the Historical and Archaeological Society of the University of Moscow*, vol. 3, 1880. Moscow: Moscow University Press. (Quoted in R. H. Charles, *The Apocrypha and Pseudepigrapha of the Old Testament*, 2:425.)

Rubenshan, Dr. *Aramaic Papyrus from Elephantine*. Sachan Publishing Co., 1911.

Terrien, Samuel. *Lands of the Bible*. New York: Simon and Schuster, 1957.

BIBLE COMMENTARIES

Clarke, Adam. *Commentary on the Whole Bible.* New York: Layne and Sanford, vol. 1, 1843.

Delderfield, Eric R. *Fascinating Facts and Figures of the Bible.* Devon, England: E.R.D. Publications, 1967.

Dummelow, J. R. *Commentary on the Whole Bible.* New York: Macmillan, 1943.

Eadie, John. *The 1862 Holy Bible:* Bible and Commentary. London: W. R. M'Phun, 1862.

Hastings, James, et. al. *Dictionary of the Bible.* New York: Charles Scribner's Sons, 1952.

Jamison, Robert, A. R. Fausett, and David Brown. *Commentary on the Whole Bible.* Grand Rapids, Mich.: Zondervan, n.d.

CHRISTIANITY

Alexander, V. G. *Christian Institutions.* New York: Charles Scribner's Sons, 1906.

Anthon, Charles. *A Classical Dictionary of the Principal and Proper Names Mentioned by Ancient Greek and Roman Authors.* New York: Harper and Brothers, 1853.

Asch, Scholim. *The Nazarene.* New York: G. P. Putnam's Sons, 1939.

Barry, F. R. *The Relevance of Christianity.* London: Nisbet and Co., Ltd., 1931.

Barker, James L. *The Divine Church.* Salt Lake City: Deseret News Press, 1951.

Bigg, Charles. *The Origins of Christianity.* Oxford: Clarendon Press, 1909.

"Book of Lost Worlds." *Horizon.* New York: American Heritage, 1962.

Brown, Henry F. *Baptism Through the Centuries.* Mountain View, Calif.: Pacific Press, 1965.

Bryan, William Jennings. *Famous Figures of the Old Testament.* London: Fleming H. Revell Co., 1923.

Burkett, F. Crawford. *The Gospel History and Its Transmission.* Edinburgh: T. & T. Clarke, 1906.

Callan, Charles J. *The Epistles of St. Paul.* London: Joseph F. Wagner, n.d.

Charles, R. H. *The Apocrypha and Pseudepigrapha of the Old Testament.* 2 vols. Oxford: Oxford University Clarendon Press, 1913, 1963.

——. *Religious Development Between the Old and the New Testaments.* London: Oxford University Press, 1936.

Danielou, Jean. "That the Scriptures Might Be Fulfilled." *The World's Great Religions.* New York: Time, Inc., 1957.

DeMille, Cecil B. *Moses and Egypt.* Los Angeles: University of Southern California Press, 1956.

Dinsmore, Charles Allen. *The English Bible as Literature.* Cambridge: Houghton-Mifflin Co., 1931.

Documents of the Christian Church. Oxford: Oxford University Press, 1947.

Edersheim, Alfred. *The Life and Times of Jesus the Messiah.* Grand Rapids, Mich.: W. D. Erdman, 1956. 2 vols.

Ellis, H. B. *Heritage of the Desert.* New York: The Ronald Press Co., 1956.

Farrar, F. W. *The Life of Christ*. London: Cassell and Co., 1903.

Faulkner, John Alfred. *Burning Questions in Historical Christianity*. New York: Abingdon Press, 1930.

Fisher, George P. *The Grounds of Theistic and Christian Beliefs*. London: Hodder and Stoughton, 1907.

Fosdick, Harry Emerson. *The Hope of the World*. New York and London: Harpers, 1933.

Fox, John. *Book of Martyrs*. London: Thomas Kelly, Paternaster Row, 1811.

Frazer, James George. *The New Golden Bough*. New York: Criterion Books, 1959.

Grant, R. M. and D. N. Freedman. *The Secret Sayings of Jesus*. Garden City, N.Y.: Doubleday, 1960.

Gregory of Nyssa. *The Great Catechism*. Wace and Schaff, the Christian Literature Co., 1890-93.

Harrison, Frederick. *The Positive Evaluation of Religion*. London: Wm. Heinemann, 1913.

Havet, Ernest. *Le Christianisme et ses Origines*, as quoted by E. DePressense in *The Ancient World and Christianity*. New York: A. C. Armstrong and Son, 1890.

Pearl of Great Price. Salt Lake City: The Church of Jesus Christ of Latter-day Saints, 1973.

Rabin, C., ed. *Textus*. Jerusalem: Magnes Press, Hebrew University, 1960.

Robinson, Christine H., *Inspirational Truths*. Salt Lake City: Deseret Book Co., 1970.

Scott, E. F. *The Kingdom and the Messiah*. Edinburgh: T. & T. Clarke, 1911.

Smith, H. S., R. T. Handy, and L. A. Loetsher. *American Christianity*, New York: Charles Scribner's Sons, 1960.

Steiner, Rudolph. *Christianity as a Mystical Fact*. West Nyack, N.Y.: Rudolph Steiner Publications, Inc., 1961.

Strong, T. B. *The Origins of Christianity*. Oxford: Clarendon Press, 1909.

Talmage, James E. *Jesus the Christ*. Salt Lake City: Deseret Book Co., 1972.

Toynbee, Arnold, ed. *The Crucible of Christianity*. New York: World Publishing Co., 1969.

Watt, William. *The History of Infant Baptism*. Oxford: Oxford University Press, 1862.

THE DEAD SEA SCROLLS

Abigad, Nahman and Yigael Yadin. *A Genesis Apocryphon*. Jerusalem: Magnes Press, Hebrew University, 1956.

Allegro, J. M. *The Dead Sea Scrolls*. Baltimore: Penguin Books, n.d.

___. *The People of the Dead Sea Scrolls*. Garden City, N.Y.: Doubleday and Co., 1958.

Brownlee, William H. *The Meaning of the Qumran Scrolls for the Bible*. Oxford: Oxford University Press, 1964.

Burrows, Millar. *The Dead Sea Scrolls*. New York: The Viking Press, 1955.

Cass, Thurman L. *Secrets From the Caves*. New York: Abingdon Press, 1963.

Davies, A. Powell. *The Meaning of the Dead Sea Scrolls.* New York: The New American Library, 1956.

Flusser, David. *The Dead Sea Sect and Pre-Pauline Christianity* and *Blessed Are the Poor in Spirit.* Jerusalem: Magnes Press, Hebrew University, 1960.

Fritsch, Charles T. *The Qumran Community: Its History in Scrolls.* New York: Macmillan Co., 1956.

Gaster, Theodore. *The Dead Sea Scriptures in English Translation.* New York: Doubleday, 1959 (hardbound ed.).

Goshen-Gottstein, M. H. *Text and Language in Bible and Qumran.* Jerusalem: Orient Publishing Co., 1960.

Potter, Charles F. *Did Jesus Write This Book?* Greenwich, Conn.: Fawcett Publications, 1967.

——. *The Lost Years of Jesus.* New Hyde Park, N.Y.: University Books, 1963.

Rabin, Chaim, and Yigael Yadin. *Aspects of the Dead Sea Scrolls, Scripta Hierosolymitana.* Jerusalem: Magnes Press, Hebrew University, 1958.

Robinson, O. P. *The Dead Sea Scrolls and Original Christianity.* Salt Lake City: Deseret Book Co., 1958.

——. *How Old Is Christ's Gospel?* Salt Lake City: Deseret Book Co., 1963.

Rowley, H. H. *The Zadokite Fragment and the Dead Sea Scrolls.* Oxford: Basil Blackwell, 1955.

Sanders, J. A. *The Dead Sea Psalms Scrolls.* Ithaca, N.Y.: Cornell University Press, 1967.

Schonfield, Hugh J. *Secrets of the Dead Sea Scrolls.* London: Valentine, Mitchell, 1956.

——. *The Bible Was Right.* New York: Signet Book, 1959.

Schubert, Kurt. *The Dead Sea Community Its Origin and Teachings.* London: Adam and Charles Black, 1959.

Sommer, A. DuPont. *Dead Sea Scrolls, A Preliminary Study.* Oxford: Basil Blackwell, 1950.

Sutcliff, Edmund F. *The Monks of Qumran.* London: Burns and Oates, 1960.

Van Der Plaog, J. *The Excavations at Qumran.* London: Longmans Green and Co., 1958.

Vermes, G. *The Dead Sea Scrolls in English.* Harmondsworth, Middlesex, England: Penguin Books, Ltd. 1962 (paperbound ed.).

Wilson, Edmund. *The Scrolls from the Dead Sea.* New York: Oxford University Press, 1955.

Yadin, Yigael. "The Temple Scroll." A special report published in Jerusalem by the Hebrew University, 1958.

——. *Masada.* London: Weidenfield and Nicolson, 1966.

——. *The Message of the Scrolls.* New York: Simon and Schuster, 1957.

ISRAEL AND JUDAISM

Comay, Joan. *Who's Who in the Old Testament.* New York: Holt Rinehart and Winston, 1971.

Cohn, Haim. *The Trial and Death of Jesus.* London: Weidenfield and Nicolson, 1972.

Collins, Larry and Lapierre Dominique. *O Jerusalem.* New York: Pocket Books, 1973.

Dimont, Max I. *Jews, God and History.* New York: Simon and Schuster, 1962.

Ellis, Harry B. *Israel and the Middle East.* New York: The Ronald Press Co., 1957.

Encyclopedia Judaica Jerusalem. New York: Macmillan Co., 1971.

Eusebius' Ecclesiastical History.

Grant, Michael. *The Jews in the Roman World.* London: Weidenfield and Nicolson, 1973.

Guignebert, Charles. *The Jewish World in the Time of Jesus.* New York: University Books, 1959.

Josephus, Flavius. *Antiquities of the Jews.* William Whiston, trans. Grand Rapids, Mich.: Kregel Publications, 1960.

Kollek, Teddy, and Pearlman, Mashe. *Jerusalem, A History of Forty Centuries.* New York: Random House, 1968.

Lewy, Immanuel. *The Growth of the Pentateuch.* New York: Bookman Associates, 1955.

Maccoby, Hyam. *Revolution in Judaea.* London: Ocean Books, 1973.

Perlmutter, Amos. *Military and Politics in Israel.* Cambridge, Mass.: Frank Cass and Co., Harvard University, 1968.

Richards, LeGrand. *Israel, Do You Know?* Salt Lake City: Deseret Book Co., 1954.

Robinson, O. P., and Christine H. Robinson. *Biblical Sites in the Holy Land.* Salt Lake City: Deseret Book Co., 1963.

_____. *Israel's Bible Lands.* Salt Lake City: Deseret Book Co., 1973.

Snell, Heber C. *Ancient Israel – Its Story and Meaning.* Salt Lake City: University of Utah, 1963.

THE TORAH

The Torah, The Five Books of Moses. Philadelphia: The Jewish Publication Society of America, 1962, 1974.

WORLD RELIGIONS

Gaer, Joseph. *How the Great Religions Began.* New York: Signet Book, New American Library, Inc., 1956.

Hesse, Hermann. *Siddhartha.* New York: New Directions Publishing Co., 1957.

Lanciani, Rodolfo. *Pagan and Christian Rome.* London: Macmillan and Co., 1892.

Michalson, Carl. *Worldly Theology.* New York: Charles Scribner's Sons, 1967.

Thompson, et al. *The World's Great Religions.* New York: Time, Inc., 1957.

INDEX

Aaronic Priesthood, in church of
Jesus, 113-4; offices of,
described by Paul, 114;
Covenantors' knowledge of,
114-15
Abraham, promised a Savior,
22; name changed from
Abram, 31; story of, 32-35;
blessing given to, 34, 215-17;
may have practiced baptism,
118. *See also* Abram
Abram, Hebrews originated
with, 31; conversion of,
131-32; story of, told in
Lameck Scroll, 156. *See also*
Abraham
Abstinence, 167-68
Adam, fall of, brought death, 47,
177; fall of, in plan of
salvation, 47; possible
baptism of, 118-19, 140-41;
free agency introduced with,
123, 212; driven from Garden,
131; devil spoke to, 140;
taught good and evil, 160
Ahikar, story of, 183-84
Albright, Professor William F., 5
Alexander the Great, 38-39
Alexandria, library in, 136
Ambassador College, 11
Amorites, 33-34
Angel of darkness, 125-26

Angels, 133
Anthon, Professor Charles, 55
Apocalypse of Baruch, origin of,
175-76; refers to destruction
of Jerusalem, 176-77;
regarding eternal life, 177;
regarding free agency, 177;
regarding resurrection, 178;
teachings of, similar to those
of Jesus, 178
Apocryphon of John, 194-95
Apollo, 170
Apostasy of children of Israel,
131
Apostles, testimonies of, 78-86;
selection of, by Jesus, 114;
warned of changes in gospel,
228-29
Arab-Israeli war, 39
Arabs, contention between
Israelis and, 39-40
Ark of the Covenant, 176
Ascension of Jesus, 58
Asher, 28
Assumption of Moses,
preexistent selection of
Moses recorded in, 46, 173;
parallels of, to New
Testament teachings, 172-73;
on impiety, 172-73
Atonement, meaning of, 50-52;
as mission of Jesus, 76-77